PETER F. BRONFMAN

Builder Extraordinaire

PETER F. BRONFMAN

Builder Extraordinaire

The Development of
EdperBrascan Corporation

Edited by Alan Dean and Frank Lochan

Printed by University of Toronto Press
Toronto   Buffalo   London

ISBN 0-9684249-0-2

Canadian Cataloguing in Publication Data

Main entry under title:

Peter F. Bronfman - Builder Extraordinaire -
    The Development of EdperBrascan Corporation

Includes index.
ISBN 0-9684249-0-2

1. Bronfman, Peter F. (Peter Frederick), 1929-1996.
2. EdperBrascan Corporation - History.
3. Executives - Canada - Biography.
4. Businessmen - Canada - Biography.
I. Dean, Alan, 1944-   II. Lochan, Frank, 1940-
    III. EdperBrascan Corporation.

HD2810.12.E36P48 1998   338.092   C98-900990-4

Printed on acid-free paper.

Printed and bound in Canada by
University of Toronto Press Incorporated 1995
Toronto   Buffalo   London

Tribute

Peter F. Bronfman 1929-1996

This book is dedicated to the life and values of Peter Bronfman, a caring man, passionate Canadian and consummate builder who lived from 1929 to the end of 1996, through sixty-seven eventful years.

The objective of this book is to capture the rare qualities of a very special and private man and to describe the way his unique character steered the development of EdperBrascan Corporation and influenced the evolution of its business values based on teamwork, sharing of credit, leading by example and fairness in its relationships with others.

In the process of building EdperBrascan, Peter Bronfman played a major role in the development of more than two hundred major office buildings, shopping centres, hydro-electric power plants, base metal mines, metallurgical facilities, forest product mills and other natural resource projects, all of which have contributed meaningfully to the growth of Canada's industrial base.

Corporate Lineage

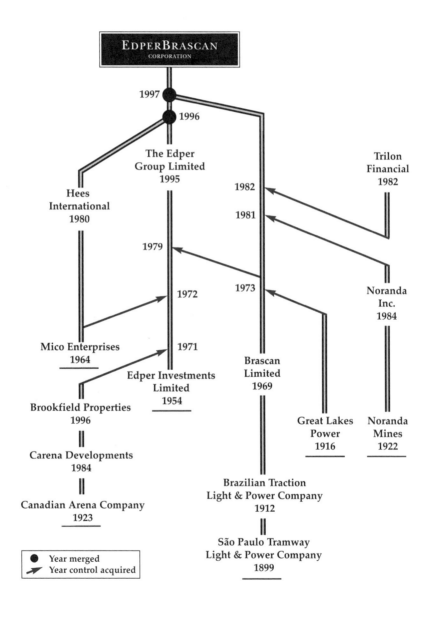

EDPERBRASCAN
CORPORATION

1997

1996

The Edper
Group Limited
1995

Hees
International
1980

Trilon
Financial
1982

1982

1981

1979

1972

1973

Noranda
Inc.
1984

Mico Enterprises
1964

1971

Edper Investments
Limited
1954

Brascan
Limited
1969

Brookfield Properties
1996

Great Lakes
Power
1916

Noranda
Mines
1922

Carena Developments
1984

Canadian Arena Company
1923

Brazilian Traction
Light & Power Company
1912

São Paulo Tramway
Light & Power Company
1899

● Year merged
➤ Year control acquired

Contents

Tribute 1

Corporate Lineage 2

Preface 5

Book One - Family Roots and Values 9

   1.   In the Beginning 11

   2.   A Caring Man 29

   3.   A Team Player 45

Book Two - Building the Business 75

   4.   Early Business Years 77

   5.   The Transition Period 91

   6.   Capturing Brascan 113

Book Three - Growth and Challenges 137

   7.   Winning and Losing 139

   8.   Preserving the Capital Base 164

   9.   The Ongoing Partnership 180

Book Four - The Legacy 201

  10.   The Initial Foundation 203

  11.   The Second Pillar 223

  12.   From Water to Energy 238

  13.   The Glue 248

  14.   Building on History 264

Book Five - The Mind of the Man 279

15. Harnessing the Unknowns 281

16. Celebrating Success 299

17. The Road Ahead 315

Appendices

  I. Closing Reflections - Words from Peter Bronfman 327

 II. Chronology - Development of EdperBrascan
    Corporation 337

III. Corporate Chart 348

Index 349

Preface

I was very fortunate to have been part of Peter's life for almost fifteen years, until his death from cancer in December 1996. How lucky for me to have had as my husband this remarkable man, who gave so much to me, to his family, to his friends, to his business colleagues and to Canada.

This book is the result of a collaborative effort of Peter's friends and colleagues in EdperBrascan Corporation as a way to pay tribute to Peter and their relationship with him, but more importantly to provide the recipients of the Peter Bronfman Scholarships with a chronicle of his life and business achievements.

Shortly after becoming aware of Peter's illness, his colleagues and I decided to establish a scholarship programme in his name at the University of Toronto with the objective of providing financial assistance each year to more than two hundred deserving undergraduate students at Woodsworth College, where Peter had, over the years, quietly become a leading patron. In 1997, this programme was expanded to introduce the Peter Bronfman International Scholarships to be awarded to children of Edper group employees embarking on graduate studies at the universities of their choice. These scholarship programmes are a wonderful way of remembering the inspiration and opportunities Peter provided to so many people in his lifetime.

This book also serves as a natural extension of *The Edper Story*, a compendium of lessons learned in building the Edper group, which was assembled by Peter's colleagues in 1996 as a gift to him. However, what follows seeks to provide a deeper insight into the man – known as a friend, colleague and partner. Peter's Foreword to *The Edper Story*, which has been included as an Appendix to this book, added his own special message and views on his journey into the world of Canadian and international business.

When he reflected on his forty years of business life, Peter drew satisfaction from what had been accomplished and pleasure from the close relationships he had enjoyed during his time at the helm. As often happens, however, there were pitfalls and occasionally individuals who let him down, but Peter did not dwell on the negatives or get stuck in wondering why. His nature was to find solutions, leaving recriminations behind, and in keeping with his ways this book deals not with regrets or those who disappointed him, but rather with lessons learned, success achieved, friendships cherished and future goals.

Special thanks are due to Alan Dean and Frank Lochan, ably assisted by Diane Horton, who were undaunted by the task of editing and cobbling into shape the individual contributions of so many friends and colleagues to make this book not only an enjoyable read for those of us who knew Peter but also, we hope, an interesting book for those who never met him.

It is not easy to label or categorize Peter's personality, business style or the gentle energy he brought to the corporate world and his community endeavours. His unique approach to life was moulded by his upbringing and early influences, combined with a strong character and determination to always do what he believed was right.

He was also a very private person, who much preferred to stay out of the spotlight. He believed his colleagues were the remarkable ones who were responsible for the group's many successful ventures and he was unselfish in giving private and public credit to others. If he were reading this book, he would, in his usual self-deprecating style, exclaim: "Who is this person? Surely not me!" He would be shyly embarrassed to be singled out for such accolades and would proceed to direct the credit to his colleagues.

This attribute for sharing credit has been passed on and embraced by his senior colleagues. However, I know Peter would want me to mention Jack Cockwell's role in working alongside him for twenty-eight years. In his last note to Jack, handwritten from home before he died, Peter had the final word on their special relationship. He wrote: "Our partnership has meant much to many and everything to me."

Peter's modesty and reluctance to take credit was a constant in his life, even in the most successful of times. He was genuinely surprised, but nonetheless appreciative, when the

University of Toronto conferred a *Doctor of Laws* degree on him and his country awarded him the *Order of Canada* in 1996. In accepting these honours he insisted in doing so on behalf of his colleagues and the business enterprise he had founded and given so much of himself to build.

Peter's greatness as a businessman was his remarkable ability to remain true to himself and his beliefs, even if they were unpopular at the time. He led by example, always showing modesty, courage, kindness and respect. He was a man of great sensitivity and compassion and was unafraid to show it in a private or public forum.

He had a giant heart that engulfed his business and personal world. After his death, I received hundreds of letters, mostly filled with stories about his unending generosity and amazing capacity to care for whoever was fortunate enough to capture his imagination and concern. His impact on the lives of those of us who knew and loved him continues to affect us today and is sure to continue into the future.

I was one of the many to be touched by Peter's strong yet gentle ways. In walking the business corridors with heart and humility, he showed that these qualities can enter the boardroom, can create successful leaders, can inspire and can make a meaningful difference.

Lynda Hamilton
August 1998

Book One

Family Roots and Values

These chapters explore the immigrant experiences of Peter Bronfman's grandparents, Yechiel and Minnie Bronfman, and their young family as they leave their tobacco farm in eastern Europe to follow their dream of establishing themselves in the New World. Their country of choice, Canada, proves at first to be a harsh and forbidding place of frozen soil, brutal winters and near poverty. It is the story of how a family with creative minds and determined spirits turn hardship into opportunity and, in so doing, better themselves while helping others along the way. The family history demonstrates the strength of character and vision which Peter Bronfman inherits from his forebears. During his lifetime, he uses his innate business acumen and caring nature to develop his own philosophy based on a strong belief in consensus building, leading by example and a commitment to sharing credit and rewards.

Chapter One

In the Beginning

How thin the thread which ties most of us to our ancestors and the conditions that led to our present state of being and yet, for the Bronfman family, how very strong that thread must have been – for so much has hung on it! All family histories spin out from some distant point – who knows where they must have started – but for the purposes of this narrative and record, we must arbitrarily decide upon a year in time from which to take the saga forward.

For Peter Bronfman and his family's story, we should travel back at least to the 1880s and their existence in eastern Europe and explore a little of the conditions in which they lived and the role of family leaders who sought improvement in their lot. We must recall a time when people existed in villages and small towns with lives closely circumscribed by religion, custom, social restrictions and limited possibilities.

We must think of a place where there was very little privacy available and the sounds, smells and contact of neighbours – not just immediate family members – were a daily fact of life. All activity turned on the duty to provide for family while observing one's faith and staying within the tightly laced bindings of social convention. Even a little prosperity could not buy much freedom or privacy.

It seemed that for most families there were only two choices. One would be to accept the situation in its entirety and live out a life according to all the local rules and conventions – praying for enough food, an absence of disease and relative peace from one's neighbours and, above all, protection from one's enemies. With few exceptions, any flicker of hope for increased stability, financial improvement or social elevation would quickly be snuffed out by the grinding oppression of getting through each day.

The other choice – should a family have produced a member capable of even imagining that they had any choices whatsoever – would be to take charge of their lives and dream about change. With a plan, with sacrifice, determination and will, a change could be possible and the long climb away from what had been accepted as the family's fate could begin.

A new world, America, hung like one bright promise in the minds of some. The immediate problem, however, was how to get through each day's practical aspects of nourishment, work and family care, while carefully formulating plans and saving enough for passage to the new land. Such an idea and its successful realization were beyond the comprehension and abilities of most.

And even if passage could be secured and the family persuaded that escape was possible, there remained two giant obstacles: the journey itself, a test of endurance, health and mental focus, and then finally establishing the family in a new and unfamiliar land, devoid of known guideposts, institutions, and social and religious networks. What courage it must have taken to embrace such an undertaking.

Imagine the severing of ties that had been in place for generations, the tossing off of all that was familiar and had seeped into the collective bones of a family for years and years – the very things which made that family what it was. Could they be transplanted – or should they be cast aside? Is a new beginning ever truly possible, or would they carry the legacy of past generations with them?

We live in an age where records of the fairly recent past can be easily found and patched together into a reasonably accurate family history. It is not difficult to discover that the Bronfman patriarch with the drive and determination to make a change was Yechiel Bronfman even though, by the standards of the day, his lot in life was better than most.

His family had acquired a tolerable level of security through the ownership of a grist mill and a tobacco plantation in Bessarabia, a former province of Czarist Russia near the Romanian border. But still, he had imagination, a dream of making life better and enough courage and fire within to think about uprooting himself and his family from their little corner of relative comfort.

Yechiel Bronfman spent many a troubled night before deciding to make the move and devising an ambitious plan to seek an improved lot in the new world which beckoned. In the icy chill of February 1889, Yechiel along with his wife Minnie and the first three, Abe, Harry and Laura, of what would eventually become eight children, bundled themselves up and departed for Canada. Yechiel had accumulated sufficient means to sponsor another couple who helped them with their children. The family was also accompanied by a rabbi, as Yechiel sought to maintain his Jewish heritage in the new land.

On the rough crossing of the Atlantic Ocean a fourth child, Sam, was said to have been born, caught in the space between old and new with no safe harbour in sight. To survive such a start the baby would have to be tough, and tough he certainly proved to be. Much later, however, Sam's sons discovered that he may actually have been born in Russia, just before the journey, although throughout his long life he enjoyed living the legend of his seaborn beginnings. Jean, Bessie, Allan and Rose, the next four children, would all be born in the new world.

Who could have ever projected that, less than half a century later, the family's name with its prophetic meaning of *whiskey man* would enter the annals of Canadian business history in so many notable ways. The Bronfman family would do exactly that, and would eventually establish residences among the mansions of Montreal and business offices in the glittering towers of downtown Montreal, Toronto, New York and other major cities of the world.

But the road to wealth and prestige would not be along a smooth highway. Nor would it be straight or without setbacks. The newly arrived immigrants, in company with about fifty other families, decided to establish themselves in the village of Wapella, which was little more than a pioneer settlement in eastern Saskatchewan, near the Manitoba border. It was grim and it was little better than nowhere.

What was worse was that Yechiel, for all his inner strength, warm dreams and happy visions of a better life, was totally unprepared for the climatic conditions of the Canadian prairies and the tests to which he would soon be put. They arrived in April to find a white and frozen landscape and learned they could not plant their tobacco seed until after the spring thaw was complete.

Even when the bleak landscape softened with the warmer weather, it was not ready to receive the Russian tobacco seed Yechiel had brought with him or the wheat grains he acquired. The land had first to be cleared of trees and ploughed using a team of borrowed oxen before the virgin ground would yield to the till and be ready for planting.

The Bronfmans were not the only immigrant family to find the environment in Wapella harsh and far from hospitable. One by one the other families turned to Yechiel for help because he at least had come with some resources and boundless energy. As a religious man and one who knew the value of neighbours and a community pulling together, he tried to assist by sharing what he had, even to the detriment of his own family.

Within ten months there were very few left in the little community and Yechiel's family, because of their sharing with others, were themselves on the brink of poverty. As a family characteristic, this strong tradition of helping the needy would re-emerge down the generations, in Yechiel's son Allan, and his grandson Peter, and many other members of this remarkable family.

❧

During the early years, Yechiel's son Harry kept a diary sporadically and it tells its own tale of hardship on the bleak Canadian prairies: "The first crop of wheat froze, and consequently father spent the winter . . . going into the bush, cutting logs, loading them on to a sleigh and drawing them twenty miles with a yoke of oxen so that when they were sold, there would be a sufficient amount of money to buy a sack of flour, a few evaporated apples, dried prunes and some tea and sugar to bring back to the family so that body and soul could be kept together."

Yechiel had not left his modestly prosperous grist mill and tobacco plantation in Bessarabia to have his family wither, starve or freeze on some desolate prairie in the new world. He drew upon whatever inner strength he had left and set off to find a town with something more to offer in the way of opportunities. He soon found Brandon, Manitoba, which he concluded might have some promise, given that it had a population of at least 3,500.

Never one to shy from change, he turned from Yechiel to the more easily pronounced Ekiel and from a struggling farmer and part-time woodsman into a Canadian Northern Railway employee who, at the very least, could count on a steady though meagre wage.

With an eager eye open for any new opportunity which might come by, he realized that the scrap wood from the houses and shacks he was clearing away for the coming railway could be reused to provide better shelter for his and other families. Each week he set aside a portion of his wages and when he had saved twelve dollars he purchased enough wood to build what today would be considered to be not much more than a tool shed.

He also bought wood to build a new home for the local rabbi and moved everything they had from their torturous exile in Wapella to Brandon. It was quite a step up, and though by today's standards their new homes were drafty and dank, they were heartened by their ability to better their lot. The real benefit to the move was as Ekiel had hoped. It put them in the path of wide-ranging opportunities which were there to be exploited by those who were energetic and had creative minds.

Brandon was a growing community and, as a man determined to improve his family's position, he discovered treasure in another man's discards. At the local sawmill where Ekiel found his next regular job, the sides of sawn logs were considered waste but he saw the potential for gain in selling them as cooking fuel. He bought them by the wagonload and sold them for a healthy profit. Before long his older sons were also in the business and the family could afford to build a more solid home.

During the winter they sold frozen whitefish for additional income. Son Abe ventured to Winnipeg to work during the summers in a tobacco factory so that he could send his wages back to the family in Brandon. Other members of the family took on contracts as teamsters for local road improvement projects. Ever eager to add to their resources, they rose early in the morning and also worked late at night in order to double up on the use of these same horses and wagons by selling loam to local gardeners.

For their versatile minds, every job held a different, yet less obvious potential for reward. It soon became clear to neighbours and friends that the Bronfman family was blessed with a keen business sense and ingenious ideas on how to make the most out of each opportunity that happened to come their way.

Very soon, the family's income and livelihood came from a veritable circus of barely related activities, each endeavour loosely hinged to the next but each contributing to the total pool of funds being accumulated to feed their growing numbers and to seed yet another venture. Before long, they were crossing the border into the United States looking for new opportunities. Soon horse trading was being added to the chain of pursuits and later wild Montana horses were herded up, broken in as cart horses and then sold to the local farmers in Brandon.

With five energetic sons at his behest and many ventures under way, Ekiel eventually garnered sufficient capital to enter the hotel business in the early 1900s. The development of the Canadian West was in full flight and the wild and rowdy crews of immigrants, railway builders and land busters often needed a temporary perch until permanent living arrangements could be made.

In time, the Bronfman family assembled a collection of hotels, not luxurious or pricey, but reasonably profitable by benefiting from the sweeping economic activity that engulfed the West. Towns like Emerson in Manitoba and Yorkton, Sheho, Leslie, Wynard and Saltcoats in Saskatchewan were all sites of Bronfman hotels. Soon Port Arthur, Ontario, and then Winnipeg, Manitoba, also had establishments owned by the Bronfmans.

The hotels were a long way from being Waldorf Astorias but they were doing good business in bed, board and bar. The experience, particularly at the bar, would lead to bigger and better things. Having entered the liquor business by accident, the family became intrigued when they discovered that the bar was the most financially rewarding part of their new enterprise.

The introduction of liquor prohibition laws in the United States and the emergence of similar sentiments in Canada, rather than being a threat to their business, became the axis on which the family's fortunes would turn. Bitter philosophical arguments between the "wets" and the "drys" had raged in Canada and the United States for some years. The temperance movement and the related laws were all it took to create a healthy and lucrative bootlegging industry.

While rhetoric raged, laws were passed to satisfy the curious demands of both sides, but were written in such a complex and circuitous fashion that they were often impossible to decipher or enforce – had the authorities held any such intention in the first place. With tacit approval assumed by the obvious lack of enforcement, the demand for alcoholic beverages was freely met, not always by conventional methods.

Potential for profit in liquor trading shone brightly for the Bronfman family, particularly since the glow of most other aspects of the hotel industry was growing dimmer every day. This led members of the family to venture to Montreal where they purchased a liquor distribution business. Before long the family had a transnational business with warehouses and distribution points strung across the country to serve a fast expanding direct customer base and even mail-order demand.

When prohibition restrictions grew stiffer and their mail-order business was temporarily snuffed out, the family hardly missed a beat. So adept had they become at adjusting to the ground shifting beneath them, that they merely switched to dealing in alcoholic beverages for medicinal purposes. The demand for bottled liquor, no matter what form it took, was truly unquenchable with ample room for profit.

While Canadian laws seemed to those entering the business to be somewhat of a deliberate muddle between federal and provincial jurisdictions, the family used the opportunity presented by the confusion to entrench its emerging pivotal position by creating a line of drinking establishments along the Saskatchewan/North Dakota border. This was done to facilitate the flow of their products into the American market. With the increasing enforcement of prohibition laws in the United States restricting the manufacture and bottling of alcoholic products, opportunities loomed large to conduct these activities north of the border. Canada as a source of liquor, with the Bronfman family fast becoming one of the principal suppliers, was ready and willing to meet the insatiable demands emanating from the country's southern neighbour.

To secure their supplies, the Bronfman family developed a process for turning crude alcohol into a palatable drink that could be swallowed and even enjoyed to some degree. From a rough and tumble kind of experimental chemistry which mixed overproof white alcohol with water, a dash of real Scotch for a trace of authenticity and then some burnt sugar caramel colouring to give the right hue to the liquid, they produced wagonloads of liquor for export.

The distilling formula was continually refined to produce more sophisticated and palatable blends. Bottling and labeling were to become yet another exercise for the creative to invent names reminiscent of old, established brands and labels that held buyer appeal. The labels did not mention the unusual distilling and blending techniques. But demand was so great that even if they had, consumers would probably have bought the mixture anyway.

In time, exclusive distribution arrangements were made with a network of characters south of the border and the relationships flourished along with the Bronfman family's profits. The steady flow of liquor across the border aided by *rumrunners*, a charming old-world term loaded with swagger and dash, was actually encouraged by the government in Ottawa as a means of improving the balance of trade between Canada and the United States. Ottawa itself also made a sweet profit from the growth of the industry by charging a validation tax for issuing federal export licenses.

∽

By 1920, however, the dissonance between the Canadian government sanctioning what bordered on being unlawful activities in the United States and the dubious roles of enforcement officers in both countries was coming to a head. A court case alleging illegal trade and bribery hurt the family's reputation and as the years ticked by the associations with some of the more colourful participants in the business began to exact a toll. Only the fact that the Bronfmans had metamorphosed from struggling Russian farm immigrants into a prosperous urban family helped them establish an impressive degree of clout in Ottawa to protect their burgeoning business interests. Some ground could be recovered and problems resolved by using the family's expanding connections, but the whiskey business was becoming more dangerous and challenging.

Bienfait, Saskatchewan, proved to be the site of the next turning point in the family's destiny, but one whose fulcrum still remains a bit of a blurred mystery. Ekiel Bronfman's son-in-law, Paul Matoff, had the unfortunate fate of being murdered in Bienfait in 1922. Whether as a retaliation for some perceived betrayal in the operation of the cross-border liquor business or whether as a result of some liquor-soaked high jinks, the result was the same – he was dead. This placed the family under an unwanted spotlight and once again their business was threatened when their warehouse operations in Saskatchewan were constrained by the authorities.

After they had scaled back their liquor export operations, it did not take long before they found their retrenched business activities relatively mundane and they thirsted for a return to the fast-paced action and opportunities they had previously enjoyed. The family regrouped and decided to operate from a new base in Montreal, where in 1924 they opened a distillery in Ville La Salle, a small town on the outskirts of the city. There they could conduct their liquor export business in a more organized way. Having had to account for their actions a few times before, they now had a much better idea of what was necessary to minimize trouble.

Through canny negotiations, they set up licensing arrangements with distillers in the United Kingdom. These agreements, which first followed an awkward and rocky path, eventually led to a highly profitable and rewarding combination of their company, Distillers Corporation Limited, with Joseph P. Seagram & Sons, an Ontario distiller with an equally intriguing history. Not only was the combined company, known today as The Seagram Company Ltd., soon selling authenticated Scotch and Canadian whiskeys, but it also became the major player in the more organized yet still equally frenzied action of the burgeoning export market.

Around this time another new front was opened beyond the shores of Canada. With a dash of bravery, a healthy dose of ingenuity and careful planning, the family developed the perfect recipe for a new distribution channel hidden behind a tangled web of export intrigue which linked Canada and Cuba in a profitable liquid embrace. When, in 1930, the Canadian government again arbitrarily decided to lower the boom, the family relocated its export operations to St. Pierre and Miquelon, two cool and fog-shrouded islands owned by France just off the coast of Newfoundland.

Hijackings by whiskey pirates, the cross-border flow of liquor and the alleged exchange of smuggled shipments of a variety of goods later led to the creation of a Royal Commission to investigate the liquor business and corruption in the ranks of the Canadian customs department. The Commission's work spread like a winter cold front across Canada, poking, prodding and questioning every shadowy and innocent aspect of the business activities conducted by any and all involved with the industry.

Adding potent fuel to the fire of anti-bootlegging and anti-smuggling sentiment was an underground swell of jealousy and resistance to change in the established pecking order of Canadian society, which soon became part and parcel of the vociferous public outcry against the industry. Even when the family managed to transcend their Canadian legal entanglements and emerged victorious from another nasty court case, it seemed that new travails were soon pounding at their door.

The 1930s brought the Great Depression, unemployment, rootlessness and abject misery, which all combined to put another crimp in the family's liquor business. Although prohibition had officially ended by 1933, smuggling charges and tax problems in the United States beset all industry participants, leading them to scramble for a safe haven. The Canadian political environment was equally unstable with liberals and conservatives jockeying for the high road and using the old wet/dry arguments as ammunition in their struggle to find a foothold which would restore equilibrium and put them firmly in power.

By 1934, the Canadian federal authorities once again had placed the Bronfman liquor operations in their sights as a fat and tantalizing target for a court case based on alleged unpaid customs duties. However, the authorities were unable, no matter how hard they tried, to substantiate their claim and the court case finished with a verdict of "Not guilty".

The process of rebuilding the family business once again began in earnest and with renewed vigour. With their names cleared and the prohibition laws repealed, more formal deals were struck with U.S. distributors, and distilleries were purchased and revamped and new ones were built. As time passed, drinking became a legal and increasingly popular pastime and the profits began to flow like spilled vats of golden whiskey.

The years of rapid expansion of the family's liquor business and continual venturing into new areas occurred while Peter Bronfman was growing up in his family's spacious Westmount home in Montreal, and would have a greater influence on him than the best reader of a crystal ball might have predicted. As his father, Allan Bronfman, and his three uncles laboured together, one brother began to dominate the stage and establish a leading role for himself. Whether through his unstoppable energy, unquestionable business acumen, natural aggression or the irresistible force of his powerful personality, there could be no question that Sam Bronfman was becoming the dominant brother, even though not the senior in age. He was determined to steer the direction of the family ship, which meant that as Seagram grew in size and influence, Sam Bronfman's power and reach grew with it.

His brothers, although they had all contributed to the success of the family business, eventually would capitulate to this force and let their brother Sam assume the role of virtual monarch. All the family members received their due respect from the community in deference to their business success, their personal generosity and roles in community activities, their political influence and the increasing recognition that they were Canadians who ranked on the international scene, but none of the brothers ranked close to Sam.

Time has a way of bringing broad issues to a head. With the brothers getting older and with their children growing up, there came a time when Sam Bronfman, like many dynamic family leaders, decided he had to assert not only his own dominance but that of his direct bloodline, his two sons. He was adamant that only they, of the next generation, should have the opportunity to take the family company into the next century.

Blood may be thicker than water, but in Sam Bronfman's mind, his nephews were not so much blood relations as they were potential competitors for the Seagram crown. He wanted to ensure that their futures were sharply directed elsewhere so that his own sons would have an unchallenged anointment as the next reigning monarchs. For a man like

Sam Bronfman, who had been through so much and repeatedly fought his way to the top, this was nothing more than a minor challenge which he needed to attend to in order to ensure his family's destiny.

Sam Bronfman's sons, Charles and Edgar, and Allan Bronfman's sons, Peter and Edward, had grown up together as close cousins, side by side, but in Sam's vision of the future their adult lives were not about to be lived as business colleagues and partners in the family business. Allan Bronfman had already reconciled himself to playing a scholarly but secondary counterpoint to the feisty and aggressive Sam Bronfman, but he had always hoped that his two sons would have a fair shot at earning a role for themselves in the management of Seagram's working alongside his nephews.

Though he never played football, Sam Bronfman seemed to have no trouble developing his own technique of block and tackle to accomplish his objectives. The Seagram stockholdings owned by Sam and Allan Bronfman had been housed in Seco Limited, a private holding company which the two families owned through Cemp Investments Ltd. and Edper Investments Limited, respectively. They had also set up trusts for each of their children to hold the shares of these two holding companies.

The ownership of Seco Limited, however, was not evenly divided, as Sam Bronfman's family held a two-thirds interest to Allan's one-third. This ensured that Sam Bronfman had the final say as to the who, what, where and how of everything the company did – and that included determining whether or not the heavy doors would slam shut on Allan Bronfman's sons' ambitions to participate in the management of Seagram. This was the block part that could keep Peter and Edward Bronfman at a safe distance.

The tackle came some years later in 1960, when Peter and Edward felt obliged to sell more than half of their Seagram shareholdings to their Uncle Sam's family's holding company. The hammer they sensed hanging threateningly over their heads and which prompted them to sell was their belief, right or wrong, that if they did not accommodate their uncle's wishes, their father could well lose his position as an officer and director of Seagram and see his standing in the Montreal business and social community diminish. They could not bear to expose their father to this risk. With love and courage and perhaps also a little fear, they sold their shares and set out together, first to get their lives in order and later to launch their own business.

While it would take another nine years before severing the last of the ties with Seagram's Montreal head office, the once cozy jostling of an ambitious immigrant family, pulling tightly together for a common cause, was over. The family dynasty had split irrevocably at the top and a new age – with two prominent Bronfman families, not one – would soon dawn. The cousins would continue to retain warm feelings for each other as their business paths diverged and they went their own ways. They would always be ready to advise and help each other, but the co-mingling of resources in jointly-owned business ventures had come to an end for this family of energetic and resilient entrepreneurs.

Chapter Two

A Caring Man

Everyone recognizes the strength of family traits, because we find so much evidence of them in ourselves and in our children, and even in relatives further removed by generations like grandparents and grandchildren. It also seems impossible to escape from the influences of countless family experiences – some dramatic and some mundane – and the lasting impact they tend to have upon the members who make up one's clan. Few can emerge unscathed by shared intimate histories. If, indeed, every person is partly a result of who and what came before, then perhaps family histories are built right into the bones of subsequent generations.

Thus, a mysterious amalgam is usually formed when the collective family experience and the characteristics of parents and grandparents take shape in a new family member. Some novel twists and changes will often occur because the times and environments which have an impact on character will have altered, but still there will invariably be that recognizable something that links a person to his ancestors through his behaviour or his actions.

Ekiel, the Bronfman family patriarch, was an adventurer who had his own vision and drive to succeed. Despite financial hardships he took his neighbours' problems as his own, shared what he had and felt a very strong need to help others around him. His children were raised in a religious household and brought up to honour their heritage. They also witnessed their father's willingness to take carefully calculated risks, tackle one challenge after another and, when necessary, make his own opportunities, all for the betterment of the family.

It is not surprising that the soul-sapping environment of eastern Europe and the freezing, wind-swept Canadian prairies fed the flames of the family's drive and inspiration to discover creative sources of income to provide for themselves and sometimes to adapt like chameleons when the environment demanded it.

The undulating fortunes of the family, through challenging decades and times of opportunity, did not change one consistent characteristic which made itself evident in each generation – the desire to help family as well as others. This characteristic of concern for others has echoed through the family from Ekiel, to his son Allan, and to his grandsons, Peter and Edward, and also through each of the other branches of the family. Once financial security had been put in place, they and other members of the family immersed themselves in helping friends, acquaintances and neighbours do better for themselves.

Starting with Ekiel Bronfman, the family members had faced many adversities including travelling a very long and difficult way, not only from Bessarabia in 1889, but also from the frozen and untilled land they found in Wapella, Saskatchewan. But by the time Peter Bronfman, Ekiel's grandson, was a young man, the challenges of putting a roof over their heads, food on the table and clothes on their backs had been well and truly addressed.

The Bronfman family had survived through ingenuity and perseverance. In fact, they had not only faced adversity but had also learned from it, been able to change course and find other ways to prosper. They had worked very hard, remained together, nurtured a family enterprise and now had most of the comforts of prosperity available to them. Life was very good for the family.

Despite some of the ragged associations that went along with the early years of the liquor business, Peter Bronfman as a young boy was, for the most part, able to live the protected life of a child born with virtually all his wants well taken care of. To a great extent his family had seen to it that he was safely insulated from the radiant heat of accusations and legal actions related to the early days of the family business. However, history is an invisible, inescapable film that somehow manages to descend periodically and cling like a fine mist.

Peter Bronfman, especially during his formative years, probably sensed that invisible mist around him. As an adult his ever-present concern that all his business affairs be conducted in a fair and proper way and his deep desire to help others and improve the world may have been inspired, at least in part, by a yearning to dispel any remaining concern about the family's early business pursuits.

Certainly Peter Bronfman was not one to waste his intelligence, his education or his financial advantages in trivial or frivolous amusements. Even as a young person, he had a serious bent to his nature. He considered the family history and other experiences he had learned about, put them together with what he had seen first-hand and began to develop his own approach to the world, to doing business, to dealing with people and to improving most things to which he applied himself.

While many Canadians are aware of some of his accomplishments in the business sphere, only the most ardent students of his career would be able to estimate their full extent. Over a period of forty years he played a role in the design, construction or financing of more than two hundred major office buildings, shopping centres, hydro-electric power plants, base metal mines, metallurgical facilities, forest product mills and other natural resource projects which contributed meaningfully to the development of the Canadian industrial base.

At the time of Peter Bronfman's death at the end of 1996, the group he founded included six of the top one hundred most profitable Canadian companies, and employed more than 50,000 people. The kind of man who could lead his colleagues to these levels of achievement was not one of singular interest but rather a multi-faceted individual whose passions and intellect encompassed business theory and practice, artistic pursuits, humanitarian interests and wide-ranging community service.

In Peter Bronfman's life – like the life of any caring and productive human being – there were many different and sometimes conflicting influences, pivotal moments and unique experiences which like so many coloured yarns were woven into the fabric of his personality. A meandering detour through some of those characteristics, moments and experiences will paint a background and fill in some important details in understanding who he really was and how he arrived at his unique business philosophy and then applied it and continuously worked to improve it in building a major Canadian enterprise. He was a rare and special individual who walked this earth and left his footprints permanently behind.

Peter Bronfman's father, Allan, was an important role model for him in developing his respect for those less fortunate and his sense of community service. On Ekiel Bronfman's death in 1919, Allan accepted additional responsibilities within the family for furthering its community service in Montreal. By his example of devoting a considerable amount of his time and financial resources to community service, Allan Bronfman passed on to his sons and grandchildren the expectation that they should be of help to others – as a moral obligation as well as a Bronfman family tradition.

It was, therefore, natural for Peter Bronfman to encourage the family tradition of community involvement in most of the businesses with which he was associated. The Montreal Canadiens hockey club, which Edper acquired in 1971, more than any other business provided him with many opportunities to go beyond traditional corporate giving and community needs. He and the club became leading patrons of the Sun Youth Organization, which helped underprivileged children participate in minor league hockey. He also helped establish the Québec Student Inter-Exchange Program, which arranged visits between minor league hockey teams in Québec and other parts of Canada as a way of fostering better relationships and understanding among young Canadians.

After his move to Toronto in 1979, his charitable work evolved even further from his early Montreal roots into a broader Canadian context, particularly in two areas which became of increasing importance to him – the disadvantaged and education. This led him to the United Way of Metropolitan Toronto, where he served as a director and Honorary Chair. Through this association he got to know and admire Gordon Cressy, who introduced him to a wide variety of organizations whose objectives matched his own sense of community service. As a result of these contacts, he became a major benefactor of Jessie's Centre for Teenagers, where he formed a warm friendship with June Callwood, and also helped support a number of other local community agencies in Toronto's inner city, including St. Stephen's Community House and Dixon Hall.

As time passed, he continued to refine his ideas about community pursuits and volunteerism, and his example made a deeply felt impression on countless individuals and organizations. This influence, like a stone dropped in a still pool, spread much further than his immediate sphere because he also persuaded many of his business colleagues to take the plunge and become actively involved in the volunteer sector. The impact of his role would have to be multiplied many times over, if it could be measured at all.

During the early 1980s, he decided to formalize his extensive philanthropic and community activities. Sheila Zittrer, one of his very best friends and a long-time community colleague who had worked closely with him on the boards of a number of philanthropic institutions, including succeeding him as President of the Montreal Jewish General Hospital, agreed to head up this function. Much liked and highly respected by all of Peter Bronfman's colleagues and friends, Sheila Zittrer continued to contribute to the group's affairs until her retirement as a director of Edper Enterprises Ltd. in 1993. Soon after, she recalled his unique approach to philanthropy with these words: "He was never content with just writing a cheque, preferring to make a personal visit to organizations and groups requesting a contribution. I always marvelled at his warm, responsive manner to everyone, regardless of their station in life and to his remarkable understanding and sensitivity to the problems of the disadvantaged."

A saying which he believed in and put into practice was one which was used extensively in advertisements seeking help for the third world during the 1950s and 1960s: "Give a family a fish and you can feed them for a day. Teach a family to fish and they can feed themselves for a lifetime." In his case, it must have fallen on a truly receptive and fertile imagination, for he took it to heart and ultimately it became a kind of bedrock for all he did in the way of helping others. In particular he believed the fishing analogy had a strong application to education in the modern world.

And what if not everyone could attend an ivy league university as a young person right out of a first quality preparatory school? Peter Bronfman's view of education, like his view of friendship, was founded on a broad framework which encompassed everyone from janitors to statesmen. It included training of all types, from university lectures at the highest intellectual levels through classes teaching poor teenage mothers the most basic skills for caring for their children and making themselves employable.

The concept of providing education at the level most suited to helping people improve their own lives and the lives of others around them was what appealed to him. Although he supported an extraordinary variety of national and community organizations, on examination practically all of them included some element of education as part of their service to those who came for help.

Peter Bronfman's growing friendship during the early 1990s with Rob Prichard, President of the University of Toronto and one of the foremost educational administrators in North America, gave him good reason to become better acquainted with the University and to find out how he could play a more meaningful role in furthering its mission. Rob Prichard encouraged him to examine any aspect of the University he chose, high profile or low, research or teaching, arts or science, in order to discover the area which might captivate his interest, and then delve deeply into it. This sweeping suggestion from a man he liked and trusted gave him the opportunity to combine his long-held belief in the essential value of education with his personal inclination to help those at a disadvantage.

Woodsworth College, which had been established by the University of Toronto in 1974 for part-time undergraduate students to ensure they had access to the full range of university services, intrigued him. He was impressed by and deeply sympathetic to Woodsworth's special role as an academic home base for people who needed to juggle work and family responsibilities while completing their university education. Alex Waugh, Woodsworth's Vice-Principal, won Peter Bronfman's admiration and was instrumental in familiarizing him with the unique qualities of the college and its students. He responded with a substantial contribution to Woodsworth's building campaign and in the process became one of the college's leading patrons.

He had appreciated Rob Prichard's energetic outreach to the many communities touched by the University of Toronto, including the business community, and wanted to support these efforts. But his efforts to do more personally were curtailed in 1996 when he learned that, due to the sudden onset of cancer, he only had a few months to live. To carry forward his intentions, his wife, Lynda Hamilton, his senior business colleagues and The Edper Group Foundation came together to make a special contribution to Woodsworth College in his memory. This gift, through various matching programs, generated over $6 million in funding for student aid at Woodsworth College as well as $2 million for a new Chair in studies in economics and international trade. Through these gifts, a scholarship program was established at Woodsworth College in 1997 to provide financial support to over two hundred students annually, a permanent testimony to Peter Bronfman's life-long commitment to helping others help themselves.

Gordon Cressy, formerly Vice-President of Development at the University of Toronto and more recently founder and head of The Learning Partnership and one of Toronto's most devoted community leaders, was particularly impressed with Peter Bronfman's philanthropy and philosophy on life: "Peter sought no personal glory. His joy came from seeing projects in action. At Woodsworth College, he had lunch with four single parents, all women, who were struggling to raise their children, go to university, find a decent job and get off family benefits. Peter took their names and addresses and kept in touch with them. Peter believed in support for those who are down and wanted to get up. This was not about the safety net – it was about the trampoline."

Along the same vein, one of his private pleasures was helping young people get a toehold in the business world. This took on an added significance, especially in the later stages of his career, perhaps because he had derived so much enjoyment from his own work and the friends he had made throughout his business life. Whenever possible he would assist youthful acquaintances, even people he did not know well or had just met casually, in getting an interview or a position in a company so that they could have a taste of business life and launch their own careers. Perhaps because he had never experienced the desperate need for a "break", he was particularly responsive to those who had no advantages, did not have special contacts and could not count on help from friends or parents. Many are the people in various businesses today who got a "leg up" from Peter Bronfman.

Jim Gray, Chairman and one of the founders of Canadian Hunter, a Calgary-based oil and gas company which became an important part of the Edper group, expressed Peter Bronfman's commitment to helping others get established this way: "Peter was always deeply interested in the human aspects of all of the businesses and associations of which he had been part. He was a natural mentor and freely lent a helping hand to countless young individuals as they considered career options and new opportunities."

As his business and work in the broader community developed beyond his initial roots in Montreal, he came to realize that the building of a country, like the building of a business, takes time, courage, strength and teamwork. Years of vision and labour can pass without seeming to make any difference and then, suddenly, one senses that something has changed and a new plateau has been reached. Tedious effort and tiny steps do eventually result in progress and sometimes dictate a new beginning to reach a goal. So, too, the growth of his concept of what it was to be a Canadian evolved.

The somewhat insular life of the close-knit Montreal business community gave him a strong foothold there during his early years. He felt very comfortable in his native city with its cosmopolitan atmosphere, its urban sophistication, its river front, its mountain and its tree-lined streets. Expo '67 was a glorious time for all Canadians but especially for anyone who was interested and actively involved in improving the city. The world was Montreal's oyster, all eyes were focused on the richness of Canada's beautiful, dynamic, multicultural city and, for a brief and exhilarating period, it actually seemed to be the centre of a thriving modern international universe. Commerce, culture and the rapid expansion of the city's reputation would have made it thoroughly understandable had he decided to remain within the boundaries of Montreal – or even Québec and the surrounding region. There would have been more than enough in that burgeoning treasure box of opportunities and delights to keep him profitably employed and challenged.

However, political developments in Québec in the early 1970s started to erase the geographical boundaries for Peter Bronfman when advocates of separation from Canada became more strident. Political strife can be a frightening and cruel eye opener for anyone, even when viewed from a position of relative safety and assumed security. Watching one's familiar and peaceful stomping grounds torn apart by conflicting ideologies is a painful experience and deeply disturbing to those who place a high value on peace and stability. When the conflict came home with explosive impact, quite literally in the form of a bomb tossed into the relative tranquillity of his home, there could no longer be any more pretending that these undercurrents did not exist.

Being advised by provincial security forces that his name was on the FLQ political activists' list of potential kidnapping targets shook his confidence in his ability to protect his family, his business and himself without making a geographical move. The political tensions had become very personal and the trust and assurance needed to foster a positive business environment in Montreal had been shattered. He knew it was only a matter of time before he would need to re-establish his business base elsewhere in order to execute and finance the many projects and plans formulating in his mind.

After making a move to Toronto in 1979, he never lost his interest and deep regard for his native province and eagerly sought out new investments in Québec. This eventually led to the Edper group becoming one of the largest investors in the province during the 1980s and 1990s, when it made major capital commitments in the mining, metallurgical, hydroelectric power and forest product industries, at a time when others were withdrawing their capital.

His deepening sense of being Canadian was further intensified by his growing business activities. The move from Montreal to Toronto quickened the pace of his expanding awareness of being a part of a great country, and strengthened his desire to have a positive impact on its development. With each passing year as the Edper group became stronger and more influential, his personal understanding of his country as a whole and all its many parts intensified and his appreciation of what could be achieved was magnified.

Travel necessitated by business investments, contact with Canadians at so many different levels of society, and time spent in the company of leaders in the arts, sports, business, education and their own immediate communities both large and small, all nourished his sense of being part of something grand, something to be proud of and something which would be of enduring significance to coming generations. He knew Canada was wonderful and respected it for what it was, but he was also convinced that it contained much unrealized potential which could only be revealed if Canadians worked together to release the country's hidden treasures.

He truly believed that he was blessed to be a Canadian and, therefore, among the most fortunate people on earth. Consequently, he felt that it was his duty to play a part to help Canada realize its destiny as a good and peaceful place for families to live productive, healthy lives within a prosperous and relatively stable economy. He had developed a deep appreciation for his country's wild vastness, its multitude of riches hidden under the earth, its sturdy, earnest people, its inherently peaceful nature and its helpful role on the international front. He wanted to see work for those with initiative, safety for the threatened and education widely available to all those who needed or wanted it. And he was thoroughly prepared to do whatever he could to bring about these conditions, since he believed they were necessary steps to achieving widespread tolerance and harmony in the country.

He was determined that any enterprises with which he was associated would help further these objectives, not only by being constantly in tune with society's needs, but also through the dedication of executive time and financial resources to improve the local economy, its non-profit community organizations and national institutions. Barney Finestone, a long-time family friend, captured Peter Bronfman's commitment very well with the following passage taken from a letter written in 1996: "His passion for the promotion and success of Canada was a golden thread that ran through his life, unbroken to the end. He believed deeply in the idea that Canadian companies could be internationally competitive and creators of employment and wealth for its citizens."

Fun and relaxation for Peter Bronfman came with the simpler, quieter pleasures that so many of us take for granted. The formality of corporate life was something from which he sought escape. It is true he disliked wearing tuxedos, or "penguin suits" as he called them, and he avoided wearing jackets and ties whenever possible. Some who did not know him well found it easy to seize upon this kind of example of his unconventionality and quickly labeled it the eccentric behaviour in which only the rich and powerful can safely indulge themselves. How unfortunate that they missed the real motive behind his style of dress in casual pants, sport shirt, sweater and windbreaker. He just wanted to be accepted as a regular person and did not want the barrier of fancy clothes to stand in the way.

Sadly, acceptance almost always stipulates that one must conform to rules of dress and behaviour and stay within certain set boundaries of self-presentation and personal associations. Those who do not adhere to the rules of conformity and those who have their own ideas about what constitutes desirable behaviour, inevitably pay a price. Peter Bronfman did pay that price, but to him it was worth it, just to be himself and to know that the friendships he made and the associations he valued had a deeper and more lasting meaning.

This same strength of character showed itself consistently through the years as he wrestled with conventional business practices and crafted the sets of values by which his business enterprises would run. As he grew older and wiser, he tried harder to conform his actions and behaviour in business, but he always remained true to his personal values.

For all his professional activities in the world of finance and industry, volunteerism and philanthropy, it was Peter Bronfman's strong preference to be unknown. His successes and good deeds, however, slowly became more widely recognized, even though the man himself was meticulous in standing as far away as possible from any credit, attention or thanks that was being given out. He preferred instead to deflect credit to others where he felt it could do the most good. To him, being part of a team and sharing credit and rewards with those around him would encourage all involved to try harder and render the toughest of challenges much easier to tackle.

Chapter Three

A Team Player

Whether the business cycle blew favourable winds as the Edper group started its journey traversing uncharted waters, or whether the larger, sturdier enterprise which it later became was being buffeted by treacherous storms, there was always Peter Bronfman's steadying hand to guide its progress. Under his leadership, the group evolved from an inheritance of about $20 million to an international enterprise comprising six significant Canadian-based companies with many thousands of employees world-wide.

In tracing the Edper group's business history, it is impossible not to notice the consistent presence of Peter Bronfman's caring personality and philosophical approach to life. From the outset, in his business and community endeavours, it was clear that he was a humanist through and through. Whether by instinct, his father's example or as a result of personal experience, he viewed every aspect of the world and all he encountered in it with the gentleness and sensitivity of the humanist's eye. This explains why he tended to regard the corporation as a kind of human organism as well, one which needed clear eyes and sharply attuned ears, a strong heart and a kindly soul all working together in order to function to its fullest potential.

In his mental construction of a living, breathing corporate entity, the eyes and ears represented the means for collecting the knowledge and information that were essential before any decision could be contemplated. The body of the enterprise comprised the men and women who contributed the technical skills, exercised the judgment and had the foresight to keep the business undertaking on track. But what body, however large and sturdy, can ever come up against a worthy and impressive challenge and emerge victorious – or emerge at all for that matter – if it is not possessed of both a strong heart and a kindly soul?

He believed that the heart of the organization, the engine which must keep pumping at all costs and under all conditions, was found in the people who provided the leadership, the courage and the stamina to get things done no matter what the odds might seem to be against achieving success. The irrepressible urge to succeed, to build and to create – this was at the heart of the organization.

The soul, that intangible essence that gives a human being its humanity, in his mind also had a counterpart in the corporate entity. The soul of the company could be found in the very essence of Peter Bronfman himself. The soul was a mystical blend of his most fundamental beliefs in teamwork, the sharing of credit, providing leadership by example, exercising fairness and decency in the conduct of business and an all-encompassing concern for others. It was also the indefinable quality that he brought to everything he did and everyone he touched.

It is, therefore, no wonder that the area of the business which excited him most throughout his career and which secured his unwavering devotion was the development of his business colleagues and staff. He dedicated much of his energy and creative thought to refining the means by which he could attract and retain the best people most suited to his style of operation, then help them operate as a closely knit team, eager to help one another and share credit without regard for self-promotion. For without the eyes, ears, body, heart and soul working together, he knew his corporate dreams would be for naught.

In every entity, from the small Edper corporate office to the Montreal Canadiens hockey club or the Toronto Blue Jays baseball team, he was totally committed to creating an environment in which the athletes and his business colleagues could flourish and perform to the best of their respective abilities.

He was quick to recognize that in the world of sports, a winning team required all players to work together, be proficient in their areas of expertise, physically honed to perform under the most difficult circumstances and mentally strong to withstand the ebb and flow of praise and failure. So too in the business world, he felt strongly that an effective corporate team had to meet the same exacting checklist if the desired financial results were to be achieved.

❧

His commitment to teamwork was in many ways a reflection of his personal modesty about everything he accomplished whether in the business world, the volunteer sector or any other area of his life. Modesty, which he believed was essential to true teamwork, is a rather old-fashioned quality, one which is not often lauded in modern times. He regretted that many people seem to feel it is essential that they receive recognition for every conceivable success they achieve – or even happen upon by accident – and it often seems that no amount of praise is ever sufficient for some individuals.

His profound discomfort at being admired, honoured or praised was very real. Having inherited a position in society and a certain level of comfort to go with it and having had the multiple advantages of good parentage and a fine education, he felt he was undeserving of being singled out for special attention and praise for having done well. It also made him rather suspicious of those who sought public recognition and was an important contributing factor in his unshifting belief in the benefits and rewards of teamwork.

The ability to work together, to share credit and to recognize large and small contributions to any endeavour appealed to him on many levels. It meant that everyone, no matter how meagre their ability or talent, could take pride in making a contribution to a larger effort and know the dignity of having had a role to perform. It meant that people with different skills could also play on the team and be confident that their best efforts also made a difference to the final outcome. And, ultimately, it meant that those with the talents to lead were expected to fulfill their responsibilities by drawing out the best in others, and be quick to acknowledge that whatever the achievement, it could never be theirs alone. In his mind, achievement was never a single-handed success but a collective effort which was to be enjoyed and shared as a group.

He recognized that, if people were to work together as a team, they needed to share common goals and values. In this regard he was a consummate consensus builder because he valued a well-rounded idea and a harmonious team effort above his own personal views. He had a gift for bringing opposing forces together, discovering common ground and then constructing a plan of action based on a firm foundation of understanding.

His innate ability to listen carefully to both sides in difficult and complex situations, combined with his self-deprecating style of questioning, concern, humour and inventiveness usually diffused potentially combustible circumstances. Whether in his business dealings or in his community commitments, individuals who associated with him were often surprised to find themselves working productively beside those whom they had once regarded as an opposing force. Many are the stories of his legendary touch and calming influence when conflicts between individuals or groups threatened to topple a good plan or idea. However, he would never accept recognition or credit for being the skillful diplomat he was, always shrugging his shoulders and saying: "Well, things just sort of came together."

Almost without fail, in any battle or argument, he took the side of the one who did not have the advantage. Maybe this came about from his early experience of being the relative underdog himself in his broader family relationships or maybe it was the natural result of watching his father positioned against a powerful brother. It should therefore be no surprise that he never identified with or took advantage of the "top dog" status that could easily have been his, once he had firmly established his interests in business, sports and a number of other fields.

The philosophy of teamwork and shared credit was as fundamental to his business life and what he looked for in his colleagues as it was to the sporting successes of the Montreal Canadiens during the 1970s and the Toronto Blue Jays during the early 1990s, of which he had been an important part. It provided each of his colleagues and the athletes on these teams with the best of all worlds because it gave them an opportunity to do something well beyond what could ever be possible as individuals, and a chance to use their own talents to the limit. An added bonus, but one not to be ignored, is that this approach happened to be very effective at truncating expansive executive egos, a benefit of which he was well aware.

∽

While the close-knit team atmosphere of the Montreal Canadiens hockey club during that era gave Peter Bronfman ample proof that his belief in team effort could also have many business applications, ownership of the club also contributed to the tide of elements that pulled him and his colleagues out of the confines of the Montreal community and onto a wider stage. The national and international aspects of owning the very best professional ice hockey team in the world, or "the winningest team" as Ken Dryden, the Montreal Canadiens' star goalie and later the general manager of the Toronto Maple Leafs called it, threw Peter Bronfman into the national spotlight and demonstrated vividly for him aspects of being a Canadian that he had not really considered before.

Owning the Montreal Canadiens was not only an important factor in his early business development, but it was also a labour of love. There was no shyness about his strong emotional attachment to the team, both as a total entity and to individual players. He paid close attention to the structure, financing and strategy involved in managing the team, and made time to become well acquainted with the executives and players. He also maintained contact with the players long after they retired from the team, visiting and offering help whenever they or their families encountered serious illness or other difficulties.

Sam Pollock is a perfect example of the depth of his relationships and the way in which his personal life became entwined with the families of those who worked with him. He first met Sam Pollock in 1971, when Edper acquired control of the Montreal Canadiens and, as their acquaintance grew into a relationship of mutual trust and respect, he invited Sam Pollock to take on a broader role in the Edper group. Over the years Sam Pollock's sound business judgment, combined with his talents in communication and sensitive management issues, were invaluable on a number of group corporate boards including Brookfield Properties and Brascan Limited. He also chaired the John Labatt board and became Chairman and Chief Executive of The Toronto Blue Jays Baseball Club.

But the association did not stop there. Sam Pollock's son, Sam Jr., also earned a senior role in the Edper group in his own right through his business skills and personal qualities – no doubt learned to a large extent from his father. Peter Bronfman was proud to have won the loyalty and confidence of Sam Pollock and was especially pleased to have had an opportunity to work closely with his son when he decided to make his career with the Edper group. Sam Pollock Jr. rose rapidly to a senior position in Trilon Financial Corporation and became one of the youngest executives admitted to the group's senior management and financial partnership.

The importance of Peter Bronfman's involvement to the Montreal Canadiens players is captured in a note from Bob Gainey, one of a number of the top-tier hockey players on those championship teams of the 1970s who made a successful transition to become equally accomplished coaches and general managers in the National Hockey League. He wrote: "I remember clearly the informal lunches I had at your home and many of the things we discussed. I appreciated your personal counsel then, but appreciate it even more today!"

Perhaps this was part of the reason why Peter Bronfman was so unusually popular as an owner of the hockey club. As with his commercial businesses, his spirit was in the dressing room and on the ice with the coaches, managers and players, not just locked away in some remote office as a cold-hearted investor. It was also clear to all that he was involved in order to promote the players and the team and not to satisfy his own ego.

From the time he was a boy, no matter where he was, he had followed the fortunes of the Montreal Canadiens, at the arena or on the fuzzy airwaves of his radio. For him, the men who poured their hearts and souls into Canada's national sport were all heroes, though none was ever as big a champion as Jean Béliveau. Although Peter Bronfman and his brother Edward bought the Montreal Canadiens just as Jean Béliveau was about to retire, the close friendship and mutual respect which quickly developed between the two men was a reward he treasured. He recognized that Jean Béliveau was far more than the great hockey player beloved by all Quebeckers. He had transcended provincial boundaries to become a national hero through his sense of fair play, outstanding leadership and sportsmanship, and the fine example he set for all the Canadian youngsters who looked up to him as the embodiment of team spirit at its very best. Jean Béliveau was for Peter Bronfman, who had followed his career with the intensity of the most devoted fan, the perfect example of what team spirit was about – an inspiration in action.

Later, when Jean Béliveau was being enticed to come out of retirement and join the World Hockey League, Peter Bronfman did not want this great hero to be lost to Montreal. He invited Jean Béliveau to join his corporate team as Vice-President of the Canadian Arena Company, the company through which he owned the Montreal Canadiens. Jean Béliveau was to assume the role of mentor to the team's younger players and become a public statesman for worthy causes related to national unity and sport in the community.

For more than twenty-five years, Jean Béliveau has served first as an officer and later as a director of Canadian Arena Company and Brookfield Properties, its successor company. He continues to be a Canadian hero not only to those who witnessed his brilliant hockey career but also to those who have come to know him through business and his tireless and devoted public service.

While in Montreal, his home town and the cradle of the Edper group's business, Peter Bronfman was in familiar territory and could take his time and pace himself carefully in putting his team together. The Montreal corporate office he assembled in the late 1960s and early 1970s was kept quite small by most standards and could best be described as tightly knit, committed and loyal. These qualities were crucial to maintaining his comfort level and confidence in the work of his colleagues because it gave him a rich opportunity to know them as individuals, to assess and value first-hand their personal and professional qualifications and to foster mutual trust and understanding.

No amount of financial success could please or satisfy him if not accompanied by a sense of fairness and camaraderie as well. He needed to be unequivocally certain of the basic human values, not just the business talents, of the people with whom he worked.

A well-defined mission and a sense of purpose were very quickly ingrained in the leading players he selected and grew stronger with every year that ticked past and with every deal that they formulated and consummated together. This sense of purpose was encouraged by Peter Bronfman, all within the strict boundaries of the rules of fair play and observance of the principles and values upon which he aimed to build his business.

He sought colleagues who had a natural aptitude for leading by example. Although he would never have used this phrase to describe his own style of leadership, it is an accurate way of illustrating how he so effectively set the tone within the many corporate concerns he touched. He would also have been the first to chuckle at this compliment and point out that he was far from perfect at anything – and certainly not a business leader to be held up as a shining example of conventional behaviour. The very notion would make him blush, shrug and turn away. But those who were in daily contact with him and who over the years came to understand how he did things, could see that he was never satisfied with the status quo and was constantly elevating the standards he set for himself.

Another key element he sought in selecting his closest colleagues was their ability to operate effectively together when the slogging was tough, budgets were missed and investors had reason to complain. His support and availability to his team never wavered with the company's fortunes, even when mistakes had been made and the success of the enterprise was threatened. No effort was too much and no time too inconvenient for him to give to the business, even though he had capable colleagues only too willing to do much of what had to be done. Working with his team rather than directing it was his style and no doubt contributed greatly to the loyalty of his colleagues.

In the early 1970s, the extraordinarily long hours spent producing the volume and diversity of work and analysis that came out of the group's Montreal office made it a rather self-selecting collection of individuals. As people, they tended to have played team sports in their youth, were disciplined, self-directed and energetic by nature. Stamina, both mental and physical, was high on the list of personal qualities required to withstand the rigours of the corporate pace set by this relatively small team in the Montreal office.

Relationships among individuals in the Montreal office grew deep and strong, partly as a result of the long hours spent together in common purpose, and partly through the important end-of-the-week sessions when they reported on their activities, decisions taken, problems at hand and recommended courses of action. Before each week was wrapped up, efforts were made to achieve a consensus on critical issues and the agenda for the next week's activities. It was very important to him for the corporate office to conduct its business in an open, candid atmosphere based on the absolute trust that everyone would act in the group's and his or her colleagues' best interests.

The experience of moving the Montreal office to Toronto in the late 1970s further cemented the loyalty of his colleagues to him and to one another, for it meant making a group decision which would uproot their families and toss them all into a new business and social environment. This environment would also be somewhat hostile, since before they completed their eventful transfer to Toronto, they had collectively challenged the Toronto business community in the early part of 1979 in a feisty and unexpected way by acquiring control of Brascan Limited, an old and well-established Toronto company. They emerged with a significant prize but were somewhat scathed in the process.

At that time, Montreal's glory days, epitomized by Expo '67, were fading fast and its time in the sun as a centre of Canadian financial power was clearly ticking to an end. Toronto had grabbed and held firmly the reigns of business influence and was not prepared to take lightly any shift in control of one of its leading companies without a fight. To the Bay Street business moguls, the issue was sharp and irritating – how utterly disrespectful it must have seemed for this small, relatively unknown group of upstart Montrealers to challenge the ruling lords of Canadian business power.

The group's saving grace and secret source of strength was, however, also a kind of Achilles' heel. The steel core was to be found in their understated style and modesty both in their corporate and individual endeavours, characteristics which tended to make them appear a little peculiar and thus different from others in the local business world. Conformity is a defence of its own, a kind of camouflage, and they did not have it. In time, this would make them unwittingly vulnerable to attack.

Having won the day in making the move to Toronto, Peter Bronfman was not one to select the regal sophistication of a luxurious suite of offices to which many others would have felt entitled by virtue of their success. Instead, he and his colleagues settled into plain and functional working quarters. The meetings they conducted with outsiders were friendly and straightforward but brief and to the point. It was no wonder that, at the time, the Toronto business community was amused and somewhat unsettled by this little knot of serious business practitioners.

With the winning of Brascan, the Toronto corporate plum, and the subsequent move to that city, a huge multi-layered hierarchical office staff was inherited. Within moments of the first meeting with the Toronto staff of Brascan, the assessment and evaluation had begun and individuals and areas of responsibility were carefully reviewed. Needs were examined and people who were thought to be readily capable of accepting Peter Bronfman's values and who were willing and wanted to come enthusiastically on board were encouraged to stay. It took less than a month after the shift of control and initial introductions to complete the assessments and trim the ranks with sharp and, for the most part, quite accurate scissors.

Adaptability, a positive attitude, a cheerful disposition, surplus energy and excitement about the tasks which lay ahead and a desire to accomplish something meaningful were among the qualities he and his colleagues sought in their new team members – the rest could be learned. It goes without saying that ability was a given – without skills and talent one held absolutely no potential as a member of the team – but attitude and self-discipline figured equally as much in selecting those who would stay and those whose time had come to go.

A shift in loyalty was also expected from each of the members of Brascan who were invited to join the Edper team. There was no doubting that it would take courage and a leap of faith for them to do this, so bitter had been Brascan's defence against Edper in the takeover battle. Peter Bronfman and his colleagues recognized instinctively that, in the end, it would be the ability to slough off the past, to make that leap and embrace shared values and objectives that would bind the newer members to the old, and make the significantly enlarged team that much stronger and capable of meeting the tests which would lie ahead.

The concept of the corporate team as shaped and applied by Peter Bronfman went well beyond just working together to solve a business problem. At a very early stage in the group's development, he encouraged his closest colleagues to practice a partnership approach in the conduct of their day-to-day work. For the partnership to have true meaning, he had come to believe that it also had to entail sharing the financial risks and rewards. This fledgling philosophy was first applied by him in the early 1960s when Austin Beutel and Ned Goodman joined Edper and were provided with opportunities to participate in the gains realized from those investments which they initiated and nurtured.

Much later, in recalling Peter Bronfman's role in building the Edper group, Austin Beutel noted the underlying objective of this partnership approach to building and managing a business: "He was an outstanding Canadian who succeeded in motivating individuals to seek superior levels of performance by sharing responsibilities and ownership."

By the early 1970s, Peter Bronfman had further refined the concept of teamwork and financial partnership, and he expected his closest colleagues to own sizeable shareholdings in key group companies and thereby, as he viewed it, become partners in the full sense of the word. To facilitate this, he helped provide much of the capital to make these purchases, but also expected his colleagues to borrow from banks. He felt that since his senior executives had assumed a measure of financial risk, they would, as part owners, be encouraged to promote their candid views on any issue. He expected, however, that once a decision was made, all team members would support the decision and give themselves fully to helping with its implementation. While every effort was made to achieve full consensus, it was clearly understood that the majority view would prevail.

The partnership approach was quickly introduced to the Edper group's new Brascan colleagues. It started with the use of the same informal reporting procedures which had been so effective in Montreal, including holding weekly management meetings for executives to make brief verbal reports on their activities and future plans. Crucial to the success of these weekly management meetings was the opportunity to ask questions of one another, thereby enhancing the knowledge level of each individual in areas in which they were not directly involved. These meetings were scheduled to last never more than an hour and were not employed as a general forum in which to debate issues or discuss extraneous matters. They were meant to bind the group together and make sure everyone was informed and shared common goals – large or small.

Any corporate executive wishing to know more about a particular activity or to increase his involvement was free to acquire additional information after the weekly management meetings. At the same time, executives were encouraged to focus their efforts and interests on their own areas of responsibility. Day-to-day reporting was generally confined to a need-to-know basis to those executives who carried responsibility for the risk, compliance and technical aspects and to those senior executives who expressed a particular interest in a matter under consideration. The given expectation was that this and everything else would be done on a timely basis.

Each executive in the corporate office was also expected to provide easy access to any other employee by practicing an open-door management style. This openness and sharing of information and business strategies was all very foreign but decidedly refreshing to Edper's new Brascan colleagues.

Since the formative stages of the Edper group's development, its corporate office, which by early 1980 included a number of senior Brascan executives, had been active and responsible for the day-to-day management of certain clearly defined aspects of the group's diversified business operations. Being at the centre of the corporate enterprise was both an exciting and a demanding place for Edper executives to work. Peter Bronfman, in selecting members of the group's corporate office, recognized that the skills required in the corporate office were often quite distinct from those required to manage the daily affairs of many of the group's operating businesses.

Given the breadth and variety of the group's activities and geographic locales, he and his colleagues decided that, if they were to be successful in owning and building their diversified business interests, they would have to create and develop competent, self-sufficient operating management teams within each enterprise. This approach to managing the overall group with a decentralized structure supported by a small corporate office would complement its financing plans. Access to capital and financial flexibility, which was particularly important in the group's early years, would be increased by operating primarily through stand-alone public companies.

Key to making such a decentralized system work in harmony with his corporate vision was the need to formulate, articulate and then communicate the group's business objectives and priorities to each of the operating companies. This task fell to his senior colleagues who participated with him as long-term owners of the group. To minimize the potential for misunderstandings within the group or by other shareholders and analysts, these priorities and the principles which were to govern the relations between the group's corporate office and its operating affiliates were set out in internal business plans and also included in public annual reports prepared by group companies.

෨

In order to expedite the process of openness and participation by all members of the team as it expanded, senior executives were partnered with junior colleagues in a mentoring role. This escalated the junior executives' progress along the learning curve and was also instrumental in broadening their range of skills. Mentoring partnerships shifted according to the needs of the various projects at hand, thereby widening the experience of the younger team members and allowing greater exposure to the more senior executives, who could pass on their knowledge, assess their apprentices' strengths and supplement their weaknesses.

Executives who only knew how to function with large support staffs or wanted to make key decisions, unfettered by the input and review of their colleagues, were weeded out. In line with Peter Bronfman's belief in teamwork and shared decision-making, executives were expected to explain their recommendations to their colleagues and, more importantly, feel unthreatened if those recommendations were challenged and ultimately improved upon when examined and massaged, often by their more junior colleagues. This sharing of views was not allowed to delay the process as urgency remained the order of the day. It took a dynamic combination of confidence and flexibility to adapt to this kind of working environment and to be productive in it. As a result, an important criterion in recruiting new team members, both from Brascan's ranks and from outside the group, was their ability not only to perform as leaders but also to function well as team members.

Peter Bronfman had come to recognize that, if his team approach was to work, given the diverse nature of the businesses the group managed and planned to own, it would become inappropriate and increasingly more difficult to tailor individual compensation packages for his senior business colleagues. Executives would need to work and be rewarded as part of a team, each doing his or her best to add value to the group's various businesses, which in turn would eventually be reflected in the value of the group's shares. Furthermore, the benefits from much of their work would by its nature only accrue over an extended period of time. Brascan's senior executives were accordingly asked to conform their remuneration programs with those used to reward the Edper team and therefore base a large portion of their rewards on the appreciation in the value of the company's shares, which they would receive help in acquiring. Only a small amount of their rewards was to be received in the form of bonus cheques, as they were expected to achieve their performance targets and, if they exceeded them, the results would, in time, be reflected in the price of the shares they held.

Obviously this required executives to have patience, as appreciation in the value of their shareholdings would be a function not only of their own and their colleagues' efforts but also of the vagaries of the economic cycle and the prevailing stock markets. Executives who had a short-term perspective and preferred to be rewarded through cash bonuses based on transitory achievements found it difficult to thrive in this environment.

❧

In adopting the partnership approach to managing the group's affairs, Peter Bronfman recognized that its success would also hinge upon all those involved having a high degree of loyalty to each other and a clear commitment to the group's stated objectives. This would require mutual trust and each partner instinctively acting in the group's best interests, rather than his own, when faced with adversity. They would need to attract and retain those individuals who found it natural to place the group's interests first and who would automatically reach out to help colleagues who experienced difficulties.

With so much importance attached to loyalty and trust, he and his colleagues came to appreciate that loyalty could not be acquired but would have to be earned over time. Trust also is a bond they found needed to be built alongside association and experience. During times of adversity, he would remind them that although these periods were trying and unpleasant, they carried one undeniable redeeming feature – they were invaluable in testing and building a strong team with deep loyalties to each other and to the organization.

He firmly believed that the quality of the people and the diversity of skills they brought to the team would make a difference in how soon and the manner in which he would attain his goals. Therefore, he aimed to make each successive appointment to his team better than the previous one. He also recognized that from time to time it would be important for him and his colleagues to make difficult decisions in order to upgrade the quality of the group's people at every level of the organization for the benefit of all concerned.

Notwithstanding the thought and care which he and his colleagues devoted to assembling their team, during the period of hectic growth in the 1980s they accepted into the group's senior ranks a few individuals who were capable in their own right but found it difficult to be truly committed team players. Fortunately, only a handful of mistakes of this nature were made. Furthermore, the younger members, for their part, excelled during the stressful early 1990s, bonded closely together in defiance of the difficulties they faced and proved to their older colleagues that they were committed team players, ready to take on more senior leadership roles.

When the smoke cleared and the group emerged from the recession of the 1990s, it was no surprise that Peter Bronfman's proudest sense of achievement was that both his long-serving colleagues and the group's younger but now seasoned executives were bound together in spirit as part of the same team, and were committed to leading by example and sharing in the conduct of the group's business.

Ekiel and Minnie Bronfman and their family in Winnipeg, c. 1915

Allan and Lucy Bronfman and their three children, Mona, Peter and Edward, in Montreal, c. 1934

Peter and Edward Bronfman growing up in Westmount, Montreal, c. 1934

Peter Bronfman, second from left, with his brother Edward and friends playing backyard hockey in Montreal, c. 1935

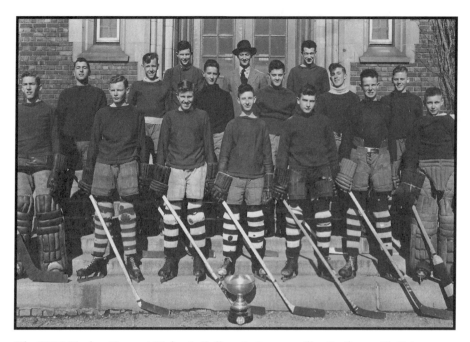

The 1946 Hockey Team at Bishop's College in Lennoxville, Québec, with Peter Bronfman, the team captain, in the centre of the front row

Peter Bronfman, second from left, graduating from Yale University in 1952 with three close friends, Charles Cane, Henry Sprague and Peter Murphy

The Montreal Forum, famed home of the Montreal Canadiens until the 1990s

Management of the Montreal Canadiens Hockey Club in 1975 with Marcel Laurin, former Mayor of St. Laurent. From the left: Jean Béliveau, Sam Pollock, Marcel Laurin, Irving Grundman, Toe Blake and Peter Bronfman

Management and players of the Montreal Canadiens Hockey Club, 1975–1976 Stanley Cup champions, with Peter Bronfman in the centre of the top row

Sam Pollock, Peter Bronfman and Scotty Bowman with the 1975–1976 Stanley Cup won by the Montreal Canadiens hockey team

Sixteen years later, Peter Bronfman with the first of two successive Baseball World Series Trophies won by the Toronto Blue Jays in 1992 and 1993

Peter and Edward Bronfman with Sheila Zittrer at the opening of a new wing at the Montreal Jewish General Hospital in 1989

Phillip Siller, June Callwood and Peter Bronfman at the 1993 "Mortgage Burning" at Jessie's Centre for Teenagers in Toronto

Book Two

Building the Business

These chapters follow the path of the two young brothers, Peter and Edward Bronfman, as they strike out to forge their own business. Starting in 1954, they invest in a variety of small, private businesses before making some daring forays into the world of public companies and high finance. As Peter Bronfman gradually develops what becomes his lifelong business philosophy of teamwork and shared values, he emerges as the leader of a young team which prepares itself carefully before making a bold move to acquire the blue-chip investment company, Brascan Limited, in 1979. This event stands out as a major step for the Edper group because it signals its entry into the fast-paced and unforgiving world of hostile takeovers. The Edper group quickly merges its corporate office with a select group of Brascan executives and together they become a cohesive team which moves on to bigger and more demanding ventures.

Chapter Four

Early Business Years

What makes a man, born to wealth and privilege, free of the necessity to get his hands soiled in the commotion of earning a living, decide to take action, to enter the stream of business life and to create and build? Peter Bronfman could have lived his life comfortably without the ups and downs of success and failure in business and without the challenges of having the viability of his decisions publicly tested. He could have elected to have a perfectly smooth and pleasant life above the fray, thereby avoiding the often harsh comments of critics, many of whom for any number of reasons would have their own axes to grind. This would not be his choice or destiny.

It is not unreasonable to assume that a number of his values, be they satisfaction from hard work, commitment to teamwork or the drive to improve, were learned not only from his family and friends, but also from the household help with whom he spent part of his time while growing up. These practical values and ideas about life, combined with his desire to prove his own worth, held great potential for an intelligent young man with some financial means at his disposal.

When he became convinced that he and his older brother would have to make their own ways in order to preserve their father's position in Seagram, he was at first deeply shaken. But he soon realized he had to face reality and construct a plan which would let him and his family hold their heads high. Love for one's father and the desire to protect him from embarrassment or reduced circumstances can be a powerful motivator for a son or daughter, and in this case Peter Bronfman was no exception.

During his formative years, there were times when he had felt somewhat remote from his parents, and from his father in particular. But he grew to appreciate that this was attributable to the demands placed on his father's time by his responsibilities at Seagram. He had come to feel a tenderness toward his father and would have done everything in his power to protect him and safeguard his dignity. If that meant finding a way to create a respectable business life outside of Seagram, then he would accept the challenge – no matter how limited his training or how tentative his taste for such a bold move.

Though young, being only twenty-five and relatively unprepared for an independent business career, he did have a compatible business partner in his brother Edward, a reasonable nest egg with which to begin, an agile intelligence which would help him learn quickly and the kind of personal modesty which would allow him to seek advice without feeling foolish about it. He was never a boastful know-all who thought he could single-handedly make brilliant business manoeuvres. He was precisely the opposite – cautious and ever eager to learn from those he felt were more knowledgeable. Fortunately his eagerness to trust others was tempered by an almost instinctive kind of self-protection from those who would try to take advantage of him. He was not without fault, but over the years he proved he had the necessary qualities to prevent him from making many bad choices in building his team and selecting his advisers.

His first investment adviser and later a full-time business colleague was Picton Davies, who joined him and his brother Edward in the management of Edper Investments Limited in 1957. Edper had been formed in 1954 to hold the interests of Allan Bronfman's three children in Seco Limited, the single-purpose investment company which owned the shares of Seagram for their family as well as their Uncle Sam's family. Picton Davies set the wheels in motion and helped carry Edper forward for nearly five years until he was succeeded in 1962 by Austin Beutel and Ned Goodman.

A notable early investment initiated during this period was the development of the Peel Centre office building in Montreal in 1957, where the Edper group would maintain its corporate headquarters until it moved its head office to Toronto twenty-two years later, in 1979. The Peel Centre was the first building in the city to include automatic elevators, air conditioning and recessed lighting. It was to be the start of a remarkable career focused on building and financing ever larger and more demanding structures – office buildings, shopping centres, hotels, apartments, hydro-electric generating stations, mines, metallurgical plants and paper mills.

Peter Bronfman's business career, however, really only gained momentum after the family had unwound the tangled umbilical cord which bound their remaining shareholdings in Seagram with those of his cousins and prevented him from gaining access to his inheritance. His Uncle Sam's long reach and perhaps careful foresight had ensured that the Seagram shareholdings to be inherited by Peter, his brother Edward and their sister, Mildred Mona, were tightly braided together with his own family's shares of Seagram in Seco Limited. As if this were not sufficient, Edper Investments Limited, the company which held the family's one-third interest in Seco Limited, was controlled by three separate trusts set up for the benefit of Allan Bronfman's three children. These trusts in turn were governed by a number of lifetime trustee appointments with strong allegiances to Sam Bronfman.

By 1960, Peter Bronfman and his brother Edward felt it was necessary to accede to their Uncle Sam's wishes and sell more than half of their family's interest in Seagram to him. Their Uncle Sam was definitely intent on securing absolute and undisputed control of Seagram and it was equally obvious he would be unwavering in this quest.

A small victory achieved by Peter Bronfman was the release of the remaining portion of his family's Seagram shareholdings from the clutches of Seco Limited so that his own, his brother's and his sister's trusts could have greater freedom in the future to deal with the shares and any dividends paid on them. This was clearly one of the defining moments in the early development of Edper, as the severing of the family's relationships with Seco Limited enabled Peter and Edward to use the dividends they then started to receive to build their own business.

～

Edper's business activities in the 1960s initially centred on accumulating a diversified portfolio of commercial and recreational real estate assets through joint ventures with more experienced partners and the acquisition of a variety of minority shareholdings in a number of relatively small private industrial and financial companies. These early investments included Apex Press, Bellevue Photo, Design Precision Castings, Halco Leasing, Investo-Plan, Laurentian Lanes, McGregor Pine Estates, Natofin, Regent Packaging and Westchester Estates. In retrospect, there was little strategic rationale for each investment and the diversity of the portfolio other than providing an apprenticeship or sampling of areas to be explored but in small doses, never too risky and never sufficiently adventurous to endanger the stability of the inheritance.

Most of the leads for the early investments came from Herb Siblin and Marvin Goldsmith, two of the senior part-ners in a medium-sized Montreal accounting firm. These relationships, drawn largely from the firm's audit clients, continued for many years and in most cases evolved into close personal friendships. Another source of business leads was Barney Finestone, the co-founder and owner of an insurance brokerage firm who, in addition to attending to a variety of Edper's insurance needs, provided business and personal advice to Peter Bronfman over the years.

In 1966, Austin Beutel and Ned Goodman, who had helped guide Edper's investment activities since 1962, decided to form their own business, which eventually became one of Canada's most successful and highly respected investment counselling firms. Their departure was viewed by Peter Bronfman as a major setback, and once again he was in search of skilled colleagues to help him with the many investment plans forming in his mind.

In 1967, Neil Baker, a young man from Winnipeg with a background in investment banking, joined Edper to help identify and evaluate new business opportunities and to spearhead the trimming and redirection of the portfolio of investments which had been assembled over the previous thirteen years. He was expected to introduce a more disciplined approach to exploring new opportunities and to managing the existing investment portfolio. Peter Bronfman had recognized that many of these investments, because of their early stage of development, would require additional funds to protect Edper's initial outlay. Since the majority shareholders in these ventures did not have the personal financial wherewithal to provide the funding, the burden would fall on Edper. A total restructuring of the holdings would be required to provide the impetus and form for future investments if the portfolio was to have a more stable and profitable base.

By the spring of 1968 Neil Baker, who had been joined by Paul Lowenstein and Lenny Spilfogel, presented a new business plan which involved two significant restructurings. First, most of Edper's commercial real estate properties were to be exchanged for a 60% interest in Great West Saddlery

Limited, a public company which was listed on The Toronto Stock Exchange. Second, Edper exchanged its recreational real estate properties for a 20% interest in Marigot Investments Limited, the predecessor of Mico Enterprises and Hees International.

The business plan to fine tune the other investments in Edper's diverse portfolio called for the sale of the shares held in the small industrial and financial companies. This had to be done over a longer stretch of time and could not be completed independently because it required the co-operation of Edper's partners who, in most cases in addition to having become good friends, were the founders and remained the majority shareholders of these ventures.

The purpose of the plan was two-fold: to improve investment returns and to reach agreement with Edper's partners to achieve greater liquidity for each investment – so that Edper at least had the option of withdrawing from underperforming investments. At the same time, by establishing Great West Saddlery and Marigot as viable publicly listed companies, their shares would be available for use as collateral for borrowings should it be decided to embark on a more ambitious programme involving fewer but much larger investments.

Great West Saddlery, which had had a checkered history for a number of years and was essentially a shell company, soon became a high-flying stock on The Toronto Stock

Exchange. During the course of twelve months in 1968, it experienced a twenty-fold increase in the price of its shares from approximately $1.00 to more than $20.00. The alchemy which transformed the public's perception of Great West Saddlery and gave it such value was the sense that the company enjoyed broad Bronfman family sponsorship and would prosper from investments recently made in four technology companies. These technology investments consisted of controlling interests in a number of unrelated computer services companies and an investment in Dr. Gerald Bull's Space Research Corporation. The lure of technological promise had been irresistible to a hopeful public.

Great West Saddlery also had an agreement in principle to acquire the commercial real estate holdings of Edper and Sam Hashman. At the time, Sam Hashman was a successful property developer from Calgary, who operated principally in western Canada and had been the development partner in three of Edper's commercial properties. The cord which tied the portfolio together and Peter Bronfman to his first business interest – the development of prime commercial real estate – was very strong, even at this early stage, and would remain unbroken throughout his business career.

The dizzying and rapid escalation in Great West Saddlery's stock price swept Neil Baker and Paul Lowenstein into further action. They hatched a bold plan in January 1969 to make a major investment in Winnipeg-based Great-West Life Assurance Company by offering to exchange Great West Saddlery shares for shares of Great-West Life. By any assessment, this was an extremely audacious act and one which provoked widespread controversy and sparked intense resistance not only from Great-West Life's management but also from the well-entrenched Winnipeg business community.

Despite the risks involved and the opposition generated, the new team at Edper was eager to take a big bite. The first step entailed Great West Saddlery acquiring a 20% shareholding in Great-West Life through open market purchases. This was executed with the deft assistance of Jimmy Connacher, who at the time was employed by Wood Gundy. In order to raise the funds required to pay for these purchases, Neil Baker and Paul Lowenstein flew to six cities in the United States in an attempt to persuade a number of mutual fund managers to subscribe for Great West Saddlery treasury shares.

The intensity of their efforts was less than convincing to the skeptical money managers, who were not impressed by the fact that commitments had been made to buy Great-West Life shares without first having put in place the necessary financing. When these efforts failed, their next step was to seek bridge financing from the Bank of Montreal, Edper's principal banker at the time. Unbeknownst to Peter Bronfman, his Uncle Sam had become increasingly disconcerted about the potential impact his nephews' aggressive investment activities could have on Seagram, and he decided to swing his own weight into the battle. He interceded with the Bank of Montreal and effectively clipped his nephews' wings by cutting off Edper's traditional sources of funding. With the primary and secondary sources of funding dried up, the ripe deal withered – and Edper was left dangling without money and with only a few days left before the Great-West Life shares would be delivered and payment expected.

A sense of urgency and indignant drive pushed the Edper team to redefine its plan. Peter Bronfman flew to Toronto to pay a call on Allen Lambert, then Chairman of the Toronto-Dominion Bank. It was a portentous move. Allen Lambert, sensing the abject injustice of the joint strength of the Bank of Montreal and Sam Bronfman and swayed by Peter Bronfman's recognition of the mistakes made and deep desire to succeed in his own business endeavours, arranged for the necessary bridge financing to complete the share purchase. Peter Bronfman never forgot Allen Lambert's accommodation, his thoughtful advice and the understanding he had extended. Fourteen years later and exactly one day after Allen Lambert retired from the bank, Peter Bronfman and his colleagues approached him for a second time and asked him to join the Edper group as one of its most senior advisers.

During those hectic few days of 1969, however, it seemed that every step forward was followed by another step back. Many of his personal advisers, for whatever their reasons – including possibly their genuine desire to protect him from excessive attention and criticism – kept urging him and his colleagues to withdraw the takeover offer and sell the Great-West Life shares which Great West Saddlery had acquired.

As yet without the experience and demonstrated success to bolster his confidence, he capitulated to the urging of his advisers and within a few weeks the 20% shareholding in Great-West Life was sold to Paul Desmarais for a small gain. Today that shareholding is the cornerstone of Paul Desmarais' Power Corporation and his family's considerable fortune. Although not exactly pleasing for the local Winnipeg business community at the time, they found Paul Desmarais' purchase of additional Great-West Life shares slightly more palatable since it was made through Investors Group – a Winnipeg-based concern. Twenty-eight years later the Edper group would sell a control block of yet another life insurance company, this time to Paul Desmarais' two sons. This occurred in the fall of 1997, when Great-West Life purchased London Insurance Group for nearly $3 billion with Edper's Trilon Financial Corporation pocketing a tidy $1.6 billion in proceeds and a $900 million gain.

Perhaps because it appeared to institutional investors that Edper had lost its nerve in retreating from the Great-West Life venture, the shares of Great West Saddlery declined precipitously in value on The Toronto Stock Exchange during 1970. The inevitable post-mortem led to the departure of Neil Baker in the fall of 1970. He quickly found a new career by acquiring and then building Winnipeg Supply and Fuel in partnership with Hambros Bank into a very profitable undertaking. Later, and after extracting a respectable profit from that venture, he joined Jimmy Connacher as a partner in Gordon Securities Limited, where over the course of the next twenty years they applied their talents to a variety of innovative business and financing endeavours. Many of these involved the Edper group and contributed significantly to its development.

Paul Lowenstein also departed from Edper and went on to form Kauser, Lowenstein and Meade, a successful venture capital and investment advisory company. This company later split into Canadian Corporate Funding Limited, which Paul Lowenstein continues to own and operate, and the Altamira Mutual Fund group, which was headed by his partner Ron Meade until 1997.

Lenny Spilfogel remained associated with Peter Bronfman until the early 1990s, confining his activities to managing a securities portfolio and advising on special investment situations largely emanating from a broad range of contacts he maintained in the United States. At a very early age he had become a successful stock and commodity market player making a good living trading actively for his own account and a few clients, including Edper.

The shifting balance of personnel in the Edper office bothered Peter Bronfman and caused him to address some fundamental questions of how he wanted his organization to be structured and staffed in the future. He was acutely aware that he would still have to accept a certain level of experimentation in order to achieve his long-held objective of a close, effective, organic unit of talented people, working as a team and committed to shared long-term goals. But he was determined to achieve a more careful and precise calibration of talents. Above all, he wanted long-term stability among his colleagues in order that momentum and progress could be achieved without repeated setbacks. His years of tentative exploration had not been wasted and, having learned some valuable lessons, he felt he had prepared himself and was ready to put his ideas about teamwork, loyalty and trust on the line to be tested.

The departure of Neil Baker in 1970 left Peter Bronfman with two younger colleagues, Jack Cockwell and Tim Price, responsible for continuing the implementation of the 1968 business plan. Notwithstanding the Great-West Life near-fiasco, this plan was essentially sound and had Peter Bronfman's full endorsement. Jack Cockwell had first become involved with Edper in June of 1968, when he led a consulting team from Touche Ross to assist Edper in preparing its commercial property assets for their planned transfer to Great West Saddlery. He joined Edper early in January 1969 on a full-time basis in the midst of Great West Saddlery's attempted takeover of Great-West Life, and was immediately thrust into the middle of the fray. As the only surviving member of this initiative, he was left for a while with sole responsibility for tending Edper's financial affairs.

Tim Price, who had also completed his professional training with Touche Ross, joined Edper a year later and took on the task of continuing the restructuring of the group's diversified investment portfolio. He had the additional responsibility of overseeing the trading operations of Geo. W. Bennett Bryson & Co. Ltd., a one hundred year old subsidiary of Marigot Investments, which eventually required a two-year stint at the company's headquarters in Antigua.

David Kerr, who had worked with Touche Ross in Canada and Australia, joined Edper in 1971 and became the third member of the team which Peter Bronfman would later fondly refer to as his "triumvirate of talent" committed to helping him in the pursuit of his business goals. David Kerr's contribution to the team and commitment to its values neatly blended with the other members of Peter Bronfman's new management group. All three had been individually recruited into Touche Ross by Don Wells, who remained a mentor and close friend long after they left the firm to join the Edper group. Touche Ross later merged with Deloitte, Haskins to become Deloitte & Touche, a leading international accounting firm, which has provided a high level of service to the Edper group for more than thirty years.

These three young accountants were to develop a lifetime loyalty to Peter Bronfman and to each other, which would be unshaken over the years and throughout many trials and external challenges. Their loyalty and unswerving dedication to the group's objectives would, in time, give him the confidence to challenge conventional business wisdom, to strike an independent plan and ultimately to carry it out despite resistance from outside the ranks. Only a minimum of turnover would henceforth take place among Peter Bronfman's closest colleagues.

Edper entered the 1970s having made a major appearance, albeit a very short one, on a larger stage. Although Peter Bronfman had been bruised, he by no means felt defeated. To the contrary, he had learned a number of valuable lessons and, though anxious to succeed in a larger arena, he would bide his time and prepare himself and his new team carefully to face the hurdles and battles which were certain to lie ahead. With three promising members of his team in place, he had a much clearer view of what he could accomplish and what he should expect from them. However, before embarking on the ambitious plans he had in mind, he intended first to carefully challenge his colleagues and watch them operate under pressure by exposing them to ever more demanding situations.

Chapter Five

The Transition Period

The early 1970s marked the end of a highly speculative investment era in North American financial markets. The crest of optimism and enthusiasm which pervaded Canada had built to a national crescendo by Expo '67, but all too soon Canada's Centennial celebrations had run their exultant course, and within two years the positive mood had largely disappeared. The waves of never-ending economic promise had spent themselves, and with them money and confidence had dissipated.

Aggressive market investors incurred substantial financial losses, and the mutual fund industry collapsed in part due to widespread governance and investment abuses. In the process, Peter Bronfman and his new colleagues learned a number of valuable lessons. One such lesson emerged when Tim Price had to wind up Edper's minority investment in a mutual fund distribution and investment management company. From this task, it became abundantly clear that in a major market correction the value of illiquid shareholdings of tightly-owned junior companies could shrink in very short order to a fraction of their former price.

Edper's net worth, which had grown steadily from about $20 million in 1954 to nearly $50 million in 1969, did not escape the rapid declines in investment values. However, there were even more pressing problems. By 1970 the immediate management challenge was to re-establish a degree of influence over the affairs of Great West Saddlery and Marigot Investments.

Great West Saddlery had changed its name to Great West International Equities Ltd. and moved its headquarters to Calgary to focus on real estate development, operating under the direction of Sam Hashman, Harold Milavsky and Ed Sardachuk. The difficulties which had arisen from the aborted Great-West Life takeover attempt and the subsequent restructuring of this company were finally resolved in 1971 when Great West International was merged into Trizec Corporation, with Edper emerging as the second-largest shareholder, owning 10% of the combined company. Trizec Corporation was one of the largest public real estate companies in Canada and the developer of two pre-eminent buildings of the 1960s – Place Ville Marie in Montreal and the Yorkdale Shopping Centre in Toronto.

Marigot Investments was a more difficult management challenge for the new Edper team, partly because Ken Patrick, the company's wily founder and chief executive, insisted on limiting Edper's board representation. Furthermore, Ken Patrick was wedded to a risky financial course in expanding Marigot's business, a track which went firmly against Peter

Bronfman's more cautious instincts. In response to a highly dilutive equity issue which was discreetly planned and placed by Ken Patrick with his friends, the Edper team worked closely with the company's institutional shareholders and eventually managed to persuade Marigot's directors to make a rights offering on similar terms to the company's other shareholders. By purchasing rights in the over-the-counter market, Edper was able to subscribe for sufficient shares during 1971 to provide it with effective board control of Marigot. It then took steps to make a number of key management changes.

At the time, Marigot operated on four Caribbean islands, where it developed land and owned a variety of wholesale and retail businesses. It also held the ski hills and other recreational holdings previously owned by Edper and two heavily indebted and unprofitable resort hotels in the Laurentian Mountains north of Montreal. The approach taken to restore the company's financial health became the model for future corporate restructurings undertaken by the group. Marigot was renamed Mico Enterprises in 1972 and reported increased earnings in each of the next eight years through to 1980, when it was merged into Hees International.

Nearly two years had passed since the attempted takeover of Great-West Life, and Peter Bronfman's new team had been busy attending to Edper's immediate needs. Edper's finances and business affairs were once again in solid shape and Peter Bronfman was feeling good about the loyalty and trust building between him and his new colleagues. He had come to feel that he was ready to make another significant move. This occurred at the end of 1971 with the purchase of a 58% controlling interest in the Canadian Arena Company, the owner of the Montreal Canadiens hockey club and the historic Montreal Forum. Edper's $20 million investment was made with two partners – The Bank of Nova Scotia and Baton Broadcasting Incorporated, which was then led by John Bassett Sr.

At Peter Bronfman's request, Sam Pollock, who was the General Manager of the Montreal Canadiens at the time, enlarged his responsibilities. Jacques Courtois accepted the Presidency of the hockey club and Irving Grundman, Edper's partner in its Laurentian Lanes joint venture, was assigned responsibility for increasing the revenues generated by the Montreal Forum's concert and other entertainment activities. The investment in Canadian Arena would prove to be an important milestone in the evolution of Edper and was destined to absorb a great deal of Peter Bronfman's interest and attention over the next few years.

In order to keep close tabs on the performance of Canadian Arena, which remained a publicly listed company, David Kerr assumed responsibility for its financial affairs, partly because of his active interest in hockey and his intuitive feel for the business. Sam Pollock, whose role continued to increase following Edper's investment in Canadian Arena, recognized David Kerr's ability to execute difficult assignments efficiently and quickly involved him in other areas of the company's operations.

Largely through the ingenuity, business judgement and dogged negotiating talents of Sam Pollock, Canadian Arena went on to produce excellent financial results for its shareholders. The Montreal Canadiens hockey team was equally successful on the ice, making history by winning four Stanley Cups over the next seven years and a fifth Stanley Cup in the season Edper sold its interest in the team. The Montreal Forum also reached new heights by broadening its operations to include a number of key events at the 1976 Summer Olympics and a variety of non-sporting events, which significantly expanded its revenue base and the value of the building itself as a versatile entertainment centre.

One hitch in the Canadian Arena success story did occur, however, and came as a surprise to all concerned. Advisers to Zöe Sheckman, Peter Bronfman's niece and the sole beneficiary under the Mildred Mona Bronfman Trust (one of the three trusts which owned Edper at the time), became concerned when Edper's remaining shareholdings in Seagram were sold in 1972 to pay down the debt incurred to acquire the investment in Canadian Arena and later to buy Baton Broadcasting's and The Bank of Nova Scotia's investments in the company. Zöe Sheckman's advisers counselled her to press for the withdrawal of the capital she had invested in Edper.

Key to the actions that followed was Peter Bronfman's concern that the wishes of the Mildred Mona Bronfman Trust be accommodated. He believed that it was essential to stabilize the ownership of Edper and satisfy the request of his niece before engaging in any further major business endeavours. The amount eventually settled upon with his niece's representatives was $25 million, which was in excess of her proportionate share of Edper's net assets. Even though a portion was payable over twenty years, this capital withdrawal placed a heavy burden on Edper. Given the group's other business needs and rising ambitions, this required a rethinking of how the group would finance itself in the future.

Following the purchase of the shareholdings of the Mildred Mona Bronfman Trust in 1973, Edper became equally owned by the trusts of Peter and Edward Bronfman – even though Peter Bronfman gave thought to and had justification for requesting a change in ownership to reflect his greater involvement and contribution to the business. The equity as well as the voting shares of Edper remained equally owned until 1979, at which time Edward Bronfman sought downside protection on the value of his family's shareholdings. Edward Bronfman had become an interested but less active participant in Edper's business activities and was concerned about the group's expansion plans related to the acquisition of Brascan Limited. In making this major accommodation to his brother, Peter Bronfman left the 50/50 equity sharing relationship intact, but received the right to purchase a few extra voting shares, thereby providing himself with a 50.1% voting interest and the necessary freedom to determine the future destiny of the Edper group.

Except for the investment in the Canadian Arena Company, Peter Bronfman wanted to bide his time during the early 1970s and pay down a good portion of the debt incurred to acquire the shareholdings of his sister's trust in Edper. He also sought to test his team a little more before embarking on another large investment initiative. This was partly because he was determined to get it right the next time he made a major move, and partly because he was thoroughly enjoying his direct and active involvement in the affairs of the Montreal Canadiens hockey club.

To evaluate the abilities of his team more intensively, he decided to give Jack Cockwell, Tim Price and David Kerr a relatively free hand in realizing value from Edper's investments in the private industrial and financial companies accumulated in the early 1960s. The collection of private companies was becoming desperately in need of financing and more intense management attention.

Peter Bronfman knew that his triumvirate would need to be constantly challenged to keep them interested and learning. Thus, he also entrusted them with expanding and broadening Mico Enterprises' activities on the understanding that they would maintain a low profile and work within the company's limited financial resources. He challenged his three colleagues to create a large, profitable merchant bank out of this collection of assets, subject only to his retaining a first call on their services to deal with Edper's two much larger investments in Canadian Arena Company and later Trizec Corporation. It was expected that these latter responsibilities would occupy less than 25% of their time, with the remainder being devoted to the business affairs of Mico Enterprises and the building of its earnings and capital base.

This arrangement suited the business and intellectual needs of all parties and became the forerunner to the more formal financial partnership which later evolved between him and the three executives. In order to acquire a meaningful shareholding in Mico Enterprises and participate with full risk as financial partners, the three executives along with Jack Cockwell's brother, Ian, borrowed $2.4 million from the Bank of Montreal to subscribe for shares of Mico Enterprises as part of a public rights offering completed in 1974. Ian Cockwell was employed at that time by an international retailing and investment group and, with its consent, he began to assist the others in expediting the recovery of capital from Mico Enterprises' Canadian real estate ventures.

The loans provided to the four individuals by the Bank of Montreal were arranged by Michael Burke, who handled their personal banking needs for the next ten years, first in Montreal and later in Toronto when he moved there to run the bank's main branch. Michael Burke was a strong believer in the group's ability to achieve its long-range plans and became a valued financial counsellor to a number of Edper executives over the years.

The shares issued by Mico Enterprises had warrants attached which entitled the four individuals to increase their ownership of Mico Enterprises after three years. In this and other ways, Peter Bronfman expected the executives to expand their ownership of Edper's existing and future merchant banking activities to 25% over time. In return for this opportunity, they were asked to make a long-term commitment to Edper and, in any event, provide at least two years' notice to him before selling their shares of

Mico Enterprises or giving consideration to leaving the Edper group.

These same ownership objectives and responsibilities also applied to Hees International, which had been spun out of Great West Saddlery in 1968 and maintained as a small company listed on The Toronto Stock Exchange with a market capitalization of approximately $1 million. Hees was subsequently restructured by selling its subsidiary, Design Precision Castings, to Alfred Holland, a well-known Toronto venture capitalist and successful stock market investor. The proceeds were used to make various investments, including the acquisition in 1971 of Edper's 50.1% interest in Halco Leasing, an automobile leasing company. This company was 47% owned by Humphrey Kassie, one of the group's most considerate and likeable investment partners. Even though he eventually acquired full ownership of Halco Leasing, he continued to be a trusted friend and a person Peter Bronfman particularly enjoyed working with on community activities.

One of Mico Enterprises' early merchant banking investments involved the purchase during the 1970s of a 25% shareholding in Boyd Stott McDonald, a prominent venture capital company headquartered in Montreal, which provided an opportunity to gain invaluable experience in dealing with institutional investors. The relationship with Michael Boyd led to Mico Enterprises, in a joint venture with Boyd Stott McDonald, acquiring a controlling interest in Westmount Life Insurance Company in 1974.

Michael Boyd also contributed significantly to the development of the group's fair sharing approach to its business dealings with partners, a philosophy which neatly fitted with Peter Bronfman's own views on how business should be conducted. Periodically relationships would be assessed and, on the conclusion of a series of transactions, the relative contribution and rewards of the various parties would be re-examined and adjusted accordingly. As well, notwithstanding the terms of the formal business agreements, adjustments were often voluntarily made or taken into account in future dealings with a partner. This approach required all parties involved to have a long-term outlook on their business relationships and a refined sense of trust and commitment to these relationships.

It was also during this stage of Edper's development that Peter Bronfman firmed up the basis of his relationship with his closest business colleagues. He continued to encourage them to acquire additional shareholdings in group companies and discouraged them from holding outside investments because he had seen how this had distracted the attention and diluted the commitment of some of his previous colleagues. He firmly believed that nothing focused attention quite like putting all one's eggs in a single basket, and this concentration and commitment were essential to him if the ambitious goals he was beginning to formulate for Edper were to be realized.

The genesis of the idea of shared ownership and singular commitment lay in the departure of previous executives to start their own businesses, particularly when Austin Beutel left in 1966. Even though a number of fairly action-packed years had passed and many successes had been chalked up, Peter Bronfman had still not forgotten his inability to retain the services of Austin Beutel, whom he considered to have exceptional investment talents and continued to value as a trusted and respected friend. Austin's departure had left a lasting impression and had made Peter Bronfman determined to achieve management stability and the long-term commitment of talented people by drawing them into the business in a very tangible way.

He definitely did not want to lose good people again and as a first step he planned to ensure that all members of Edper's new management team aligned their long-term financial interests with his, which meant requiring them to invest and think and act as partners in every sense. These concerns and objectives, more than anything else, led to the special relationship he developed with his colleagues and in time involved not only sharing the financial rewards but also seeking a consensus on all major business decisions.

Later this evolved into a broader policy of emphasizing the ownership of shares by management throughout the group, with the introduction of formal share ownership plans for senior executives in most of the group's public operating companies. It also meant that he would attract executives who were individually strong enough to keep their eyes on the distant horizon of achievement while maintaining a sharp focus on the daily tasks at hand. There would be no room for executives who preferred to be rewarded on an individual basis for each transaction they were involved in, as this would not foster teamwork. Salaries were kept at a modest level. If he and other shareholders did not find their investment in the group growing, neither would the executives charged with the responsibility for managing the group's affairs.

∽

The next major milestone in the development of the Edper group arose in 1976, when English Property Corporation, a British real estate company and the frustrated absentee controlling shareholder of Trizec Corporation, approached Peter Bronfman and asked him to consider increasing Edper's investment in Trizec beyond its then 10% holding. Peter Bronfman agreed to do this on the condition that Edper be given board and management control of the company and the right to introduce a new management team more responsive to the interests of the company's shareholders.

Given Edper's earlier success in the real estate business and continued dedication to the industry, this was exactly what he had been looking for. This investment initiative was concluded by Carena Bancorp Inc. (the successor company to the Canadian Arena Company and the predecessor to Brookfield Properties Corporation) and English Property Corporation pooling sufficient shares of Trizec in a new partnership company to provide Carena with a 50.1% controlling interest in the holding company, which in turn held a similar ownership position in Trizec.

All but $10 million of the $50 million required by Carena to bring its interest up to the 50.1% controlling position in the partnership company was borrowed from The Bank of Nova Scotia on a long-term, limited recourse basis with the encouragement and support of its chairman, Cedric Ritchie. This was only one of a number of times that he and his successor, Peter Godsoe, were most helpful to the group at critical points in its development. The balance of the funds needed was provided by the Mercantile Bank of Canada.

At the time, Trizec's finances were in such strained condition that, shortly after Carena increased its investment in the company, Trizec could not meet its payroll commitments from its own financial resources. It took two years of concerted effort by Harold Milavsky, Ed Sardachuk and Michael Cornelissen, assisted by Jack Cockwell on a full-time basis during the initial stages, to place the company on a sound financial footing. It was a challenging and difficult task, taking equal parts of talent and faith to keep the company viable.

Fortunately for the Edper group, shortages of office space and inflationary pressures during this time materially increased commercial rental rates and property values. As a result, in a very short period Edper's investment in Trizec multiplied in value almost tenfold. This rapid and very large escalation in value provided Peter Bronfman and his colleagues with a new sense of confidence. It also supplied the crucial impetus, given Edper's significantly expanded financial base, to start thinking about seeking another large investment in order to diversify Edper's predominately real estate-related business base.

✦

From 1977 onwards, Jack Cockwell, Tim Price and David Kerr stepped up the pace of expansion of Mico Enterprises' merchant banking operations, utilizing as capital the proceeds received from the sale of many of Mico Enterprises' Caribbean trading businesses and diverse Canadian assets. Ian Cockwell, in a consulting capacity, continued to help with the liquidation of Mico's real estate assets, and also provided valuable assistance in managing a number of its more troublesome non-core investments.

Tim Casgrain, who had joined the group in 1976 initially to assist David Kerr with some of his Canadian Arena responsibilities, moved to Antigua to manage Mico Enterprises' Caribbean operations. This allowed Tim Price to return to Canada to focus more intently on Mico Enterprises' growing merchant banking operations, in particular the investment in Westmount Life. The financial performance of this latter company was substantially improved, making it possible to conclude a sale later in 1976 for a meaningful gain.

In addition to the investment in Westmount Life, other successful merchant banking investments made during the late 1970s included numerous transactions with S.B. McLaughlin & Company and the acquisition of a 25% interest in Canadian CableSystems. Laurentian Lanes was restructured and eventually sold to Edper's partner, Irving Grundman. Astral Communications was acquired and subsequently merged with Bellevue Photo to form Astral

Bellevue Pathé, a new public company operated and controlled by four brothers, Harold, Ian, Harvey and Sidney Greenberg. The warm and mutually supportive business relationship with the Greenberg family continued even after they purchased the group's shareholdings in Astral in 1993 in accordance with a handshake agreement reached fifteen years earlier.

Although Mico Enterprises increased the level of earnings it reported in each year, this was overshadowed by the sizable unrealized gains which were steadily accumulated throughout the second half of the 1970s from its merchant banking activities and structured partnerships. David Kerr's work in operating and eventually disposing of the La Reserve and Far Hills resort hotels in Québec was of particular importance in raising the group's confidence in dealing with complex operating issues and extracting value from troubled operations. These and other initiatives resulted in Mico Enterprises' equity base growing from $3 million in 1971 to nearly $70 million in 1979, including $50 million of unrealized investment gains.

As exceptional as this performance was, given Mico Enterprises' modest start, it was only a small indication of what was to come. As with many of Edper's investments over the years, the idea of examining an entity to see how assets might better be deployed became a hallmark of Edper's style. In a figurative sense, dissecting an investment and reassembling it in a variety of shapes and forms to find which configuration could best utilize what was available for the advantage of all – shareholders, employees, partners and the public – became an important Edper *modus operandi*.

These skills, which were practised in Mico Enterprises in the 1970s and honed through Hees International in the 1980s, have now been effectively applied by the group for more than twenty-five years.

By 1978, as a direct result of the substantial increase in the value of Edper's real estate holdings, including in particular its investment in Trizec and the very profitable sports and entertainment business centred around the Montreal Forum, Peter Bronfman and his colleagues started to take definitive steps to establish more balance to the group's asset base. For a variety of reasons, the decision was made to execute the diversification efforts from Toronto. David Kerr was chosen to conduct the exploratory work and moved to Toronto in 1978 to set up a merchant banking office and a listening post to seek out a substantial investment opportunity for the group to pursue. These initiatives also facilitated the eventual move of Edper's head office from Montreal to Toronto early in 1979.

Since Peter Bronfman and all concerned felt a strong desire to maintain Edper's business focus within Canada, it was agreed that the natural resources sector should be the area where they would concentrate their search. They believed it best reflected Canada's long-term competitive strengths. Part of the overall vision of remaining in Canada was not to confine all activity to the Canadian scene, but rather to keep Canada as the home base and primary beneficiary of the group's projected worldwide expansion.

Once the natural resources sector had been selected as the next area of focus, David Kerr started to build his knowledge base of the industry and, early in 1978, began to develop a business plan directed at an acquisition in this sector. The group's objective was to acquire a controlling interest in an established public company which would provide a degree of financial leverage as well as the necessary technical skills to develop large-scale natural resource projects that would be competitive in the world markets.

Peter Bronfman and his colleagues recognized, even at this early stage of their diversification studies, that success in this highly cyclical and capital-intensive sector would require access to a substantial amount of long-term capital. The importance they came to attach to long-term equity capital in entering and then building a successful natural resources business caused them to give serious consideration to employing a financial structure similar to those used in other countries which have natural resource-based economies. This would in time involve having a number of separate business units operating as stand-alone public companies, each with direct access to the capital markets.

In anticipation of the diversification of the group's interests into the natural resources sector, Edper began to increase its cash reserves through a variety of initiatives. Although the $50 million investment in Trizec had paid off handsomely, increasing nearly tenfold in value on paper, Edper was still cash poor as it had borrowed most of the capital required to make the investment in Trizec, and Trizec was busily re-investing most of the cash it was able to generate.

One of the more significant steps taken to generate cash was the sale of the Montreal Canadiens hockey club, whose main asset was the premier franchise in the National Hockey League. Over the previous seven years, Sam Pollock had displayed considerable business acumen in operating the hockey team and in promoting initiatives to increase the returns from the Montreal Forum. This was in addition to developing the Montreal Canadiens hockey club to a pre-eminent position in its league, matching sporting success with sparkling financial results. It was generally recognized that Sam Pollock's involvement was critical to this success and, when he began to give serious consideration to retiring, it expedited Peter Bronfman's thinking on the possible sale of the group's investment in the hockey club.

By the fall of 1978, the Montreal Canadiens hockey club had been sold to Montreal-based Molson Breweries, largely because Peter Bronfman considered Molson Breweries to be the appropriate owner given its Montreal origins and operating base. His love for his native city and his respect for the team's unifying role within Canada superseded the opportunity to promote a competitive, price escalating bidding war, surely the dream of most people with something to sell.

He believed that it would be better for the city of Montreal and Canada itself if the team were sold to a Montreal-based company. He sought a transaction that was right for the team and right for Montreal and was willing to accept a lower price – but one which he believed to be fair considering all the circumstances. Thus, he short-circuited a potential bidding war, and a price, fair in his estimation, was settled upon quickly and quietly with Molson Breweries and with minimal posturing and fanfare.

∽

The more deeply David Kerr explored the financial requirements of the natural resources industry, the more convinced he became that the amount of capital required for the group's diversification into this sector would be considerably higher than they had previously contemplated. The proceeds from the sale of the Montreal Canadiens would not alone be sufficient if the group was intent on becoming a major participant in the industry. This started the process of realizing additional cash from a number of the group's other investments and a search for an investment partner able to contribute a portion of the additional equity capital required. To this end, Trevor Eyton, who had worked closely with the Edper group on a number of its larger investment initiatives since the mid-1960s and had provided valuable assistance with its corporate and other relationships in Toronto, introduced Peter Bronfman to the Patiño family, which had accumulated a substantial fortune from its Bolivian tin mines.

Pat Keenan and Jamie Ortiz-Patiño, the two senior Patiño group representatives, were also in a position to provide useful information on the natural resources sector in North and South America, including particularly Brazil. They agreed to invest $50 million of equity through Patiño N.V. in a new partnership company, Edper Resources Limited, formed for the purpose of acquiring an active natural resources operating company. Edper in turn committed to invest $100 million of equity capital for a 66% interest in the partnership company. The Bank of Montreal and The Toronto-Dominion Bank provided a further $150 million of financing in the form of ten-year preferred shares without recourse to either Edper or Patiño N.V. Notwithstanding the subsequent sale by Patiño of its shares in this partnership company, Pat Keenan continues to play an important role in the group's affairs as one of its longest-serving non-management directors.

Having agreed to contribute $100 million to the partnership company, Edper set out to garner the additional financial resources required by selling a number of other investments which had increased substantially in value during the 1970s, including its shareholdings in Canadian CableSystems, S.B. McLaughlin and Boyd Stott McDonald. The new investment initiative was expected to be very large in relation to anything Edper had contemplated before, and recent investment successes had to provide the financial fuel for what could be a very long haul. The equity investment made by Edper in Edper Resources Limited was eventually fully financed from the proceeds of investment sales and realizations of profits, and without incurring any new borrowings. This was considered important as the risks taken were likely to be larger than anything previously encountered and it would not be a good time to add further risk through bank debt.

Early in 1979, just when Peter Bronfman and his colleagues were ready to step up and start buying shares in Brascan Limited, the target company identified through David Kerr's work in Toronto, Olympia & York became involved in a hostile takeover bid for English Property Corporation, Edper's partner in the ownership of Trizec. This suddenly placed Edper's investment in Trizec in jeopardy, requiring that serious consideration be given to mounting a competing bid for English Property Corporation. This idea was abandoned when the opportunity arose to enter into a friendly joint venture with Olympia & York which confirmed a number of the previous partnership understandings, including an option entitling Carena to purchase an additional 10% interest in Trizec. The new partnership arrangements did, however, give Olympia & York the right after a five-year standstill period to require Carena at any time thereafter to buy them out or arrange a sale of both of their blocks of Trizec shares to a third party.

At the time, it was considered necessary to grant the forced-sale concession, otherwise Olympia & York, in its position as the new owner of English Property Corporation, may have wished to reassess many of the critical understandings and the working relationship that had become an important part of Edper's successful partnership with English Property Corporation. Notwithstanding the fact that the forced-sale provision hung out there like a trap-door lever waiting to be pulled, Edper developed a constructive working relationship with Olympia & York. Peter Bronfman and his colleagues also came to enjoy good and mutually helpful relationships with the Reichmann family, the sole owners of Olympia & York, beyond their jointly-owned Trizec investment and endeavoured to be of assistance to them after they experienced financial difficulties early in 1992.

However, an important lesson was learned. Thereafter it was considered essential that Edper avoid forced-sale provisions in all agreements involving its core holdings. This was taken to be especially relevant in pursuing the group's diversification objectives in the natural resources sector, which were steadily taking shape.

Having resolved the immediate threat to Edper's real estate interests, the way was cleared for Peter Bronfman and his colleagues to launch the major initiative they had been intensively working on under tight wraps for the previous nine months. The years of toiling away at smaller businesses to make them profitable and to build the group's financial reserves, combined with the efforts made to cement good business relationships with the country's major banks and institutional investors, were about to help catapult the Edper group to the next stage of its business development.

The group's public profile had been relatively quiet, apart from the Great-West Life takeover attempt in 1969, and the acquisition of the Montreal Canadiens in 1971, which had brought a different kind of attention to Peter Bronfman as an individual and to the group as a whole. Public attention, however, was about to suddenly swing in their direction with the announcement of Edper's plans to acquire a major investment in Brascan, an important corporate icon firmly established in Toronto. There would be no way of avoiding the spotlight, which would soon place Peter Bronfman and his colleagues under its intense and unavoidable glare.

Chapter Six

Capturing Brascan

The opportunity to acquire a meaningful foothold in the natural resources sector was first identified early in 1978, but really only started to crystallize towards the end of that year as a result of the announcement by Brascan Limited that it had finally reached agreement to sell its South American electric utility operations to the Brazilian Government. In addition to its other Brazilian holdings, Brascan had a number of North American mining and oil and gas properties and had publicly stated that the company was committed to the natural resources sector.

Brascan had long been an aberration in the Canadian business landscape. It began in 1899 with adventurers who left the cold Canadian shores to stray as far away as hot, exotic Brazil, where they founded what would become, in 1912, Brazilian Traction, Light and Power Company Limited, Brascan's original name. The mere mention of Brascan would immediately bring a fanciful smile to the lips of those who heard it, carrying with it images of Rio de Janeiro's curving white sandy beaches, samba music and, of course, the bronzed and leggy girl from Ipanema. This ever-youthful, ever-beautiful beach fantasy quickly blossomed in the minds of businessmen attired in dark blue suits and black brogues. Who would not want to be a part of all that Brascan had to offer – offshore, away from the snow and the cold?

The real story behind the beginnings of Brazilian Traction, Light and Power was no doubt obscured by all the attendant fantasy and magic that came with the two-syllable latchkey word – *Brazil*. In fact the company enjoyed an excellent reputation in this large South American country, as did Canadians, who were seen as industrious and ingenious folk who brought public transit, electricity and telephones to Rio de Janeiro and São Paulo in the early years of the twentieth century. But the company, which at one time had large teams of engineers in Toronto designing power stations and planning the expansion of its network of Brazilian holdings, had endured many changes since the time of the first financial adventurers.

As Brazil itself matured as a country and political entity, it underwent a metamorphosis and began to realize its potential as an economic power in South America. As in many other countries at the time, the need to own steel mills, telephone systems and power plants also began to assert itself. Canada and Canadians remained well liked and popular and in fact Brazil was grateful for the technological advancements made possible by its northern partners. But there could be no doubt the exotic butterfly had finally emerged from its chrysalis, and independence and nationalization of the utility businesses were to be the order of the day.

Brascan sold its tramways to the government, as well as its telephone lines, both for fair prices. But Brazil, not anxious to lose capital or Canadian investors, usually attached strings to at least some of the money from the sales, requiring a good proportion of the proceeds to be reinvested in Brazil. While the need to reinvest could not be questioned, somehow Brascan had managed to assemble over time a collection of unrelated assets including cattle ranches, tin mines, sardine factories, meat packing plants, tomato paste manufacturers, armament facilities and a brewery, to name but a few. The portfolio was in flux, in that once money was recovered from one investment there was never a shortage of new and exciting projects which were unearthed to consume the sale proceeds.

Despite all this, one glorious jewel of an investment still remained at the end of 1978 and that was Light-Serviços de Eletricidade S.A. Known everywhere in Brazil as *The Light*, this mighty hydro-electric company lit up the shorelines, streets, public parks and glittering night skies of Rio de Janeiro and São Paulo. The entity was a huge one and so tightly woven into the fabric of Brazil that the writing was on the wall. Either *The Light* was going to be nationalized by the leaders of the country at their price – an act which would hobble future foreign investment in Brazil because *The Light* was well known internationally and its contribution to the development of the country was recognized to have been fundamental – or it was going to be slowly bled to death as rate increases were deferred or denied, despite the rampant inflation of costs. There was, however, a slim but real chance that Brascan, with deft handling, could sell *The Light* to the Brazilian Government for an almost fair price.

This slight possibility, at first a fragile bubble of a dream, was slowly and painstakingly forged into a deal. Jake Moore, Brascan's Chairman and Chief Executive at the time, and Antonio Gallotti, President of *The Light*, and their teams carefully worked their way across the minefield of potential disasters, picking their path with delicacy and trading on personal associations, favours owed and Old World honour. Finally, in January 1979, and with a great sense of mission accomplished, Brascan announced that it had sold its Brazilian electric utility operations to the Brazilian Government for US $380 million. This was far less than a fair price, but under the circumstances it was considered a coup, particularly because all of the money could be repatriated. It was real money and it was destined to come home to Canada.

It is said that the finish line of one race is really the starting point for the next challenge. Such was the case with the sale of *The Light*. While Brascan's executives in Toronto congratulated themselves on their adroitness and celebrated their victory over potential disaster for the company and its thousands of long-standing shareholders, the external picture of the new Brascan was coming into much sharper, and quite delectable, focus for some interested outsiders.

At first hoping and praying, then finally knowing that a great wad of cash would soon be winging its way to land with a pleasing thud in Brascan's elegant 48th floor Commerce Court Toronto head office, senior management of the company had been looking into what it might do with all that money. To sit on a fat and juicy bank account for any length of time would make Brascan a plump chicken, a perfect feast for an aggressive predator. But to make an unwise choice – or choices – would be equally disastrous.

A team of newly hired investment analysts had been beavering away on the 49th floor, one floor above the company's senior executives. Independent of mind and personal preference, most of the analysts spent week after week researching pet projects and talking in enigmas when asked to account for their time. Many projects were reviewed, but, in the end, the best they could do was come up with a poorly thought out proposal to make a monumental investment in the somewhat tired and cumbersome U.S. five-and-dime store, the F.W. Woolworth Company. Brascan's management had set its target and felt, as major players on the Toronto scene, an entitlement to win whatever they wanted.

Soon after announcing the triumphant sale of its Brazilian utility operations, Brascan's board authorized the company to launch a hostile takeover bid for the F.W. Woolworth Company, as much as anything to ensure that Brascan itself did not become a tasty morsel of a takeover target. Many Americans were outraged over the nerve of the clumsy Canadian swipe at one of their favourite, if shabby, national institutions. Some were deeply offended by the move while others were simply perplexed. Woolworth itself took to the courts to keep the upstart predator at bay.

On the Canadian side of the border, reaction to the announcement was also mixed. Some saw it as courageous, inventive, a sign of Canadian business coming of age, unafraid to test new borders and conquer previously untouchable territories. Others, less swayed by the immediacy of action, saw it as badly thought through and a reckless step made only to stave off other stalkers temporarily. Relatively few favoured the move, and the least impressed were Brascan's larger shareholders.

One has to imagine the enormous shift in thinking required by shareholders to flip in the course of one bold-faced announcement, without consultation, from holding stock in what was viewed as basically a steady earning, high-dividend paying utility company with its major assets in Brazil and some interesting North American natural resource holdings, to owning shares in America's largest five-and-dime chain, strung like a chipped and broken multi-strand necklace from one side of the North American continent to the other and touching innumerable points in Canada and the United States in between. From lighting up the romantic subtropical skies of Rio de Janeiro and São Paulo and providing energy for the throbbing industrial hum of a massive, young, vibrant country with immeasurable promise, Brascan was to become a company which sold dish-racks, cheap lipstick and screwdrivers – with lunch counters on the side. Is it any wonder that many of Brascan's most faithful shareholders balked at the proposed acquisition?

Suffice it to say that Brascan's previously supportive and tolerant shareholders reacted negatively to the proposed investment in Woolworth. With the remittance of the utility sale proceeds from Brazil to Canada still being subject to some political risk, Brascan's shares traded on the stock market at a substantial discount from their underlying asset values. Strong doubts were beginning to form about whether or not the phoenix had the wings to rise from the ashes. The worm had turned – and it was against Brascan's management.

This was the backdrop against which Brascan's institutional shareholders were measuring the company's prospects when they began assessing the opportunities to sell their shares. Having purchased approximately 2% of Brascan's common shares in late 1978, Edper was patiently watching this strange story unfold, while at the same time diligently accumulating its cash and lining up partners to intercede when the right opportunity presented itself.

Edper's management had spent countless hours familiarizing themselves with Brascan and its assets. They believed that if only they could persuade Brascan's board of directors to abandon the massive frivolity of the Woolworth takeover, Edper would be able to justify paying Brascan's shareholders substantially greater value than the trading price of Brascan's shares at that time or the price at which they were likely to trade if Brascan was successful in its Woolworth quest. The gleaming possibility of using Brascan as a sturdy financial vehicle to fulfill Edper's diversification plans lay in the obvious financial leverage which Edper would acquire by owning a 50% controlling interest in a well-established and easily financeable public company, rich in tangible assets which could be readily deployed in the natural resources sector.

Trevor Eyton and Jack Cockwell respectfully approached Jake Moore, Brascan's Chairman and Chief Executive, with Edper's vision and tried to convince him that abandoning the Woolworth offer would be the wisest course of action for his shareholders. Jake Moore had scarce interest in giving an ear to the upstart group from Montreal and brusquely dismissed their proposal with a heavy shrug of his massive shoulders. Unsurprised and equally undaunted, the Edper team approached the Ontario Securities Commission to obtain its approval for a takeover offer by Edper, conditional on the Woolworth transaction being aborted by Brascan. Loyalty in establishment circles at the time ran wide and deep, particularly in conservative Ontario, and the idea was rejected out of hand by the powers in place.

Edper then regrouped and decided that the most effective means of persuading Brascan's board of directors to reconsider their position would be to become a much larger shareholder in the company while letting it be known that Edper would oppose Brascan's offer to acquire Woolworth.

The Edper group moved into action early in March 1979 when Tim Price, accompanied by Jimmy Connacher, flew to New York and purchased a 14% shareholding of Brascan in a single day. Tim Price had gambled that there were plenty of disgruntled shareholders who, if given a firm bid with a limited time period for acceptance, would vote with their feet and an avalanche of share certificates would follow. He returned to Toronto that same day with his mission accomplished, having set a new record for the largest transaction ever executed on the American Stock Exchange.

When even this bold step failed to persuade Jake Moore to reconsider the course he had chosen for Brascan, and after he refused to provide Edper with an audience before his board of directors, Tim Price returned a few days later to New York and once again aggressively bought shares as investors eagerly dumped theirs. This brought Edper's ownership position in Brascan to 33%, completed in what at the time constituted two separate days of truly unprecedented share trading.

Jake Moore and Brascan's board of directors suddenly found that they had fallen into the uncomfortable and strategically unsound position of conducting battles on two separate fronts with an unseasoned army of corporate head office staff. It seemed there were no allies and not even enough time to read reports from the front. When asked by Woolworth's lawyers what he thought of a disparaging report on their company prepared by an outside consultant for Brascan at great expense, Jake Moore – the general of the battle – replied that he had not read it. When asked why not, he countered: "I pay people to read things like that for me." The pressures began to mount, with the result that other senior officers gave similar terse responses in the course of the legal manoeuvrings which ensued.

It was proving to be an eventful spring. Never before had the celestial calm of Brascan's 48th floor head office seen so much turbulence and activity. The boardroom, a dark inner chamber lined with polished wood and dominated by a huge, sleek wooden table surrounded by stylish and uncomfortable modern chairs, had been renamed "command central" and was the point from which all orders emanated. A giant black and white poster of the landmark Woolworth Building in New York was tacked on the wall at one end of command central – for inspiration. In the gloomy depths of this room voices rose and fell in argument as strategy was debated, fists were slammed on the table and hands slapped together in noisy rebuttal to points made. Advisers slipped in and out bearing stack upon stack of paper and more paper – often plans which participants were told to memorize and destroy.

No sense of daily rhythm could be detected within command central's walls because the vision of a rising or setting sun could not permeate its windowless confines. Meetings were called at any time in any twenty-four hour period because senior team members were constantly being prepared by the company's Canadian lawyers to fly off in different directions to give depositions and testimony all over the United States, since Woolworth had launched dozens of counterattacks in defending itself against the rash Canadians. The rumpled and weary executives often came home only to pick up a freshly packed suitcase, fall back into a limousine and catch a flight to another courtroom in a remote little town somewhere in the United States.

As Brascan's chances of emerging victorious from the raging battles grew slimmer, and with the company's executives forced to survive on snack foods, their waistlines expanded as did their fears that the game was over. It was. A number of them had already started thinking about the time they could go home to tend their wounds and consider their futures with the support of their families. What some did not guess was that for those with the right attitude who were prepared to stay, the real fun and rewards were not far ahead.

The vivid contrast in the management style of the protagonists would have been amusing to any privileged outside observer or even a fly on the wall. At command central in the Brascan camp could be found numerous executives and support staff. Committees and subcommittees were abundant as were phone calls, advisers and lengthy deliberations and written reports.

At the other end of the scale was the Edper team, consisting of Peter Bronfman's three central players, Jack Cockwell, Tim Price and David Kerr, a few carefully selected outside team members led by Trevor Eyton and including Pat Keenan and Jamie Ortiz-Patiño, and always at the very centre, the clearing point for any major decision, Peter Bronfman. The critical path for any action was mercifully short and efficient – and as time would prove, ideal for executing rapid-fire business decisions.

The weeks unfurled during the spring of 1979, and as tulips and daffodils popped up out of the frozen earth, so did new problems for the Brascan contingent. An acrimonious legal battle in New York bubbled away with Brascan suing

Edper to reverse the two days of unprecedented stock trading on the American Stock Exchange. How this was to be accomplished was anyone's guess, since the sellers of the shares certainly did not want them back. The future of Brascan and its team hinged on the decision of Judge Pierre Laval, a highly respected member of the New York State judiciary. At the end of the day, he alone would decide whether Edper's forays on the American Stock Exchange would be allowed to stand.

When it was given, the New York court ruling was rendered overwhelmingly in favour of Edper, which immediately led to Brascan abandoning its offer to purchase Woolworth. In a gesture of peace and in an attempt to appease the Toronto business community, Edper agreed to support the reappointment of Eddie Goodman, Lew Harder, Peter Hardy, Peter Widdrington and a number of other Brascan directors. Edper then let it be known that it would proceed to make a follow-up offer to increase its ownership to the 50% level. While waiting for the follow-up offer to run its course to completion, Noranda Mines Limited, in a show of solidarity with Jake Moore and the Brascan old guard, considered topping Edper's offer. But Noranda Mines then shied away when it realized that a short-term gain held no appeal for the Edper team, which was unequivocal in its refusal to stray from its much larger objectives. After Edper Resources Limited increased its ownership in Brascan to approximately 50% in June of 1979, Peter Bronfman replaced Jake Moore as Chairman and the process of integrating Brascan with Edper's quite different style was quickly launched.

The Brascan annual meeting, delayed that year because of the events of the spring, saw the changing of the guard in a ballet of formality and decorum broken only by the persistent flash and buzz of press cameras and microphones thrust millimetres away from the faces of Peter and Edward Bronfman. Ted Freeman-Atwood, outgoing President of the company, a tall, distinguished man who usually spoke in extraordinarily long and complex sentences, was asked by a shareholder what the cost of the legal bills had been to fight the Woolworth and Edper battles. He took a deep breath, paused a moment, surrendered his usual intricate syntax and rich vocabulary to give a two syllable reply: "Five mill".

Jake Moore, the powerful outgoing Chairman of Brascan, was nowhere to be found, though reporters checked inside and outside the hall. Jake Moore had chosen not to attend what he called the "closing ceremonies". The evening before, in an emotional and tender parting of executives and loyal support staff, the office bar was opened for the last time and stories were told. Compliments were paid, thanks given and affection confirmed as the reminiscences of the many years of his tenure were sentimentally reviewed. He had said the most personal of his good-byes there in private, after hours.

Jake Moore had left once and for all his spacious, airy, ultra-modern office, which would have made a good sized board room – with plenty of light. He turned his back on his oversized desk with the special inlaid slip for his telephone – a phone which more than once had been flung across the room when he had been displeased by someone or something proposed. He would never again sit in his custom-designed steel blue suede sofa, set just so to provide an impressive view of the vast and equally blue expanse of Lake Ontario visible through the wall of floor-to-ceiling glass windows. His final words when asked what the press and shareholders should be told about his absence from the annual meeting were: "Tell them I've gone fishing." Jake Moore did, however, continue as a well-informed and helpful director of two key Brascan affiliates for a number of years afterwards.

The annual meeting finally came to a close. Brascan's employees had a chance to look at their new colleagues eye to eye for a change instead of through newspaper and magazine photos. Somehow the Edper contingent did not seem quite as bad to the Brascan executives as they had been told or expected. In fact, the Edper team came across as quietly determined, reservedly friendly and surprisingly understated. Rather than the bucket of snakes they had expected, these people gave every impression of being rather decent and serious about their business. Going back to work after the holiday weekend would be an interesting rather than a terrifying experience, that is, if appearances could be counted upon.

To implement their acquisition plan, Peter Bronfman had relied on a carefully devised division of labour. David Kerr had been responsible for identifying and researching the target, Jack Cockwell for ensuring the financial resources were in place, Tim Price for executing the stock purchases and Trevor Eyton for managing the complex legal aspects of the transaction, with the final call on each of these areas resting with Peter Bronfman. The efficiency with which these individuals completed their inter-related tasks reconfirmed in Peter Bronfman's mind that more could be accomplished by compatible individuals working together, but still retaining full responsibility for their specific tasks, than by any one individual or by forming a traditional committee-type task force.

Around this time Peter Bronfman asked Trevor Eyton, who was one of the few members of the Brascan acquisition team not already an Edper executive, to take a two-year leave of absence from his position as a senior partner at the Toronto law firm of Tory Tory DesLauriers & Binnington to help Edper restructure Brascan. Peter Bronfman knew he wanted to avoid spending his own time dealing with the public side of managing the transition because his real interests lay in seeking a balance among the group's various investments and in ensuring that the expanding team stayed true to his values and the group's strategic objectives. At the same time, the group badly needed someone to protect and further its external interests and to be a credible public representative for the company.

Trevor Eyton agreed to commit a portion of his time to the group on the basis that he would be free to pursue his outside business interests, which were and would remain unrelated to Edper's business activities. He also brought to the group a level of flamboyance not shown by Peter Bronfman or his other colleagues. This arrangement was acceptable to Peter Bronfman even though it was a departure from the low-profile, full-time commitment required from his other colleagues, because it was expected to have a limited duration and it was the only basis on which Trevor Eyton, who enjoyed a multitude of personal and business relationships, could be attracted to the group.

In August 1979, after preparing a new business plan setting out the group's strategies for expansion in the natural resources sector, which was quickly endorsed by Peter Bronfman and Brascan's board, Trevor Eyton and Jack Cockwell were appointed President and Chief Executive Officer and Senior Vice-President of Brascan, respectively. Other management changes were also made to ensure that they had a clear mandate and the necessary support to realize the group's diversification objectives.

Trevor Eyton enjoyed his new corporate role and remained President of Brascan until his appointment to the Senate of Canada in 1990. Following this appointment he continued to serve the group as a representative to a number of its public constituencies, an activity ideally suited to his broad-ranging political, social and community relationships, which were once described as "a vast and seamless web." This included playing a pivotal role in the development of the SkyDome stadium in Toronto, which received significant financial sponsorship from three Edper group companies.

As 1979 wore on, the work at Brascan intensified and the hours were long and difficult, but there could be no denying the excitement that permeated the place and charged the players with remarkable energy and determination. Evaluations were made of the Brascan personnel as the two groups got to know one another and potential team members were carefully assessed. By the end of 1979, the team had been selected and those who were to be let go had been given generous severances. Most departed feeling well compensated with their termination arrangements and looked forward to new careers in a booming economy.

By the spring of 1980, Brascan's operations had been substantially restructured with its Canadian and Brazilian corporate offices scaled down to less than a quarter of their previous levels. While the company still had all of the 48th floor and part of the 49th for months to come, many of the offices became empty. At first, it seemed for many of Brascan's personnel as though the ghosts of departed colleagues prowled the corridors. Echoes and memories of past, more relaxed times seemed to haunt the quiet halls and spaces. Jake Moore's modern art collection and his personally owned pieces of bright, primitive Brazilian art which had decorated the office walls were returned to him, and faded marks on the wallpaper reminded those who stayed of what had once been there and of those who had left.

These were not the only changes with which the Brascan staff were confronted. Gone were the days spent in endless committee meetings studying and re-studying the same issues over and over again. The Edper team had long before drawn a leaf from IBM's management book which required problems to be "solved quickly, right or wrong. If wrong, you will soon know and then you can solve them right." This had been the credo at Edper for some time and it soon became common practice at Brascan.

There would be no going home until all issues were dealt with, or at least a starting point and frame of reference set to make the decision the next day. Going over old ground was not permitted, time was of the essence and the corporate office would no longer have the right to sit on problems hoping they would fade away. General Electric, which practises a similar management style, is even more rigorous in forcing decisions, setting aside one meeting to study a problem, and then requiring an action plan to come out of the next.

Any unsettled and shifting feelings in Brascan's corporate office soon evaporated because there was exciting and challenging work to be done, and it had become obvious to those who chose to remain that they had a great opportunity which they could either blow away or dig in and make the most of. A crucial part of the assessment of individuals had not only covered their technical abilities but also their attitude to life in general, so what remained was a collection of people who could adapt to swift changes in circumstances and get on with a positive frame of mind.

The core group of senior personnel from Brascan who joined the Edper team included Lowell Allen, Wendy Cecil, Gill Churchill, Bob Dunford, Bill Farmilo, Ed Kress, Frank Lochan, Duncan McAlpine, Paul Marshall, Bob Simon and Bob Yeoman, most of whom went on to play important roles in Edper group activities for many years. Brascan's corporate office team was eventually rounded out with Alan Dean taking on responsibility for the group's public and corporate affairs including The Edper Group Foundation, Blake Lyon for finance and accounting and Harry Goldgut as legal counsel with corporate development responsibilities for the group's power generating business.

It was rare to find senior executives in a company just taken over in a bruising battle who were as willing as Paul Marshall and Bob Dunford, as well as Roberto de Andrade from Brascan's Brazil office, to provide the leadership necessary to get on with the healing and tasks at hand. They were instrumental in melding the two teams together. It was Peter Bronfman's ability to gain the respect and loyalty of people of this calibre that enabled his other colleagues to learn a great deal from them. This proved to be invaluable as the group was entering new businesses where it was necessary to gain new expertise and technical knowledge before they could become successful.

Paul Marshall, who passed away in 1997 after a courageous battle with cancer, provided immediate and invaluable guidance to the Edper team as they wrestled with the many technical and market-related challenges of the natural resources industry, which was basically new to Peter Bronfman and his Edper colleagues. He was heading up Brascan's Canadian natural resource operations when Edper acquired its interests in Brascan in 1979 and was uniquely qualified to provide valuable guidance to his new colleagues, having had extensive business experience in the mining, forestry and oil and gas industries prior to joining Brascan. Soon thereafter, he was appointed to the Brascan board, became Group Chairman Natural Resources in 1983, and later Vice-Chairman of Brascan. As Group Chairman Natural

Resources, he served as a director of Noranda, Chairman of both Norcen Energy Resources and Westmin Resources, and a director of a number of other group companies.

In response to a request made to the group by the Canadian Federal Government in 1984, Paul Marshall, with Peter Bronfman's blessing, took on the added responsibility for two full years of working for his country for $1.00 a year to oversee the government's privatization program. As President and Chief Executive of Canada Development Investment Corporation, he arranged the sale to the private sector of de Havilland, Canadair, Eldorado Nuclear Corporation, Saskatchewan Mining Development Corporation and the dismantling and sale of Canada Development Corporation. Following Paul Marshall's death in 1997, his colleagues and senior group companies decided to commemorate his long service to the group by funding the refurbishing of the teaching theatre at St. Michael's Hospital, which will be named in his honour.

Bob Dunford was another Brascan executive who also performed a key role in the development of the Edper group as it entered new businesses which required a higher level of specialized expertise than Peter Bronfman and his other colleagues had at that time. As Group Chairman Power Generation, Bob Dunford became a driving force in the development of what soon became a thriving business. He was also responsible for negotiating the finer details and documentation of all of Brascan's major business transactions during the 1980s and early 1990s. In the process, the group benefited immeasurably from his skills in crafting clear legal agreements which were easy to read and understand. This included reviewing all major new initiatives at an early stage to ensure compliance and consistency in the group's dealings. Another important role involved Bob Dunford acting as an accessible and astute sounding board in providing business counsel to senior Edper corporate executives.

Roberto de Andrade, who had been with Brascan in Brazil since the 1950s, was made a director of Brascan in 1981. He was accustomed to a changing of the guard in Canada and had been spared the battle pains of the Edper takeover of Brascan. Roberto de Andrade had been instrumental in overseeing the re-investment in Brazil of funds received from Brascan's earlier sales of utility assets. It was therefore a natural decision to appoint him Group Chairman Brazilian Operations to lead the development of Brascan Brazil into a successful diversified operating company. Under his direction, Brascan Brazil created a new management team and continued to prosper despite the extremely difficult economic environment that persisted until the early 1990s in Brazil. As a prominent and respected business leader in the country, he developed strong commercial and community relationships which continue to serve the Edper group well in the expansion of its Brazilian and other South American operations.

Besides the three Group Chairmen drawn from the ranks of Brascan personnel, two other Group Chairman appointments were later made to oversee the group's financial services and real estate operations.

Early in 1982, Allen Lambert was asked to join the Brascan management team following his retirement as Chairman of

The Toronto-Dominion Bank. Although his initial involvement was with Brascan, he soon took on a much larger role as Group Chairman Financial Services, which also encompassed advising and watching over Hees International's rapidly expanding merchant banking activities. Allen Lambert's guidance, impeccable reputation and constant input proved to be invaluable in helping the group work its way through the difficult business environment which touched all financial businesses in the early 1990s.

Allen Lambert's other special contribution to the Edper group involved his unique ability to identify young management talent and encourage its early development. Like Peter Bronfman, Allen Lambert believed that any great organization needed a certain number of people who were constantly striving to stimulate change in order to improve performance. He likened them to the grit in the oyster which creates the pearl. To really play this role, he felt they needed to be young, energetic, creative and open-minded. Based on this belief, Allen Lambert had recommended the appointment of Dick Thomson, while still in his thirties, as the President of The Toronto-Dominion Bank.

Allen Lambert shared this gift for spotting eager, young talent with Peter Bronfman and relished the opportunity to promote young executives from well down in the ranks and then provide them with the guidance and confidence to assume key leadership roles at very early stages of their careers. A recent example was Allen Lambert's endorsement of Bruce Flatt as President and Chief Operating Officer of Brookfield Properties in 1995 to work with Gordon Arnell in restoring the group's fortunes in the real estate sector. In the Spring of 1996, the group named the magnificent atrium, which is the centrepiece of BCE Place, *The Allen Lambert Galleria* in lasting recognition of his many contributions to Edper and its affiliates, the City of Toronto and the Canadian business community.

Harold Milavsky rounded out the team of Group Chairmen with responsibilities for the real estate sector, serving not only as Chairman of Trizec but also as a director of London Life, where he chaired the company's audit committee and provided advice on its extensive real estate holdings. Gordon Arnell, who joined Edper in 1984, succeeded Harold Milavsky and later assumed responsibility for all of the group's real estate activities. He faced five extremely challenging years in leading the restructuring of the group's real estate operations when property values declined precipitously in the early 1990s and a new approach had to be adopted to owning, financing and managing real estate. In addition to providing strategic advice on real estate initiatives throughout the group, he mentored a number of the group's younger real estate executives, including Bruce Flatt, Bill Pringle, David Arthur, Alan Norris and Steve Douglas as he promoted them rapidly through the ranks. Shortly after concluding the relaunching of Brookfield Properties to the public equity markets early in 1997, twenty-five of Gordon Arnell's most senior colleagues honoured him for his exceptional leadership and recognized him for having excelled under extraordinarily difficult circumstances and for creating substantial value for the group.

The appointment of Group Chairmen with extensive practical industry experience in their respective sectors allowed Edper to remove a number of layers of management and helped meld the Edper and Brascan teams together. This in turn enabled high-level responsibilities to be assigned over time to a new generation of executives charged with driving the expansion in these industries, which to a large extent were new to the original Edper team. Through these initiatives and the clear definition of responsibilities, Edper changed Brascan into a smaller and more focused management group. No longer was it a big, cumbersome bureaucracy, but instead it had become a responsive, hands-on team which could assess and act speedily on investment opportunities.

Pleased with this outcome, Peter Bronfman was very comfortable in arriving at the decision to use Brascan as the principal vehicle for the next stage in the expansion of Edper's business activities. This entailed giving Brascan the mandate to achieve not only the group's objectives in the natural resources sector but also to seek out one or two other industries which would be chosen for their more stable earnings profiles.

Book Three

Growth and Challenges

These chapters trace the group's history after the acquisition of Brascan Limited as it expands its base of operations beyond the real estate sector. This phase encompasses building a major ownership position in the natural resource sector through Noranda, expanding the power generating operations of Great Lakes Power and forming Trilon Financial to manage and develop the group's investments in the financial services sector. But just as the group is ascending to new peaks of achievement, a severe recession strikes hard throughout Canada. Although a destructive and painful experience to endure, the recession strengthens the bond between Peter Bronfman and his team as they face many challenges together. Once the recession is behind them and the financial aspects of the business are restored, Peter Bronfman puts in place long-term management and ownership succession plans. With a strengthened foundation, new goals are set to achieve improved operating results throughout the group.

Chapter Seven

Winning and Losing

With a well co-ordinated management team in place and with aspirations rising, the search for additional equity capital once again came into sharp focus. Brascan wanted to obtain a meaningful ownership position in one of the leading natural resource companies being studied by its corporate development specialists and then play a role in building it into a world-competitive enterprise. To accomplish this, Brascan would need to expand its capital base, which in turn would require Edper to subscribe for additional Brascan shares in order to maintain a dominant ownership position in the company.

Since Edper itself was a private company with limited financial resources and no direct access to the public equity markets, a plan was developed to expand Edper's home-grown financial arm in tandem with Brascan's planned growth in the natural resource sector. The objective was to strengthen Edper's financial capability fast enough so that it could contribute part of the capital and share the financing burden which the natural resource sector was expected to soon place on the group.

To accomplish this objective, David Kerr, Tim Price, Tim Casgrain, Don Marshall and Tony Rubin assumed responsibility for building on the already highly profitable merchant banking base established through Mico Enterprises. An important structural step was completed in 1980 by merging Mico Enterprises into National Hees Enterprises Limited, which was subsequently renamed Hees International Bancorp Inc. Then, having secured a Toronto Stock Exchange listing for the merged company, Tim Price and David Kerr proceeded with the group's plans to build a much larger capital base for this business.

Over the next ten years, the Hees International management team grew to include Don Craw, Bob Harding, Brian Kenning, Brian Lawson, Bill L'Heureux, Terry Lyons, Bryan McJannet, George Myhal, Grant Sardachuk and Manfred Walt. Together this dynamic team of merchant bankers was successful in building Hees International's equity base from less than $100 million in 1980 to $2.4 billion by 1990, and in the process amply fulfilled the group financing role assigned to this key business unit. During this period, Hees International expanded its client base and became a preferred financial partner for a broad range of private investors and corporations. This included providing bridge financing to a number of investment dealers at critical points in their development or when stock markets turned sour.

Along with the expansion of its capital base, Hees International's earnings increased dramatically from approximately $10 million in 1980 to more than $200 million in 1990. Commensurate with this solid financial performance, the market value of its shares also increased, rising from $1.85 to

$30.00, which ranked Hees International among Canada's best-performing companies during the 1980s.

With its increased capital base, Hees International was able to provide a steady stream of long-term capital to Edper's two major areas of investment by subscribing for common as well as senior preferred shares in the two holding companies formed by Edper Investments Limited to finance its investments in Carena and Brascan. The risks associated with these investments were largely underwritten by Edper, in return for the financial leverage it received from these arrangements.

This structure and form of financing was appropriate while Edper remained a private company. However, when Edper became a public company some years later in 1989 under the name Edper Enterprises Ltd., shareholders found it difficult to understand the arrangements for sharing the earnings and cash flows of these jointly-owned holding companies. To address this and eliminate any room for confusion, Edper subsequently transferred all of its economic interests in Carena and Brascan to Hees International. This was one of the first of a number of major restructuring steps implemented by Bob Harding and Brian Lawson between 1993 and 1997 to simplify the group's corporate structure.

Notwithstanding the intense focus, time and effort devoted during the 1980s to expanding the group's operations and capital base, Peter Bronfman remained ever sensitive to building and strengthening his management team. This involved attracting individuals capable of adding new skills and above all being comfortable with a team approach to tackling issues. While his direct involvement in the day-to-day business of the group never diminished, his interest in the development of the team around him tended to increase over the years as a means of keeping his finger on the pulse of the organization and its future. He took great personal delight in watching tested and capable business leaders emerge from the fast-paced environment of Hees International, where he kept his office.

Thus, in addition to its financing role, Hees International assumed primary responsibility for developing a practical fast-track executive training program to prepare selected individuals for senior management roles. This helped to develop the business skills of a number of younger executives, including George Myhal, Bob Harding and Manfred Walt, who were subsequently appointed to leadership positions in Trilon Financial, Hees International and Edper Enterprises, respectively, at early stages of their careers. Manfred Walt also became one of Peter Bronfman's closest advisers, helping him with his personal financial affairs. The programme which produced these key executives in the 1980s was reinstated in the early 1990s resulting in the emergence of Bruce Flatt, Brian Lawson, Aaron Regent, John Tremayne and Sam Pollock Jr. in senior operating roles in Brookfield Properties, Hees International, Brascan and Trilon Financial, respectively, by the mid-1990s.

This ongoing executive training programme afforded Peter Bronfman a first-hand opportunity to know his newer colleagues well, to assess their abilities and shortcomings and to become confident of their loyalty to his values. He also wanted to be sure that, as each new generation of management came through the ranks, they would be learning from one another and developing an intimate understanding of each other's strengths and weaknesses. This in time allowed them to conduct much of their business in a kind of verbal shorthand, so thorough was their perception of what each was expected to do and their knowledge of each other's capabilities to contribute to the group's overall goals.

By the mid-1980s, the group had forged the management teams of Edper, Hees International and Brascan into a fairly cohesive unit. By working together, these companies had assembled meaningful investment positions in the real estate, natural resource and financial services sectors as well as interests in a number of other non-core businesses, such as consumer products, which were intended to help balance the group's exposure to its more cyclical operations.

Throughout most of the 1980s, the group's rapid growth and business strategies closely matched the economic conditions prevailing in Canada. The first half of the decade began with a severe recession fueled by high interest rates and inflation, a situation which provided multiple opportunities for those with capital to make new investments with limited competition from other strategic investors. As a result, assets could be acquired fairly swiftly by well-financed companies, without the competitive frenzy of an auction process. Another contributing factor was the ability of companies to accumulate large share positions in target companies through the stock market, since it was not until the late 1980s that more restrictive regulations were introduced. These factors helped the group accumulate a number of its more significant investments and increase its holdings in its major operating companies during this period.

The group's principal business objective in the early 1980s was to further its expansion plans in the core natural resources sector. This had been at the very heart of the reason for the acquisition of Brascan. Primary responsibility for this lay with David Kerr, Trevor Eyton, Jack Cockwell, Paul Marshall, Bob Dunford and Bob Yeoman. The difficult financial environment in the early 1980s, which included bank prime interest rates rising to the 20% level, had not weakened Brascan's financial resources or Peter Bronfman's resolve to achieve his objectives.

In comparison with others, Edper in fact had strengthened its consolidated financial position and was well equipped to seize an opportunity to acquire a 13% shareholding in Noranda Mines, which owned a diverse mining and forest product asset base. Noranda was led at that time by a high-profile management team which included Alf Powis, Bill James, Adam Zimmerman and Ken Cork.

Soon after this key block of Noranda shares was acquired from Conrad Black's Argus Corporation, Brascan stepped into the market and purchased additional shares. Noranda's management then implemented their own unique poison pill by issuing a block of Noranda treasury shares to Zinor

Holdings, a company established for the sole purpose of providing Noranda's incumbent management with the votes attached to these shares, without any financial risk to themselves. After considerable challenges and counter-attacks, Brascan completed its acquisition of a controlling interest in Noranda in October 1981 through Brascade Resources Inc., a 70/30 partnership company formed with Caisse de dépôt et placement du Québec, the giant Québec pension fund.

The investment in Noranda signalled the beginning of an important association between Conrad Black and Peter Bronfman and his colleagues. Peter Bronfman held him in high esteem throughout their relationship and was pleased to be invited to sit on the board of directors of Conrad Black's principal public company, the only external corporate board he ever joined despite many requests from others. Their acquaintance grew into friendship over the years as he found many unique qualities to admire in Conrad Black, among them his rapier wit and skill at fashioning honest, incomparably eloquent responses to even the most probing and complex questions in the flash of an instant. Peter Bronfman often referred to him respectfully as "the last of the great Shakespearean men". As well, Conrad Black was unwavering in his loyalty and encouragement of Peter Bronfman and his colleagues and always generous with his time and energy in giving candid, incisive analysis whenever they encountered problems or experienced difficult patches in the group's development.

For the Brascan employees who had thrown in their lot with the Edper group, the acquisition of Noranda was an unusually sweet new experience as they found themselves wearing the winning colours. It served to cement the loyalty even of those who still harboured a few remaining reservations or jitters about their choice. Never ones to gloat or celebrate for long, the members of the Edper team did not slow down to catch their breath after securing control of Noranda because Peter Bronfman was prodding them to get on with the next challenge while they still had the wind behind them. As each success was planned, worked for and attained, a new goal would rise to the top of the list and efforts to achieve the group's objectives were redoubled.

Once control of Noranda was in hand, repeated attempts were made to apply a new approach to managing Noranda's many diverse businesses. Noranda's senior executives, however, found it difficult to accept change. Eventually, their prolonged resistance necessitated the appointment of David Kerr as a senior officer of Noranda so that the group's objectives could be properly enunciated and steps taken to strengthen Noranda's asset base and financial performance. With David Kerr in place, concerted efforts were made to upgrade Noranda's existing mining and forest product operations. Its oil and gas interests were enlarged through the acquisition and expansion of Norcen Energy Resources and North Canadian Oils. Mining operations were also expanded through the acquisition of Falconbridge Limited.

Another key strategic objective incorporated in Edper's business plans during this period involved building a complementary business base in industries with more stable earnings profiles in order to balance the impact of the cyclical natural resources business. The areas which were viewed as having the best potential for stable earnings were power generation, financial services and consumer products, since they were generally thought to be relatively non-cyclical. The group's interests in these sectors were expanded accordingly by adding to the generation capacity of Great Lakes Power, an electrical power generating company based in northern Ontario, and by increasing Brascan's ownership in London Life, an insurance and retirement savings company, and in John Labatt, a brewer and food processing concern. New investments were made in Scott Paper Company, a producer of tissue and fine papers, and in Royal Trustco, a personal financial services company and mortgage lender.

By the end of 1985, the second phase of Edper's diversification plan was substantially completed. The group had established a broad business base with diversified natural resource interests to supplement its other core business activities in the real estate sector. In addition, it held a number of other non-core investments to provide a stable component to the group's earnings base. The group had achieved a position of strength, was well financed and had a management team which was battle tested with proven performers.

To all eyes it appeared as though Peter Bronfman and his colleagues could easily have shifted to automatic pilot, so well were their plans unfolding. From the knot of young, enthusiastic Montrealers had emerged a more rounded and seasoned team, forged in its own style and tightly dovetailed with the new Toronto players. But they still had not been completely accepted into the ranks of the Toronto business community, partly because they had been too busy and absorbed in their own plans to participate fully in the community and social side of the Toronto scene. If ever there was a group that practised the concept that the business of business is business, this was it. Work time was most of the time, with sight being lost of the many other aspects required to build supportive relationships with their newly-adopted community. In their view, opportunities abounded and there was no time to waste, but in the long run there would be a heavy price to pay for this oversight.

Business activity continued to heat up during the second half of the 1980s as many companies competed aggressively with each other to expand their operations through acquisitions by using borrowed funds. Corporations bumped head first into one another as they jostled to acquire more and better assets than their competitors, almost without regard for the cost and their mounting debts. Edper's objectives were carefully considered and quite restrained by the wild and reckless standards of the mid-1980s.

Peter Bronfman wanted each operation to be committed to conservative financing principles and to rise above fleeting market trends and the often quirky actions of competitors, notwithstanding media urgings or the impact that inaction on the part of the group could have had on short-term industry rankings. While other pots were bubbling and the steam rose, Edper chose not to participate in the massive leveraged buy-outs of the day but rather to keep the group's own pot on a carefully controlled simmer. The focus throughout this period remained on pursuing internally generated growth and building a significantly larger equity base.

By running contrary to the prevailing business wisdom of the day, the group and its executives appeared to be out of step with the frenzied business activity at the time. But the philosophy, unconventional as it was, did have the distinct advantage of providing the group with the opportunity to add to its financial resources and brace itself for the impending severe disruptions in the financial markets which would inevitably arrive. By the end of the decade, poisonous clouds were imperceptibly taking shape just beyond the horizon and once they appeared would remain overhead in suffocating density throughout the early 1990s.

The equity financings completed during the second half of the 1980s, more than any other factor, differentiated the group from most of the other family-controlled Canadian enterprises which expanded rapidly during this period using debt. Peter Bronfman's strong aversion to the popular but precarious nature of leveraged buy-out transactions, as well as the restraint exercised by the group in resisting the abundant temptations during the late 1980s to overpay for business assets, provided the group with its own identity, relative financial strength and considerable staying power.

In the second half of the 1980s, while the group's combined capital base expanded to well over $10 billion, the operational focus at the Edper corporate level was directed towards the development of management talent to assist in implementing the group's strategic initiatives. The expansion of the group's merchant banking activities enabled Hees International to fulfill this role as it became a growing power in the financial arena and there was a never-ending array of challenging assignments in which to become immersed. Hees International had established sufficient financial strength and reputational clout to engage in considerably larger assignments for third parties than it had ever contemplated before.

These assignments were structured so that they could be effectively accomplished and then wound down within a short time frame, should the capital employed be required elsewhere in the group. This enabled Hees International to free up both financial and management resources for redeployment in the group's operating affiliates, should they be needed. The merchant banking business was demanding, intense and lucrative, but above all it provided financial flexibility and a well-stocked reservoir of management talent which was invaluable to the group as it expanded in size and diversified geographically.

Although it should not have taken a crystal ball to foresee the coming financial trauma, few companies were fully prepared for the severity of the storm which rapidly descended on the Canadian business scene in the second half of 1990. The lethal impact of the economic collapse, when it did eventually occur, was far greater than Peter Bronfman and his colleagues could have anticipated in even their bleakest predictions. The storm broke with full fury quite suddenly, and the buoyant economic growth in which Canada had been luxuriating during the second half of the 1980s came to an abrupt and brutal halt.

A number of factors converged simultaneously which inflicted serious, long-lasting damage to the Canadian business community and had an unprecedented impact on the confidence of Canadian bankers. With little warning, many of the banks started to withdraw the money they had eagerly lent, leaving corporate borrowers scrambling to find replacement funding.

The introduction of tough monetary and fiscal measures, coupled with reduced consumer demand, tipped Canada into a severe recession. The recession itself was then aggravated and prolonged by the contraction in the credit previously made available by the banks to corporate borrowers. This occurred first in the real estate sector, then in the forest products industry, and later it applied to most Canadian corporations. It was as though, with the arrival of the new decade, in one burning moment a hot wind had blown and dried into dust all pools of credit which only hours before had sat full and glittering in the sunshine of a healthy economy. The environment became arid and hostile and the acrid odour of panic permeated everything.

The high real interest rates and unfavourable exchange rates which prevailed throughout the early 1990s crippled Canada's international competitive position and rendered the country a floundering entity on the international economic scene. Domestically, an unprecedented implosion in commercial and residential real estate values greatly reduced both corporate and individual net worths and plunged many into economic ruin and despair.

The inescapable deterioration in the business environment was grim, and by early 1992 the gloomy severity of the suffocating recession had placed considerable strain on most Canadian companies, including the Edper group. This strain, combined with the group's rapid growth, size and diversity and its low-key, tightly knit management style, created an easy target for those seeking a scapegoat to blame for the predicament in which virtually all Canadian companies found themselves.

To a large extent, the group had brought upon itself some of the troubles it would soon face. With its growing success and increased presence in the Canadian business community, the media focused an inordinate amount of attention on the group's activities. Coupled with its rapid expansion across such a broad spectrum of businesses over the previous ten years and its growing desire to be accepted by the Toronto business community, the group had retained within its ranks a few high-profile executives who, while talented and capable, had never fully embraced the team approach promoted by Peter Bronfman. Unfortunately for the Edper group, they were also a rich source of provocative comments about the group both on and "off the record". The refusal of Peter Bronfman and his closest colleagues to engage in public dialogue to counter the comments of these executives inadvertently added credibility to their remarks.

Fortunately, Peter Bronfman and his colleagues knew when to backtrack and trust their instincts. The vast majority of the executives in the companies acquired during the 1980s had adapted well and demonstrated that they were committed to their companies' new direction and wholeheartedly endorsed their relationships within the group both publicly and privately. The challenge was to deal as graciously as possible with the few who had distinctly different agendas.

Roles were changed for some executives and others were encouraged to leave. Slowly the group began the tedious and painstaking process of repairing the damage that had been done, mending the breaks in reputation and relationships and re-establishing throughout the group the real meaning of teamwork. Peter Bronfman led the way in returning to what he felt was right, that is to let the work and results speak quietly for themselves and be of benefit to the shareholders and not just to satisfy any individual's need for personal recognition.

While attention had always been paid to the overall performance of management teams, early in the 1990s a more detailed examination of each leader's performance, motivations and commitment to the group's objectives and values was made. Peter Bronfman's objective was to ensure that the senior personnel in each business unit devoted their full and total energies to the hands-on management of their respective businesses while, at the same time, being supportive of the group's overall strategies and business objectives. He believed that a non-hierarchical management structure which provided talented individuals with a good deal of flexibility and freedom to manage also required absolute commitment to the business and the goals of the group as a whole. Otherwise the base would crumble and with it the value of the entire enterprise.

∽

The recession also brought out the best and the worst in some of the Edper group's external relationships. Although a few organizations and individuals used the group's perceived weakness for their own gain, many others went out of their way, often at considerable cost to themselves, to assist the group in dealing with its challenges. Foremost among the financial institutions which provided exceptional support were the Canadian Imperial Bank of Commerce, which had had a close relationship with Brascan from its earliest days, The Toronto-Dominion Bank and The Bank of Nova Scotia and their respective investment dealer subsidiaries, as well as Gordon Capital, Goldman Sachs, Merrill Lynch and CS First Boston.

The relationship with the Canadian Imperial Bank of Commerce was renewed and strengthened by Don Fullerton when he became Chairman and Chief Executive of the bank in 1984, and continued with his successor, Al Flood, who made a point of gaining an in-depth knowledge of Edper and the capabilities of its senior executives. In even the most trying circumstances, Al Flood ensured that the bank assigned individuals of the highest calibre to work with the group and made it known that he would be available personally to assist when needed. John Hunkin and John Bowden were two of the bank's senior officers who were particularly helpful in providing guidance and support for the group's refinancing initiatives during the early 1990s.

Similarly, the solid relationship that had begun with Allen Lambert at The Toronto-Dominion Bank so many years before remained strong through Dick Thomson's tenure as Chairman and Chief Executive. This association flourished further with Charles Baillie, the bank's current Chairman and Chief Executive, who continues to build on the sense of trust and understanding so essential to productive, long-term business associations.

Jon Corzine and Jack Curtin, two senior partners of Goldman Sachs, helped prepare the group to enter the financial markets in the United States to refinance maturing debt in the early 1990s when a number of Canadian banks were cutting back and corporate bond financing was generally unavailable in Canada. They also gave freely of their time to provide advice on strategic initiatives and broader world financial trends.

Prem Watsa was one of several self-made business leaders who won the loyalty of Peter Bronfman and his colleagues through their consistent confidence in the Edper group. Their ready availability with wise counsel and thoughtful analysis particularly during difficult times helped the group restructure and rearrange its affairs.

Though the group did not have direct business dealings with Gerry Schwartz, founder and Chief Executive of Onex Corporation, and his equally accomplished wife, Heather Reisman, founder and Chief Executive of Indigo Books and Music, they were among the friends who in the toughest of times expressed confidence in the group's ability to rebuild once the recession ended. Peter Bronfman particularly admired how they had balanced their corporate achievements with their political and community work.

There were also a number of outstanding individuals who served as directors on the boards of group companies, who provided generous support and on whom Peter Bronfman relied for guidance during this and other critical periods in the group's development. These included Bill Davis, former Premier of Ontario; Peter Lougheed, the former Premier of Alberta; Governor Jim Blanchard, former U.S. Ambassador to Canada; Isabel Bassett, currently a Minister in the Ontario Government; André Bérard, Chairman and Chief Executive of the National Bank of Canada; John Scrymgeour, founder of Westburne Resources; Roy Maclaren, the current High Commissioner to the United Kingdom; Michael Nesbitt and Lionel Schipper, two highly skilled investors; Saul Shulman, an experienced real estate lawyer and senior partner of Goodman and Carr; and Bill Dimma, chairman of a number of major companies and a leading advocate of corporate governance.

Peter Bronfman also recognized that it always took more than just the leaders and senior executives to make a success of any venture. His direct involvement with and concern for all employees resulted in long service and stability from support staff at the corporate office who ensured that reports were produced efficiently and that deadlines were met. Their work was constantly acknowledged in many meaningful ways by Peter Bronfman as an important part of the corporate team's accomplishments.

Throughout the darkest days of the recession, there were other friends who demonstrated loyalty and support to Peter Bronfman and his colleagues through telephone calls, letters and thoughtful advice. While many of these individuals were themselves feeling the impact of the downturn in the economy, their faith in him and his colleagues and their ability to achieve their objectives manifested itself in much-welcomed words of encouragement. Friends who stand the test of time and tribulations are precious, and Peter Bronfman and his colleagues were most grateful for their support during this most challenging period in the group's development.

❧

In response to the recession, key members of the group pulled even more tightly together, relying on the integrity and intimate trust between Peter Bronfman and his closest colleagues. The financial partnership which they had embraced meant that their personal financial interests, though also badly affected by the recession, remained closely aligned throughout this critical time with protecting the group's interests and laying the groundwork for future success.

The members of the team drew heavily on the understandings and bonds which had always served them well in the past. The team was considerably larger, the problems more complex and the stage on which they had to perform broader and more closely watched than before. However, their mutual trust and well-tested values held firm as the storm raged around them, and they did what they had always done when weather and tide had turned against them – they battened down the hatches and set about tackling each problem, issue and challenge and settling them, one at a time.

The rapid tumbling of real estate values in the early 1990s had a severe impact on the group. They were not alone in confronting a destruction of value in the real estate sector. In fact many individuals and companies were hurt to such an extent that they were completely eliminated from any significant future participation, so mortal were their wounds. Edper's managers refused to contemplate taking a final and fatal bow and exiting the industry. Wounded but still alive, they devised and implemented a fallback plan to prepare for recovery once better times returned.

It began with the refocusing of Hees International's resourceful merchant banking team with its extensive workout and restructuring experience. Very few other corporate groups were so fortunate in having a home-grown in-house team of specialists skilled in working out structural and financial problems. This team quickly wound down many of its third-party assignments and turned almost all of its attention to the group's real estate affiliates to help them sort out their options. As time passed and the storm clouds still remained overhead, Hees International provided the group's real estate affiliates with well over $1 billion of cash to cushion the adjustment to their reduced and rapidly deteriorating circumstances.

Most painful among the decisions made to ensure that the real estate group could withstand even the direst predictions was the decision in 1994 to withdraw from Trizec Corporation. The pain notwithstanding, parting with Trizec was acceded to in order to secure a solid and more valuable future base in the real estate industry for Brookfield Properties, which held a 32% interest in Trizec at that time. This base had to be strong enough to enable the group to add to its directly-owned premium quality commercial properties, once it was felt the bottom of the real estate market was approaching and the cycle was about to turn. Every effort was made to ensure that Trizec, for its part, continued as a successful public real estate company. This has occurred under Peter Munk's capable management and control, with Bill L'Heureux using Brookfield Properties' withdrawal from Trizec as an opportunity to establish a new career overseeing Trizec's international expansion plans.

The withdrawal from Trizec had been a difficult decision which left Peter Bronfman, Gordon Arnell, Sam Pollock and a number of their other senior colleagues disappointed for a long while. They found it difficult to shake the sense of failure from having to part with a large portion of the group's first business focus, commercial real estate, under strained circumstances.

The group had reached a crossroad in the real estate sector – they could fold their tents and withdraw from the business, or they could dig in and redouble their commitment to their long-held belief that they could prosper through building and managing commercial real estate properties. They chose to set a new course of action and began to re-launch their real estate dreams. This led to the group finding ways to conserve and then build its financial resources within this sector, so that it could acquire the very best commercial properties and in the very best locations when others had no choice but to throw in the towel.

The wreckage from the financial storm which rocked the real estate sector spread far and wide. The decline in real estate values was also the precipitating factor in the equally painful restructuring of Royal Trustco, one year earlier in 1993, as a result of its real estate lending activities in the United Kingdom and the western United States. As a major shareholder and having played a key role in bringing Royal Trustco back from the brink of failure years before, the Edper group was again called upon to provide the essential capital needed for Royal Trustco to complete an orderly sale of its operating subsidiaries to the Royal Bank of Canada where they could ride out the unprecedented global decline in real estate values.

Notwithstanding the demands for cash at that time from a number of the group's other operations, Peter Bronfman was in favour of providing financial support for a restructuring and sale that ensured the continuing operation of Royal Trustco's intermediary and investment businesses, insisting that this be done without disruption to the deposit holders and investment clients. Although this was ultimately achieved, the Royal Trust sale, like the group's withdrawal from Trizec, came at a cost to shareholders and to the group's reputation, severely hurting the morale of Peter Bronfman's team – many of whom had by that time worked together for more than two decades without a significant setback.

❧

By any measure, the withdrawal from Trizec and Royal Trust were major blows. However, spurred on by Peter Bronfman's constant encouragement, his colleagues drew heavily on their own sense of mission, revised their business plans and determined never again to place any part of the group's destiny in the hands of people who did not share their goals and have the same commitment to their businesses.

One team of colleagues concentrated on pursuing operating efficiencies in every corner, nook and cranny of the group. Cost containment and cash conservation were the watchwords of the day. They also refocused on business strategies, making them more refined and responsive to the times, and once they knew what was expendable or what could later be replaced, they initiated a massive capital recovery and refinancing program.

As a result, by the end of 1995, $25 billion of cash was raised by the group through equity issues, asset sales and long-term bond financings, much to the amazement of doubting, then startled, observers. Most of these financings were accomplished outside of Canada, principally in the significantly larger and more sophisticated capital markets in the United States. A portion of the funds was used to repay the domestic banks, to lengthen the term of institutional borrowings and to complete a multi-billion dollar property development programme commenced by BCE Inc. in 1989 and taken over by Brookfield Properties in the early 1990s.

Among the assets sold was the group's 38% shareholding in John Labatt. With the growth of Great Lakes Power, the stable portion of the group's earnings base was rapidly rising, placing less importance on the continued ownership of John Labatt. Furthermore, John Labatt faced a potential competitive threat from larger brewers in the United States should they ever decide to exploit the new opportunities provided by the Canada-U.S. Free Trade Agreement. This possibility cast a shadow over the long-term stability of John Labatt's future earnings.

With the help of George Taylor, who had proved to be a dedicated and exceptionally capable Chief Executive of John Labatt, steps were first taken to surface value from the company's food businesses. This was a key factor in enabling the group to sell its shareholdings in John Labatt in 1993 for a gain of nearly $400 million, through a record Canadian stock market distribution arranged by CIBC Wood Gundy. Since this sale, George Taylor has continued to contribute to the group's affairs as a director of both EdperBrascan and Great Lakes Power.

The sale of John Labatt represented the final step in the Edper group's withdrawal from the consumer products sector. Earlier it had sold its remaining interests in two other investments in this sector, Scott Paper and M.A. Hanna, in 1989 and 1991 respectively, for total gains of more than $450 million. Most of these proceeds found their way into the core natural resources sector. Skip Walker, the Chairman and Chief Executive of M.A. Hanna, had overseen a major remake of this company by building a highly regarded specialty chemical company virtually from scratch. He ranked among the most effective executives the group ever had the pleasure to work with, and after the sale of the group's investment in M.A. Hanna, he continued to provide invaluable advice and support.

Having restored the group's financial position, Peter Bronfman knew only too well that maintaining a strong capital base in the senior corporate entity was imperative to ensure investor and banking support. Without a broad, firm capital base, no amount of careful planning would have been sufficient in the face of the financial malaise that had befallen Canada in the early 1990s. He and his colleagues knew that, for an enterprise to be successful, it would need strong roots and, in the financial world of the time, this meant an unshakeable, permanent capital base.

Chapter Eight

Preserving the Capital Base

Peter Bronfman and his colleagues had come to appreciate at an early stage of the Edper group's development the importance of having the confidence of the financial markets. This became particularly relevant as the group entered the 1990s and many of its operations were thrown open to international competition for the first time and, in some cases, were about to face costly structural problems. At the same time, increasing amounts of capital were being withdrawn by family members. Furthermore, ominous dark financial clouds had started to gather on the horizon.

None of this was particularly new for Peter Bronfman and his colleagues. A constant challenge in the development of the Edper group since the early 1970s had been the need to keep adding to its capital base in order to finance the orderly growth in its businesses while maintaining the confidence of the financial community. He and his colleagues were well aware that capital would also have to be set aside in anticipation of further withdrawals of cash by family members. In this regard the only questions were – how soon and how much?

The withdrawal of the Mildred Mona Bronfman Trust's capital from the business in 1973 had been the first wake-up call, since it had shrunk the capital base of Edper Investments Limited by more than a third at a time when the group's financial resources were already stretched to pay for the investment made in the Canadian Arena Company.

The ongoing concerns over the appropriate size and the periodic need to expand the capital base led the group to seek equity capital from a variety of sources. These included three different approaches – joint-venturing major investment initiatives with partners, operating through stand-alone public companies, and utilizing preferred shares with specially designed attributes as an alternate form of permanent capital.

Early corporate joint ventures involved The Bank of Nova Scotia and Baton Broadcasting to purchase Canadian Arena Company, Boyd Stott McDonald to acquire Westmount Life, Patiño N.V. in the acquisition of Brascan, and Caisse de dépôt et placement du Québec as a partner in securing control of Noranda.

Later, as Edper's operations continued to grow and capital requirements increased still further, the group adopted a corporate structure which allowed a number of its major business units to raise capital by operating as stand-alone public companies. This structure enabled each of the public operating units to secure its own independent access to the capital markets, without its debts having recourse to Edper.

Furthermore, since the group's affiliates were only partly owned, a dollar of equity capital invested by Edper in an affiliate permitted a similar or larger amount of capital to be raised from the public for investment in the group's expanding array of buildings, power plants, paper mills and mining projects.

By spreading the sources of capital and the financial risks associated with entering these new businesses, the group's combined capital base, including the investment made by minority shareholders in group companies, was steadily expanded from less than $1 billion in the early 1980s to well over $10 billion by the early 1990s. A necessary by-product of this method of adding to the group's capital base was the three-fold growth in the number of public companies within the Edper group. In time, this resulted in the group's corporate structure being considered too complex and difficult by North American standards for investors to analyze.

In the careful piecing together of the group's corporate structure, the potential for an unflattering portrayal of that structure had been largely overlooked by Peter Bronfman and his colleagues, and certainly had not been foremost on their minds as they implemented their plans to expand the size and nature of the group's operations. The benefits and practicality of the structure seemed so obvious to them, having observed that it had worked successfully in other countries with large natural resource interests, that they were genuinely surprised by the persistent criticism of the uniqueness of the structure itself.

∽

It took a while for Peter Bronfman and his colleagues to recognize that the time had arrived to reformulate the group's financial architecture by simplifying it wherever this could be done without placing a strain on the group's financial resources. It became clear to them that, notwithstanding its merits, its uniqueness in relation to other companies in North America would, unless painstakingly and repeatedly explained, continue to spark critical comments, and these would generally be uttered at the most inopportune times. Beginning in 1992 under the leadership of Bob Harding, a concerted effort was made, first to explain the less understood merits of the group's financial strategies to investors and, second, to outline the plan they proposed to follow to bring the group's structure more in line with prevailing practices.

Commencing in 1993, the simplification process began in earnest as group companies were merged, surplus cash was used to repurchase their own shares, assets were sold and the cash realized from these sales was used to increase the ownership of their affiliates. It took a few years, but by the end of 1997 these actions had resulted in the elimination of five private holding companies and six public companies. Throughout the course of implementing the step-by-step simplification process, painstaking care was employed to avoid weakening the financial ratios of each corporate entity or the group itself.

With this two-pronged approach of explaining and simplifying, the group gradually won over the majority of its critics. Group executives had learned the hard way, and at great cost, that a high priority had to be assigned on a continuing basis to providing adequate explanations whenever the group's corporate structure and business actions differed from the accepted norm. Throughout the early 1990s, as the economy continued to change for the worse, they increased their vigilance in responding promptly to public and media anxieties and by opening the doors and explaining the group's plans and actions. Time was also spent with government representatives explaining the group's role in the economy and the depth of its commitment to Canada. Ed Lumley, a former federal trade minister and a director of Trilon Financial, provided invaluable guidance in dealing with this area of communication which had been badly neglected.

Above all, the group learned that by designating senior executives in each company to take these tasks seriously and by responding quickly and accurately to media and other inquiries, they could solve many potential problems before they arose. In the process, they were able to establish good working relationships with those who were responsible for analyzing the activities of the corporate world for investors and the general public through investment reports and media commentary.

In addition to supplementing its capital base through investment partnerships and operating through partly-owned public companies, the group became a major issuer of preferred shares to provide another layer of permanent capital.

The reliance on preferred share capital also came under close public scrutiny in the late 1980s as some critics tried to make the case that the group relied too heavily on these securities.

George Myhal, in his previous position as Treasurer of Hees International, played a pivotal role in developing the preferred share market in Canada. He was particularly effective in advising group companies to issue preferred shares with perpetual attributes through the mid-1980s when this market failed to ascribe a cost factor to this valuable characteristic. As a result, the overwhelming majority of preferred shares issued by group companies had this perpetual feature. Doubly trained as both a chartered accountant and an engineer, George Myhal applied the discipline of one to the precision of the other and became a constructive and moving force behind the Canadian preferred share market's five-fold growth from 1980 through 1987.

Suddenly and without forewarning in 1987, the Federal Government pulled the carpet out from under the feet of corporate preferred share issuers by changing the preferred share rules. This effectively eliminated new preferred share issues as a viable financing alternative for most companies, other than banks and utilities. The preferred share market had become an important source of long-term equity capital for many Canadian companies, and even more important it had helped them offset the fiscal and other financial disadvantages which handicapped domestic corporations simply because they were based in Canada.

The market had been lucrative and huge. Preferred shares distributed by way of public offerings by numerous

Canadian companies during the 1980s totalled approximately $30 billion. Of this total, Edper group companies had issued $4.5 billion, representing approximately 15% of the total amount of preferred shares issued. At the peak, preferred shares accounted for 20% of the group's combined capital base and represented the lowest-cost permanent equity capital available to the group. By the end of 1997, through conversions of preferred shares into common shares and redemptions, group public preferred share issues had declined to less than $2 billion.

During the 1980s, group companies were not only issuers of preferred shares but also investors in these securities. Mico Investments Limited was one such company formed for this purpose by Hees International in 1975 in partnership with the Mercantile Bank of Canada. Over the years it steadily grew to hold $700 million of assets, all funded by equity capital, and paid out more than $750 million in dividends to its shareholders, which consisted primarily of group companies. In addition to enhancing group earnings by more than $250 million since its formation, Mico Investments Limited continues to provide a source of liquidity for group preferred share issues by being a participant in the after-market for these securities.

In the mid-1980s when the group was applying great energy to building and strengthening its capital base, Peter and Edward Bronfman's six children, who were then young adults, began to increase the frequency and amount of their capital withdrawals. And, as the time approached when this generation of family members would become entitled to withdraw their shares of Edper Investments Limited from their respective trusts, there were indications that times and attitudes were changing. Different interests among the next generation were emerging, and the organization would have to balance the group's growing capital requirements with the families' needs.

In order to anticipate and accommodate the desires of the various family members, the business plans formulated through the late 1980s included provision for the two family trusts each to withdraw $50 million of capital from Edper Investments Limited over a five-year period starting in the 1990s. These plans changed when Edward Bronfman, on the recommendations of outside advisers, decided that it was in his family's best interests to exercise his right to launch Edper Investments Limited, the brothers' original private investment company, as a public company. This was done in the second half of 1989, shortly after the company was renamed Edper Enterprises Ltd. Edward Bronfman's concern was the fast-waning strength of the capital markets. Understandably, he wanted to strike while the iron was still hot. But it became a problem for his brother and his colleagues, because the request came at an inopportune time since there was still much to be done to prepare Edper Enterprises Ltd., the most senior company in the group, for the public equity markets.

During most of the 1980s, Edward Bronfman, by choice, had continued to play a limited but helpful role within the Edper group. He was a member of several group company boards including Brascan, Hees International, Trizec Corporation and Edper Enterprises Ltd. He also expanded his involvement in community work, emulating his father's role in Montreal. In the late 1980s his children began to take a more active interest in their family's affairs and in developing their own business interests. Paul Bronfman, Edward's eldest son, at the time was investing successfully in the entertainment field, building an integrated motion picture services company.

The timing of the requests for additional cash was unfortunate because the best part of the business cycle was rapidly coming to an end and much of the work in bullet-proofing the capital base of Edper Enterprises Ltd. had yet to be done. If ever there was a time for the Edper group to conserve its resources, this was it. Every dollar counted heavily as the anticipated market downturn quickly approached. As a compromise and an alternative, it was proposed that a substantially larger dividend payment be made to Edward Bronfman's family over a number of years. This was accompanied by a commitment to merge Edper Enterprises Ltd. with Hees International to enable Edper to acquire an operating base and a stable source of cash flow. The plan was to do this as soon as the necessary preparatory work could be carried out and the business cycle turned for the better.

When this proposal was rejected early in 1989, an urgent search was commenced for long-term equity investors to strengthen Edper Enterprises Ltd.'s financial position prior to launching the company in the public stock markets. A basic requirement which complicated the process, but which was viewed as crucial to the acceptance of any deal, was the retention by Peter Bronfman of his voting control, even though his effective economic ownership interest would fall to less than 25% after an injection of additional capital into Edper Enterprises Ltd. Needless to say, the combination of this voting structure and the issuing of shares in a holding company with no operating base was not especially palatable to many investors and consequently reduced the universe of potential investors prepared to make a major capital investment in Edper Enterprises Ltd.

After completing an exhaustive search for private investors and concluding that there were no compatible candidates within view, Peter Bronfman decided that the financial partners he was searching for to solve the capital problems created by his brother's withdrawal from the business were in fact the colleagues with whom he had worked for many years in building the business. Ever confident of the abiding trust they shared among themselves, Peter Bronfman proposed to twelve of his long-time Edper colleagues that they pool their group shareholdings, which had a value of more than $300 million at that time, and use these securities as collateral to borrow $100 million from the Bank of Montreal. This was accomplished through a company called Partners Limited, which had been formed in 1987 and was subsequently expanded and renamed EdperPartners Limited.

The cash borrowed by EdperPartners Limited from the Bank of Montreal early in 1989 was used to purchase control of The Pagurian Corporation Limited, a publicly listed company which had no meaningful operations but ample cash resources. This company was purchased from Christopher

Ondaatje and Hees International for the purposes of leveraging the amount of equity capital which could be invested in the financial partnership with Peter Bronfman. Hees International had acquired voting control and a 4% common equity interest in Pagurian a few months earlier as a result of a workout assignment which revolved principally around Canadian Express Limited.

Once EdperPartners Limited had acquired control of Pagurian, a $280 million equity issue was made to bolster Pagurian's existing cash resources. Two key participants in the equity issue were the Canadian Imperial Bank of Commerce and The Toronto-Dominion Bank. In addition, senior executives of the Edper group, both individually and through EdperPartners Limited purchased $120 million of the issue.

These two Canadian banks were key to the success of the equity issue and remained steadfast supporters of the group notwithstanding the steep decline in the price of the Pagurian shares when the business environment and the stock market subsequently deteriorated. Through their investment in Pagurian, they acquired a thorough knowledge and understanding of the group's long-term business plans, which enabled them to take a long-range view of the business cycle and the group's prospects. This support was greatly appreciated by Peter Bronfman and his colleagues.

Over the course of 1989, Pagurian used $500 million of its cash to acquire a 49.9% senior ranking equity position in Edper Holdings Inc., a partnership company formed by Peter Bronfman to hold his controlling interest in Edper

Enterprises Ltd. Tom Allen, a prominent and well-respected Toronto lawyer, played an important role in advising Peter Bronfman on setting up Edper Holdings Inc. and the partnership sharing arrangements. Peter Bronfman held Tom Allen in high regard for his sensitivity and judgement in dealing with this transaction and a number of other issues relating to the group's development.

Edper Holdings Inc. used a portion of the funds received from Pagurian to strengthen Edper Enterprises Ltd.'s capital base and to make certain that Edper Holdings Inc. retained ownership of a majority of Edper Enterprises Ltd.'s shares after the planned public issue. Later on, the balance of the funds was used by Edper Holdings Inc. to purchase additional shares of Edper Enterprises Ltd. both in the market and from Edward Bronfman's family.

The introduction of Edper Enterprises Ltd. and Pagurian as two new public companies exacerbated the already prevalent view that the group was excessively complex. By 1990, when the impact and misery of the recession had investors in its crushing grip, what had begun as a poor and unenthusiastic investor reception of Edper Enterprises Ltd.'s debut as a publicly-listed holding company turned decidedly acidulous as the stock market price of the company's shares dropped. Although most Canadian companies were suffering to some degree from the recession which had begun in earnest in 1990, the Edper group, with three new additions to its corporate structure – Edper Enterprises Ltd., The

Pagurian Corporation Limited and Edper Holdings Inc. – sticking out like three sore thumbs, attracted criticism from a variety of sources.

By 1991, for the first time in more than fifty years, Canadian-based businesses were simultaneously burdened with an overvalued domestic currency, high real interest rates, record low commodity prices, reduced business volumes and a major contraction in credit available to the business sector. Two generations had worked their entire business careers without having been challenged by such a thick and complex stew of negativity. The Canadian business community had little experience, collectively or individually, in navigating their way out of the mess they were in. Peter Bronfman and his colleagues, however, knew that no business environment lasts forever and cycles do turn. The trick was to be ready and, if they were not ready and got caught short, they had to adapt and adapt they did.

As a result of numerous painstaking initiatives, the shares of most group companies started to rise slowly but steadily in value in 1993. Still, by the summer of that year, Peter Bronfman's three children, Linda, Bruce and Brenda, continued to be deeply concerned about the difficulties facing the group as a result of the recession. Understandably they, like many others, found it difficult to hang on indefinitely. They sought and accepted the counsel of outside advisers, who determined that their best course of defence against the prevailing economic situation and the tepid stock market for group securities was to crystallize the value of their investment in Edper Holdings Inc. and withdraw their capital from the group.

In order to accommodate the requests of Peter Bronfman's children, group executives once again increased their investment in EdperPartners Limited, this time by raising the cash needed through bank borrowings as well as by selling shares they held directly in Hees International, Great Lakes Power and Noranda and reinvesting the proceeds in their partnership with Peter Bronfman. It was a difficult stretch, but by now most of them knew that when things were bad, they had better be prepared for them to get worse before they would get better. The only way they could ensure that things would improve for their partner Peter Bronfman, for themselves and for all the other shareholders, was to pull together, and if this required putting all their eggs in one basket – so be it.

⌘

While Peter Bronfman may at one time have harboured thoughts of his interest in the business being passed on through generations of blood relatives, he felt a compelling responsibility to accommodate his children's wishes, given the uncertain economic environment at the time of their request to withdraw their capital.

In many respects, the sale by his children of their remaining shares represented an important turning point in the Edper story. It hastened the last few steps in the process of Edper's evolution from a family-controlled investment company to a more broadly-owned enterprise with formal provisions in place to ensure orderly ownership succession. These provisions would facilitate future exchanges of shares between the partners, an association which was soon to grow from twelve to twenty-five senior group executives. Among the new members of the partnership were Aaron Regent, Sam Pollock Jr. and John Tremayne, each of whom emerged from an expedited management leadership program in the early 1990s to play important roles in the recapitalization of the group. Their admission to the senior ranks helped to double the number of third-generation executives in the partnership.

The next step was to change the name of The Pagurian Corporation Limited to The Edper Group Limited. This was a signal that the group was intent on furthering the simplification of its ownership and corporate structure, first through a combination of The Edper Group Limited with Edper Enterprises Ltd. and then with other companies in the group ownership structure. The final step in the process occurred in December 1995, when Peter Bronfman exchanged his shareholdings in Edper Holdings Inc. for shares of The Edper Group Limited and then exchanged a portion of these shares for shares of EdperPartners Limited, to become one of the largest shareholders of this company. Through this private holding company, he and his longstanding business colleagues then shared control of The Edper Group Limited with a much simplified ownership structure.

These initiatives prepared the way for two further important simplifications of the group's corporate structure. At the end of 1996, The Edper Group Limited merged with Hees International Bancorp Inc. and in August 1997, the merged company amalgamated with Brascan Limited to form EdperBrascan Corporation. With these changes, EdperBrascan emerged as the group's senior public company, managing its investments in four core areas of business. Bob Harding was appointed Chairman of EdperBrascan because of his role in bringing these companies together and his group-wide responsibilities for governance, compliance and communications.

Peter Bronfman's primary objective in combining his shareholdings in the Edper group with those of his long-standing business colleagues was to put in place an owner-ship structure which would survive external and personal stresses and provide the ownership stability he considered so essential to the well being of the enterprise he and his col-leagues had built. He was a firm believer that meaningful value should be attributed to stable ownership as it enabled the executives in the group's operating companies to concen-trate on implementing their growth strategies undistracted by potential corporate raiders. There was still much to be done and stability of ownership and common purpose would be essential if these goals were to be achieved.

Peter Bronfman had also come to believe that for any business to succeed, it required deep passion and commit-ment on the part of its leaders. He recognized this commit-ment would have to grow in magnitude in proportion with the size and diversity of the group. His own sense of respon-sibility to shareholders and to his colleagues dictated that he place the company on the firmest, safest base possible. With the expansion of EdperPartners Limited and the combination of his controlling position with his colleagues' shareholdings, he was confident that his lifework of building the Edper group would continue in experienced and committed hands.

Chapter Nine

The Ongoing Partnership

The seed of the enterprise had been Peter Bronfman's and his brother's and sister's inheritance, a nugget of about $20 million. The Bible story of the ten talents provided sufficient incentive for him to put this money to work. To sit on it, to simply consume it over a period of time or invest just enough to keep him and his family in comfort, would have been a waste of a gift and opportunity. Instead, he and his brother chose to take responsibility for actively deploying these funds to launch and nurture a major new Canadian enterprise.

He recognized from the outset of his career that he would need skilled colleagues alongside him. When he found and subsequently lost some of them to more appealing environs, he quickly revised his notions of how to manage his affairs by introducing a plan which encouraged his colleagues to think as well as act as partners and made it possible for them to acquire meaningful ownership stakes in the enterprise.

With each new obstacle he encountered, he and his colleagues endeavoured to find ways through or around it. The periodic withdrawal of capital by other members of his family, which seemed to occur at inopportune times, led to his conviction that a strong permanent capital base was essential for future growth and the long-term stability of the enterprise. Thus began a relentless effort to create an unshakeable financial foundation.

With his own capital tied to the appreciation in the value of his shareholdings and the bulk of his income derived from dividends paid by Edper, Peter Bronfman truly appreciated the contributions made by his colleagues and business partners. Shareholder value, its protection and its growth were regarded as a basic trust and obligation among himself, his colleagues and the increasing number of investors who came to share in the many business ventures he helped to found and build.

When a person has devoted a lifetime to building a business and poured years of energy and thought into assembling a team committed to growth, the longevity of the enterprise becomes increasingly important. Personal satisfaction is not the only motivator. Indeed, a sense of responsibility for thousands of employees and shareholders adds impetus to protect the future of the organization.

From his many years of refining the ideas he had about partnerships, whether with external associates in structured deals or with his colleagues within the Edper group, Peter Bronfman became well experienced in the complexities of fashioning effective partnership arrangements. He felt that when the time arrived to combine his investment in the Edper group with his partners' shareholdings, it would be important to set out in writing how he wanted the Edper partnership to work in the future. He also intended this document to contain guidelines on how his partners should relate to each other in order to enhance the group's ability to survive and prosper over the long term.

It was during 1995 that he turned to one of his closest colleagues, Bob Dunford, to assist him in framing a definitive partnership agreement to govern the ongoing ownership and management of the group. The objective was to prepare a document which would withstand the test of time, be faithful to his values, provide financial flexibility within the partnership and incorporate guidelines to help in resolving the potential problems which could lie ahead.

In preparing the Edper partnership agreement, Bob Dunford drew heavily on partnership documents governing some of the leading Canadian professional firms as well as a number of investment banking partnerships in the United States. The shareholders' agreement which eventually emerged differed, however, in a number of material respects from these other agreements. Key among these differences were provisions which facilitated the renewal of the partnership and protected its capital base.

Another important requirement was the size of the partnership agreement, which was kept to ten pages as Peter Bronfman wanted it to be a document of clarity and simplicity. It had to be practical and easy to read and understand.

Above all, and most telling of the depth of his belief in his partners and the mutual trust he expected among them, was his willingness to sacrifice precise provisions covering every possible eventuality in the interest of having a document that was intelligible and provided a guide rather than too many iron-clad rules.

The emphasis in drafting the agreement was therefore placed on trust and expectations, because he believed that if partners were dictating "you shall" to one another or were ever tempted to test the legal enforceability of any provision of the agreement, the partnership would by such actions severely weaken itself. Confidence and trust in each other would by that point have diminished and would take considerable time and effort to restore. Instead, he would encourage the partners to take great care to settle their differences by using their energies to reach a consensus rather than resorting to legal challenges. This had always been his preferred way of conducting business.

For this approach to be successful, he knew the partnership would need to continue the practice of placing a high priority on the selection of new partners. Since the introduction in the early 1970s of a partnership approach to managing the group's business, he had paid close attention to the hiring of each of the executives who worked closely with him. High among the attributes he looked for was a natural aptitude to work as part of a team and the potential to qualify for admission to the partnership.

Before being admitted to the partnership, executives would be expected to accept that the bulk of their personal financial resources would henceforth be dedicated to their ownership of shares of the group. There was an explicit expectation that, for the most part and only with few exceptions, partners would not hold outside business investments, not only to avoid potential conflicts of interest but also in order to better manage distractions and to enable them to devote their full attention to the group's affairs. Any exceptions to this practice would have to be approved by all partners.

Also high among the matters to be addressed, before transferring his voting position in the Edper group to EdperPartners Limited, was his desire to make sure that his colleagues were prepared for and committed to fulfilling the ownership responsibilities he would henceforth be sharing with them. Foremost among these responsibilities were the benefits they would enjoy through the special voting rights provided by the group's capital structure.

For this reason, he sought a commitment from his colleagues that they would collectively maintain a meaningful ownership position in all classes of common equity issued by the most senior public company in the Edper group. Although he realized that the size of the shareholdings of each partner would vary and change from time to time, as partners retired or reduced their involvement for whatever reasons, he expected the younger partners to increase their effective ownership of Edper group shares each year by electing to receive the major portion of their rewards in shares rather than cash.

It was his view that EdperPartners Limited's special voting position, which in 1996 was reconstituted to limit it effectively to appointing half of the board of the group's most senior public company, should never be justified solely on the basis of his and his colleagues' historical role in building the group into a multi-billion dollar enterprise. These rights would need to be continuously earned by the partners, who would be expected to have the vast majority of their personal assets and income closely tied to the future of the Edper group.

In his view, being a partner not only conferred the privilege of being in a position along with the other partners and directors of EdperBrascan to influence the overall direction of the group and thus their own business destinies, but also entailed a major responsibility to strive for top-level performance and an absolute commitment to always act in the best interests of all shareholders.

To assist partners and other group executives in increasing their ownership of the group, all major operating companies were encouraged to adopt management share purchase plans which enable senior executives to trade off salaries and bonuses for increased opportunities to accumulate larger shareholdings in group companies. These directly-held shareholdings provide the executives with a greater degree of liquidity than their shareholdings in EdperPartners Limited. They are free to sell these shares into the market should family needs dictate, whereas they are expected to hold their shares of EdperPartners Limited throughout and possibly long after their active careers with the group ended. It was not critical to him whether his partners held their shareholdings in EdperBrascan through EdperPartners Limited or directly in their own hands or through family members.

Growth and Challenges

∽

In handing over the leadership reins of the partnership in 1995, Peter Bronfman selected David Kerr and Jack Cockwell as co-chief executives of EdperPartners Limited and nominated Tim Price to succeed him as Chairman of both EdperPartners Limited and The Edper Group Foundation. For nearly thirty years, the three of them had worked side by side with him, recording many victories as well as enduring their fair share of discomfort when the dogs of adversity were snapping at their every step. Perhaps because they were by nature quiet and reserved and their trust in each other was so great and their shared beliefs and values so strong, they never felt the need to demonstrate in an obvious way how harmonious their partnership had always been. Over the years the friendships matured and encompassed personal and professional experiences and concerns, resulting in relationships which were deep and all-embracing in their commitment to each other. For them it had become a lifelong friendship without boundaries, based on mutual respect, understanding, shared values and trust, a friendship that was truly personal and important in each of their lives.

Having dealt with the immediate leadership change, Peter Bronfman also wanted the partnership agreement to deal thoughtfully with how they would effect leadership changes in the future. Because the Edper group operated in a number of industries, he believed that it was simply too diverse to be led effectively by any one person. Besides, he had shown over the years that a smoothly functioning team could always outperform even the most capable individual.

Although he believed the appointment of a corporate chieftain who would operate as a one-man band was clearly not appropriate for the group he had built, he did recognize that from time to time the team might be in need of a different form of leadership to strike a new course and drive ahead with renewed vigour. The necessity for new leadership could present itself when a change of direction was required, when it became important to refinance the group in a different way, when it was opportune and appropriate to focus on sowing new seeds for future growth, or when group values needed to be re-examined or reinforced.

As times changed and different scenarios presented themselves, he felt it was important to have mechanisms in place which would allow those partners best suited to the task to assume positions of leadership in the group and that this be done with minimal disruption. However, he was well aware that situations could arise where the incumbent leadership would be the last to acknowledge the need for change.

To address these concerns, the partnership agreement incorporated the democratic principle of voting for the officers of EdperPartners Limited, and hence the group's most senior leaders, based on a show of hands. Each partner would have an equal say in the choice of the group's leaders, regardless of the number of shares held. Similarly, the partners assigned with leadership roles in the group could be replaced by a show of hands irrespective of their shareholdings. An overriding understanding was that, should the partners deem it appropriate for whatever reason that a leader step down, he would do so gracefully. Under the terms of the partnership agreement, partners could also be asked to leave the group and be required to sell their shares back to EdperPartners Limited at their fair value at the time.

Peter Bronfman's convictions relating to the group's need for a strong permanent capital base were also reflected in a number of specific clauses contained in the partnership agreement. At several critical junctures in the life of the group, large amounts of capital had been withdrawn. These transactions had been conducted well within the legal rights of those wishing to do so, but in some cases seemingly without regard for the consequences to the group and its stability, or to the eventual impact of these withdrawals on the group's remaining partners, employees and shareholders. It was his goal that each partner make a long-term commitment of capital which would remain with the group to some extent even after that partner retired or wound down his active involvement with the group's business.

Therefore, the partnership agreement included a clause which stipulated that, at the end of every five years, only 20% of the shares of EdperPartners Limited could be offered back to the partnership, with the company reserving the right to defer buying back shares for financial reasons. The purpose of the clause was not intended to reduce the liquidity of any individual's investment, because there were no limitations placed on the ability of shareholders to buy or sell shares of EdperPartners Limited amongst themselves. Furthermore, each year a formal auction was expected to be held to distribute shares offered by retiring partners or others wishing to sell to existing shareholders or new individuals being admitted to the partnership. These provisions were designed to ensure the long-term stability of the capital base within the partnership and thus for the group as a whole.

Integral to the concept of a lasting partnership, a clause was included in the partnership agreement to reflect the expectations placed on longer-standing partners to extend financial assistance from their personal resources to newer, younger partners. This was to be done in order to enable younger partners to acquire meaningful investment positions in the partnership company at an early stage of their careers and thereby facilitate the ownership continuity of the group. Furthermore, given the objective that EdperPartners Limited would continue to hold its controlling interest in the Edper group indefinitely, no value was to be attributed to control premiums inherent in the group's corporate structure when shares were issued to new partners or cashed in by retiring partners.

To guard against future partners succumbing to the temptation of liquidating the group or a major component of the group in order to realize a quick short-term gain, the partnership agreement requires that, should a control premium, for whatever reason, be realized by EdperPartners Limited, the premium is to be shared with both current and previous shareholders of the partnership company, and in certain circumstances with other group executives and the communities in which the group operates.

Though he recognized that it would take time, Peter Bronfman hoped that eventually the most senior executives of each of the major operating companies within the group would want to become shareholders alongside his long-standing colleagues in EdperPartners Limited. The gradual maturing of the group was expected to make this a natural step in its evolution, particularly if the culture of teamwork, trust and commitment was successfully transferred to each of the group's principal operating companies – which was, in any event, an important long-term objective in itself.

True to his commitment to the ongoing partnership, Peter Bronfman gave a great deal of thought to the lasting message he wanted to leave with his partners. The opportunity arose when his colleagues told him that they had commissioned a portrait of him to hang in the group's main boardroom. They asked him to help them compose an inscription for the brass plaque to be attached to the portrait.

He rejected all suggestions which honoured him or described him as "the founder" of the Edper group as he felt that this would separate him from his colleagues. Instead the inscription he chose to be remembered by reads as follows: *"True partners work together in their colleagues' best interests."*

These nine carefully selected words would be his last gift to his partners. They reflected the standard he had set in building the partnership over more than twenty-five years, and it was clear that he expected no less from those who would follow him.

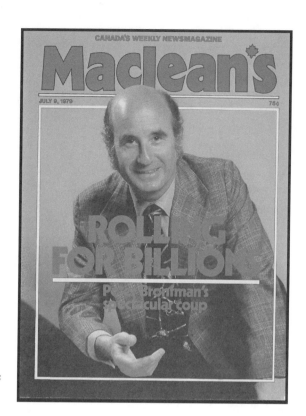

Peter Bronfman on the cover of the July 9, 1979 issue of Maclean's *recording Edper's acquisition of Brascan*

Peter Bronfman, centre, flanked by Edper Group Chairmen in 1987. From the left: Bob Dunford (Power Generation), Allen Lambert (Financial Services), Harold Milavsky (Real Estate) and the late Paul Marshall (Natural Resources)

Peter Bronfman's office filled with family photographs and memorabilia in Toronto in the 1980s

BCE Place in Toronto, headquarters of the Edper group since 1992, was selected in 1997 by other building owners as the finest office complex in the world

Three prestigious office buildings in World Financial Center, New York, developed by Paul Reichmann and acquired by the Edper group in 1996

Republic Plaza, Denver, acquired by the Edper group in 1990. Gordon Arnell, while with Oxford Properties Limited, played a role in the development of this premier office property

Peter Bronfman, on the left in the back row, with directors and staff of Westmin Resources at a company outing in Vancouver, c. 1990

A visit to the Brunswick zinc mine in Bathurst, New Brunswick, in 1988. From the left, Trevor Eyton, Brian Flemming, Jack Cockwell, Antoine Turmell and Peter Bronfman

The new Raglan nickel mine in northern Québec started production in 1997

The Collahuasi mine in northern Chile, one of the largest copper mines in the world, started production in 1998

David Kerr and Jim Gray in 1998 visiting a drill site in the Elmworth Deep Basin, one of the largest gas fields in North America

With natural gas reserves and production facilities in Alberta and British Columbia, the Edper group became one of Canada's largest explorers and producers of natural gas during the 1990s

The Edper group is the third-largest producer of oriented strandboard in the world

A typical working lunch at Hees International in the early 1990s. From the left: Steve Douglas, Bruce Flatt, Tim Price, Brian Lawson, Manfred Walt, Tony Rubin, George Myhal and Bob Harding

The Edper group started expanding its power operations in 1980 with the construction of the Clergue Generating Station in Sault Ste. Marie, Ontario

Since 1980, the group's power generating operations have more than doubled, including the recently acquired Waltham Generating Station in western Québec

São Paulo Tramway, Light and Power, the earliest incorporated predecessor of EdperBrascan, hauling penstock steel for the construction of the first hydro-electric generating station in Brazil, c. 1900

By 1908, electric power was being provided to light the parks and streets of São Paulo

Brascan Brazil's Rio Sul shopping centre in Rio de Janeiro, with its head office located in the adjacent office tower

A picture taken by Peter Bronfman of his colleagues on a business trip to Rio de Janeiro in 1995. From the left: Roberto de Andrade, Jack Cockwell, Bob Dunford, Trevor Eyton and Jacky Delmar

Book Four

The Legacy

These chapters retrace the story of the development of each of the business sectors which now comprise EdperBrascan Corporation. Real estate was the group's initial foundation and is represented today by Brookfield Properties, one of North America's premier office property companies. Natural resources became the group's second pillar after the acquisition of Noranda in 1981. Power generation, Brascan's principal business before selling The Light to the Brazilian government in 1979, re-emerges as an important part of the group in the 1980s through the expansion of Great Lakes Power. Financial services, now conducted through Trilon Financial Corporation, have from the beginning been the glue which holds the various parts of the group together. While the group is primarily North American-based, it also conducts extensive operations in South America arising from Brascan's long involvement on that continent.

Chapter Ten

The Initial Foundation

Property development is said to be spurred either by the growth in demand for accommodation or by the burning drive that seems to exist in human beings to build, to improve, to leave some visible and lasting structure behind as evidence of their accomplishments. This urge to build goes back to the beginnings of time, with each civilization struggling to outdo the previous one. The pyramids of Egypt, the Parthenon in Greece, the Colosseum in Rome, St. Paul's Cathedral in England and Mt. Rushmore in the United States all stand as witness to the dreams of glory of pharaohs, emperors, kings, presidents and ordinary people.

Peter Bronfman always believed that for any building to have lasting appeal and commercial value it needed a touch of, or better still a big dose of, both a commercial rationale and that additional element which comes from the developer, architect or city planner who wants to leave something new and special behind for others to admire and enjoy.

Peter Bronfman's earliest business dreams centred on building prime commercial properties as well as acquiring properties from others and then finding ways to improve them and provide better services to the tenants. At first he started in a small way, not much different from many other successful property developers before him, by acquiring unserviced land, subdividing it and building homes. Utilizing the experience and confidence gained, he began to build low-rise apartment units and office properties, bringing the latest mechanical systems and other technological improvements to the buildings he developed in Montreal in the early 1960s. He also learned financing techniques and honed his property management skills.

Within five years of striking out with his brother, he had assembled or had access to most of the skills necessary to develop and manage the most sophisticated commercial properties. To enter new geographical areas, partnerships were struck with local developers, with Edper providing additional financing and technical support when needed. Properties were sold and others bought with the constant objective of upgrading the portfolio.

Having started out in the property business, it is understandable why it always had a special place for him and invariably received a first call on his attention. Even with the excitement and distractions provided by the Montreal Canadiens hockey club or the Toronto Blue Jays baseball team, and after numerous other businesses had been added to the Edper group, he always found time to pore over and become engrossed in the intricacies of any new property development being considered by the group. It therefore seemed natural for the surplus cash generated during the 1970s by the group's investment in the Montreal Forum and the Montreal Canadiens hockey club, both held through the Canadian Arena Company, to be directed into the real estate sector. And when the chance came along to acquire a position in Trizec, which at the time was one of Canada's largest public real estate companies, it was no surprise that Peter Bronfman would be very interested.

The opportunity to purchase a controlling interest in Trizec arose in 1976 when English Property Corporation, Trizec's principal shareholder at the time, sought a Canadian partner to help restore the company's financial health and initiate management changes. Carena Properties Inc. was formed by Canadian Arena to hold a 51% interest in Trizec. Canadian Arena, which was subsequently renamed Carena Developments Limited in 1984 and Brookfield Properties Corporation in 1996, invested $50 million in return for a 50.1% controlling interest in Carena Properties Inc., including the right to appoint Harold Milavsky, Ed Sardachuk and Michael Cornelissen as the new senior management team in Trizec. Following the sale in 1978 of the Montreal Canadiens hockey club, additional capital was invested in Trizec to facilitate its expansion into the United States shopping centre market through the acquisition of The Hahn Company.

The steady escalation in commercial property values which took place over the next ten years provided the capital base to expand the group's residential land development and home building activities. In 1985, Brookfield Properties acquired a 50% interest in Coscan Development Corporation (renamed Brookfield Homes in 1996) from the U.K.-based

Costain development group. Substantial additional capital was invested in Brookfield Homes as it acquired a number of large scale master-planned residential land development projects located in California, Maryland, Virginia and Ontario in order to broaden the geographic spread of the group's home building operations.

In 1987, following the bankruptcy of numerous real estate companies in western Canada, Brookfield Properties acquired a 45% interest in Carma Corporation from several Canadian financial institutions. This company proved to be one of the group's most profitable and well-managed real estate operations, producing double-digit profit margins in each year since it was acquired. The investment in Carma, which was subsequently increased to an ownership position of nearly 80%, was recovered in full within six years. It continues to generate attractive returns and still holds a twenty-year supply of prime developable residential land.

Gordon Arnell, who joined the real estate group in 1984, was appointed President and Chief Executive of Brookfield Properties in 1988 with responsibility for co-ordinating its various real estate interests and establishing a real estate merchant banking capability. As Group Chairman Real Estate, he was also assigned responsibility for providing strategic advice on real estate issues involving other group companies. He led the real estate group through a number of extremely difficult years, restructuring its asset base when real estate values started to decline rapidly in 1990 and new organizational and management practices had to be introduced. He drew on his extensive career in the industry, which covered all facets of property development and management, to provide valuable mentoring to Bruce Flatt, Bill Pringle, David Arthur, Alan Norris and Steve Douglas as he moved them rapidly through the management ranks.

Brookfield Properties took the first steps towards upgrading and expanding its directly-owned office property operations in 1990 when, at the request of BCE Inc., it agreed to manage the financial restructuring of BCE Development Corporation (BCED). This eventually led to Brookfield Properties acquiring full ownership of BCED's principal operating subsidiary, which was renamed Brookfield Commercial Properties Ltd.

In the process of completing the development projects taken over from BCE Inc., Brookfield Properties obtained an early warning of the impending credit contraction about to sweep north and engulf the Canadian real estate industry. This led Gordon Arnell to implement a major review of the company's real estate interests in mid-1990, long before most Canadian real estate investors had given much consideration to the collapse about to take place in real estate values. As values plummeted, it became evident that real estate properties would no longer be able to support the same levels of debt as they had in the past and that property mortgages would have to be paid down to much lower levels when they matured and needed to be refinanced. Another concern was that the traditional bank lenders would reduce the corporate credit facilities they had very generously extended to companies in the Canadian real estate industry throughout the 1980s.

With this market intelligence in hand, Gordon Arnell expedited the refinancing of Brookfield Properties by eliminating short-term bank debt, paying down mortgage borrowings and preparing for sale those properties which were not in prime locations, as well as properties which did not have premier quality environmental and business support systems. These lesser-quality assets were quickly sold in order to generate cash to strengthen Brookfield's balance sheet. This would enable the company to acquire prime properties should others be required to dispose of their best assets because they had failed to restructure their affairs in time. Brookfield Properties also steadily reduced its ownership in joint ventures and real estate affiliates, which required the refinancing of substantial amounts of debt within the following five years.

After a gruelling five-year period of operational and financial restructurings, Edper emerged at the end of 1995 with its continuing direct and indirect interests in the real estate sector repositioned for growth. The objective had been to structure the group's real estate operations to effectively eliminate any potential financing risks through to the year 2000, by which time it was expected that rental rates would recover and property cash flows would once again be rising.

Edper, by investing counter-cyclically, increased its ownership of Brookfield Properties from approximately 50% in December 1990 to 94% by December 1996, and in the process increased the group's effective beneficial interest in prime office space and residential land holdings by more than a third. This was accomplished despite Brookfield's withdrawal from Trizec in 1994. As a result, when real estate values started to rise in 1996 and 1997, which was much earlier than most people expected, Edper more than recovered the substantial losses it had suffered in the early 1990s in this sector of its business.

Across the industry most seasoned real estate executives were unable to cope with the dramatic changes experienced by their industry in the early 1990s. They either went into denial believing it was the beginning of a normal cyclical downturn or were not disciplined enough to close down costly development offices, cut overheads and turn their focus to tenant service. Many also found it difficult to cull their portfolios and hold on to the proceeds for reinvestment in prime commercial properties when these later became available at a fraction of their replacement values. These executives either voluntarily left to pursue different careers or had to be removed to make way for the appointment of new executives who were capable of responding constructively to the structural changes occurring in the industry.

To fill the gaps in Brookfield's executive ranks, Gordon Arnell seconded Bruce Flatt in 1994 from a senior role in Hees International to oversee the group's real estate finances and to work closely with him on strategic initiatives. The objectives were to increase Brookfield's equity base and to pursue a new growth-oriented business plan founded on high-quality office properties. In 1995, Bruce Flatt's responsibilities were increased, with his appointment to President and Chief Operating Officer of Brookfield Properties, to include acquiring additional premier office properties and achieving a closer co-ordination of the group's various real estate operations. Gordon Arnell also persuaded Ian

Cockwell, who had worked with the group as a consultant from time to time during the previous twenty years, to become a full-time senior member of the real estate team.

Brookfield's new management team quickly executed a remarkable turnaround in each of the company's operations. In the twenty-four months ended December 31, 1997, the new management team completed $4 billion of long-term property financings at significantly reduced interest rates, acquired over 15 million square feet of prime office space, built one of the largest Canadian property management services companies, increased the company's capital base from $1 billion to more than $3 billion and generated earnings of $109 million in 1997. Even more significantly, they set the stage for doubling the company's earnings and cash flows within two years.

One of the most difficult, costly and challenging, yet in the end rewarding, assignments involved Brookfield Properties' relationship with BCE Inc. In the fall of 1989, The Toronto-Dominion Bank suggested to BCE Inc. that it seek assistance from the Edper group in rationalizing BCE's real estate interests held through BCED. Since time was of the essence, it was agreed that Brookfield Properties would rely on BCE's assessment of the amount of cash required to complete the major property development programme which was then under way.

Based in large measure on BCE's assurances that it would compensate Brookfield Properties on completion of the assignment should BCE's estimates prove too low, Brookfield Properties agreed to invest $208 million in return for a 50% ownership interest in BCED's principal operating subsidiary, later renamed Brookfield Commercial Properties. These funds were designated for the completion of the development program. An important factor in Brookfield's acceptance of this assignment was BCE's enthusiasm at the time for increasing its involvement in the real estate industry and selecting Brookfield Properties as its preferred partner for pursing these goals.

Soon thereafter, BCE appointed a new management team and its business strategy changed dramatically as it refocused on its core telecommunications business. This meant that BCE was no longer interested in pursuing its earlier plans to add to, or continue funding, its real estate holdings. With the change in BCE's focus, and having already advanced more than previously contemplated, the management of Brookfield Properties concluded early in 1991 that they had no choice other than to proceed alone and fund the development projects under way solely from the group's own resources. There were five major office towers in the process of construction, leases to be signed and municipal development rights which would be placed in jeopardy if construction did not continue. The state of uncertainty over the funding of this portfolio continued until the fall of 1993, placing substantial pressure on Edper's financial resources.

Were it not for the intercession of Red Wilson and Gerry McGoey, BCE's new President and Chief Executive and Senior Financial Officer, respectively, the consequences for Brookfield Properties could have been very serious. Under the direction of these two executives, BCE undertook a thorough review of the contributions of both parties to the joint venture, resulting in the transfer of full ownership and responsibility for these properties to Brookfield Properties on acceptable terms early in 1994. Bob Harding played a key role working with BCE in bringing this transaction to a satisfactory conclusion for all parties.

The investment in BCE's real estate portfolio, which started as a high-profile workout assignment, became a major consumer of the group's cash and management at a time when these resources could have been better deployed elsewhere within the group. In this respect, the intangible costs, which included being unjustly subjected to criticism from BCED's various security holders, were substantial. On the positive side, Brookfield earned a special relationship with BCE and acquired full ownership of a portfolio of high-quality, well-located office properties in Toronto, Denver and Minneapolis.

It was in the context of the severe contraction in credit available to the real estate industry in the early 1990s that Brookfield Properties reluctantly allowed its effective ownership in Trizec to decline to a nominal level in 1994. That same year, Brookfield Properties increased its ownership of Brookfield Homes to 90%, Carma to 75%, and Brookfield Commercial Properties to 100%. Hees International provided much of the capital to accomplish these ownership changes and in the process increased its effective ownership of Brookfield Properties to 94%.

Brookfield's decision to withdraw from Trizec was a particularly difficult one for Peter Bronfman and his senior colleagues as they had participated with Harold Milavsky and later Kevin Benson for more than eighteen years in developing Trizec into one of the most respected commercial property companies in North America. Brookfield Properties had exercised joint control over Trizec, first with English Property Corporation from June 1976, and after March 1979 with Olympia & York. It had been a rewarding investment for Brookfield Properties, yielding approximately $200 million in dividends. The market value of its shareholdings appreciated at one point to well over $1 billion compared with the $350 million of capital invested.

Unfortunately, Trizec had never established an effective and easy working relationship with the senior executives of its largest subsidiary, Bramalea Limited, in which it held a 65% interest. As a result, when Bramalea encountered financing problems in March 1992 as part of the fallout from Olympia & York's financial collapse, it took time for Trizec's management to address these difficulties.

In the process of stabilizing Bramalea's finances, the international banking community's attention was drawn to the fact that Trizec was partially owned by Olympia & York. Thus, many of the major financial institutions withdrew their support pending resolution of Olympia & York's bankruptcy proceedings, making it very difficult for Trizec in 1993 to refinance or extend the terms of its maturing debt.

The problems faced by Trizec were compounded when, despite the company's available cash resources, it decided in the fall of 1993 not to pay the amount owing on one series of corporate debentures, based on advice it had received that this would facilitate an extension of term on all of the company's debentures. Instead, the institutional holders of these securities called a default, which in essence gave all of the debenture holders a voice in deciding the terms of any restructuring unless the company repaid them in full. Many of the debentures soon changed hands from the international banks and institutional investors to U.S. vulture funds, which came to dominate the restructuring discussions.

These problems were further aggravated by the course chosen for raising the additional equity capital required to refinance the company's debenture debt. Unknown to Peter Bronfman and his colleagues at the time, certain Trizec representatives had been working directly with Horsham Corporation, a holding company owned by Peter Munk, making it difficult for others to become involved. Consequently, Brookfield Properties and other prospective investors faced difficulties in sponsoring competing refinancing plans. It later became clear that the company's Canadian investment advisers had, from the outset, favoured Horsham for a variety of reasons.

The lesson learned from Brookfield's withdrawal from Trizec was the need to have the necessary resources readily available to become actively involved in any major corporate initiative undertaken by a corporate affiliate in circumstances where there are divergent interests which are not necessarily conducive to maximizing shareholder values.

Kevin Benson, Trizec's Chairman and Chief Executive at the time, earned considerable credit for his integrity and sense of responsibility in seeing the restructuring of Trizec completed in the face of difficult circumstances created by others. Without his commitment, the result would have been even more painful for many of the parties involved.

Brookfield Properties' acquisition of the World Financial Properties office portfolio, similar to the BCED portfolio, had a difficult and costly beginning. In December 1989, Paul Reichmann approached Brookfield Properties about a potential investment in Olympia & York's prestigious World Financial Center properties in New York as he was in the process of raising cash to complete the massive Canary Wharf office project in London, England. Partly because the Reichmann family had been very good partners in a number of ventures and partly because of the group's concerns over Olympia & York exercising its forced-sale rights covering their joint investment in Trizec to raise cash, Brookfield Properties agreed to help by purchasing a one-third interest in three World Financial Center buildings. The equity component of this investment amounted to US $240 million, and was made on the understanding that these three buildings were in the process of being sold to a group of foreign investors and that this sale would be completed within six months.

Towards the end of 1991, it became obvious that Paul Reichmann was making little progress with the sale, leaving the group with a large amount of capital tied up in an illiquid partnership. The situation deteriorated further in March 1992 when the partnership's cash reserves were diverted, placing in default $1 billion of mortgage loans secured by the World Financial Center properties and ranking ahead of Brookfield Properties' equity investment.

Equally significant to the group were the investor relations problems created by its investment in these assets. Brookfield Properties, at the request of Olympia & York, had agreed that it would maintain the confidentiality of the transaction as their intention was to sell the properties within six months. However, when circumstances changed and Brookfield Properties requested approval to disclose the terms of its investment to its shareholders, this request was declined. It was only after Olympia & York's bankruptcy filings that Paul Reichmann released Brookfield Properties from its confidentiality undertakings, enabling it to explain the rationale for its original investment in these properties.

At the time of Olympia & York's default in 1992, Brookfield Properties had other priorities and did not have the resources immediately available to play a proactive role with respect to its investment in the World Financial Center. However, late in 1993 as the challenges to Brookfield's partnership interests began to mount, Gordon Arnell assembled a multi-disciplined team to address these challenges. The team eventually included Joe Killi, Bruce Flatt, Bob Harding, Ed Nordholm and Manfred Walt. The accomplishments of this team under Gordon Arnell's leadership represent one of the group's most significant business successes. While Brookfield Properties owned important partnership positions in the three World Financial Center office buildings and was therefore critical to the ultimate reorganization of Olympia & York's assets in the United States, the adversarial positions of many parties taken together became a serious threat to Brookfield's investment.

Over a period of almost two years, numerous joint-venture agreements, creditor settlements and nearly $2 billion of new financing arrangements were negotiated with more than thirty major financial institutions, as well as with Olympia & York's unsecured creditors. These agreements were necessary to permit Brookfield Properties to become the lead sponsor of World Financial Properties Inc., the corporation formed to acquire Olympia & York's principal U.S. office building assets.

Brookfield would not have been able to perform its sponsorship role with respect to these arrangements and emerge as the largest shareholder without Joe Killi's diligence and careful attention to the transaction's many complexities. In the process, the Brookfield Properties team earned the respect of the New York financial community for its role in achieving a consensual reorganization of the largest and most complex real estate bankruptcy ever experienced in the United States.

Merrill Lynch also played a crucial role by facilitating the refinancing of the defaulted mortgages on two of the World Financial Center properties. They structured two of the largest securitized mortgage financings on record in North America based largely on their long-term leases and their top-tier credit rating.

Early in the formulation of the reorganization plan, it was recognized that Brookfield Properties needed to build alliances to win support for its position. First it turned to Dick Shiff, an experienced and successful Canadian real estate developer and investor with whom the group had worked effectively on a number of other investments in the past. Then in early 1995 Brookfield Properties formed an important alliance with the Canadian Imperial Bank of Commerce which, along with one of its key clients, Li Ka-shing, later agreed to become significant financial partners in the ownership of World Financial Properties Inc. The relationships with the Canadian Imperial Bank of Commerce and Li Ka-shing were mutually advantageous, and the intense period of negotiation was productive and positive. Ken Davidson, Paul McFarlane and Brian McDonough were particularly constructive in pursuing the bank's position and extremely helpful in dealing with the numerous creditor claims and other competing interests.

With the active participation of the Canadian Imperial Bank of Commerce, Brookfield Properties was in a position to commence negotiations with the other substantial party involved, Apollo Real Estate Fund. However, after failing to come to terms with Apollo, Brookfield Properties sought out Citibank as an important local investment partner because of Citibank's knowledge and the respect with which it was held in New York. This solidified the sponsoring group led by Brookfield Properties and made most of the parties involved with the reorganization recognize that Brookfield Properties had substantial support for its position. By November 1996, the partnership emerged as the owner of World Financial Properties Inc., with Brookfield holding a 46% investment in the partnership.

Throughout the intense negotiations, the group was intent on building a reputation in the New York financial community for fairness in its dealings, and was committed to working with partners in a collaborative manner to protect its own as well as their interests. This was extremely important to the numerous outstanding individuals involved. These included Judge James Garrity, who oversaw the many legal proceedings, his appointed mediator, the former Secretary of State Cyrus Vance, and John Zuccotti, Olympia & York's Chief Executive Officer and former deputy mayor of New York City. John Zuccotti, who later agreed to serve as Chairman of World Financial Properties Inc., continues to be of immeasurable assistance in providing local market knowledge and in helping Brookfield Properties enhance the value of its office properties.

Between the time substantial agreement was reached by Brookfield Properties with Olympia & York's creditors and the date of final court approval of the World Financial Properties restructuring in late 1996, property values had begun to increase. The improvement in values more than restored the value of the Canadian Imperial Bank of Commerce's original loan position and its additional investment. Having achieved this, Brookfield was able to purchase the bank's and Li Ka-shing's 25% interest in World Financial Properties Inc. in June 1997, bringing Brookfield's ownership to approximately 70%.

The successful restructuring of World Financial Properties Inc. was instrumental in Brookfield Properties completing a record $1.7 billion of equity issues in Canada during 1997. Early in 1998, Brookfield Properties used a portion of this capital to purchase most of Citibank's shareholdings to increase its ownership of World Financial Properties Inc. to nearly 90%, and shortly thereafter changed the name of this important business unit to Brookfield Financial Properties Inc.

With the completion of the restructuring and refinancing of World Financial Properties, Brookfield Properties emerged in 1997 as one of North America's premier office property companies. Another strategic move was completed later that year with Brookfield Properties' acquisition of the 43% interest in Gentra Inc. held by Trilon Financial. This was done to align all of the group's real estate operations in North America under a single company.

After completing the acquisition of Gentra, Brookfield Properties emerged with a portfolio of 55 commercial properties containing 32 million square feet of rentable area, in which Brookfield Properties holds a net beneficial interest of 24 million square feet. This portfolio included four major office properties acquired in 1997 – Exchange Place in Boston, Fifth Avenue Place in Calgary and the Exchange Tower and Queen's Quay Terminal buildings in Toronto.

In rebuilding Brookfield Properties, Peter Bronfman had encouraged the company's board and management to focus on acquiring and owning premier-quality properties. As a result, the Brookfield office property portfolio today surpasses the one the group previously controlled through Trizec and ranks among the very best in North America. BCE Place in Toronto, Brookfield Properties' flagship office complex in Canada and the location of the Edper group's head office, compares favourably with the group's previous flagship properties. The three office towers Brookfield Properties owns in the World Financial Center complex in downtown Manhattan are among the finest in New York, and Brookfield's office towers in Boston, Minneapolis, Denver and Calgary are also landmark buildings in each of those cities.

As Brookfield Properties rebuilt its wholly-owned operations, it also developed a leading property management business, not only to provide the highest quality of service in its own buildings but also to other property owners. By the end of 1997, Brookfield Properties managed nearly one hundred million square feet of property and was recognized for the high-quality services it provided. That year, it received an unprecedented three prestigious awards from the internationally recognized Building Owners and Management Association – the first for BCE Place, the second in the historic category for its office property at 320 Bay Street, Toronto, and the third for Republic Plaza in Denver.

While Brookfield's primary emphasis remains on the ownership and management of commercial properties, it also conducts residential land development operations through Brookfield Homes and Carma Corporation. Master-planned communities are under development in a number of major housing markets across North America, including Toronto, Calgary, the Washington D.C. area, Denver, San Francisco and southern California. The current residential land inventory, when fully subdivided, will provide over 50,000 building lots. Although Brookfield Homes is not yet an industry leader in this segment, considerable progress has been made to increase sales, improve returns and generate capital for reinvestment in its core commercial property business.

The re-emergence of Brookfield Properties in 1997 as a leading office building company was met with considerable enthusiasm from the investment community, coinciding as it did with a renewed interest in those few real estate companies, like Brookfield Properties, which had survived the recession and used the downturn to significantly upgrade the quality of their assets. This positive response enabled Brookfield to triple its capital base during the year, an extraordinary accomplishment in an industry that was considered unsuitable for institutional investment only a few years earlier. EdperBrascan participated in these equity issues to maintain its interest in Brookfield Properties at approximately 50%.

With the strengthening of its operations and the improved business environment for the real estate industry, Brookfield's cash flow rebounded to over $160 million in 1997 compared to only $35 million in 1996. Moreover, the assets and tenant lease contracts had been put in place to ensure significant growth in Brookfield's future earnings and cash flows.

While Peter Bronfman was not alive to witness the extraordinary resurgence of Brookfield Properties in 1997, he would have been very pleased that the business which was the initial foundation on which Edper's growth was built had once again become a major pillar of strength for the group.

Chapter Eleven

The Second Pillar

The rapid rise in the value of Edper's real estate holdings in the latter part of the 1970s led to the search for another major area for investment. Peter Bronfman sought a new business sector in which Canada enjoyed meaningful competitive advantages, since he was determined to maintain the group's headquarters in Canada and wanted to play a bigger role in the development of the country's industrial base. He had built apartments, office buildings, shopping centres, industrial parks and residential communities and derived great pleasure from the finished products. They were useful assets which added to the well-being of his fellow citizens.

There were good reasons why his search led to the natural resources sector. He had come to realize that Canada, by any measure, was blessed with a vast, varied and potentially valuable array of natural resources which were waiting to be developed. But to do so would require a high degree of technical competence and a heavy dose of upfront capital – much like the real estate business.

By 1979, the group's expertise in real estate had been built steadily over more than twenty years. However, if the group entered the natural resources sector, Peter Bronfman wanted to move up the learning curve a great deal faster. Perhaps turning fifty added a degree of impatience to his enthusiasm for action. To compress the process would mean taking on added risk, unless Edper could acquire the necessary technical expertise through the acquisition of a company which was already well established in the business. However, as with most things in life, there could be no shortcuts and Edper's entry into the natural resources sector would prove to be no exception to this rule.

Brascan had been acquired as a stepping stone to enter the natural resources business in a meaningful way. Brascan itself had accumulated a number of smaller holdings in this sector, including oil and gas and coal properties in western Canada and a 51% interest in Western Mines Limited, which was immediately expanded and renamed Westmin Resources Limited. But none of these was large enough to provide the basis for the type of entry into the natural resources sector which Peter Bronfman and his colleagues wished to make.

By the fall of 1979, the new Brascan team was firmly in place, busy supplementing its financial reserves and actively searching for opportunities to multiply its existing investment in the natural resources sector. Several companies were analyzed in order to achieve the group's goals, with primary interest centring on Falconbridge, Hudson Bay Oil and Gas and Noranda Mines.

In October 1979, Conrad Black was in the process of liquidating a number of the investment holdings he held through Argus Corporation, including a 13% shareholding in Noranda Mines, the predecessor to Noranda Inc. This was the chance the Edper group had been searching for – a meaningful entry point into one of Canada's better-respected natural resource companies. Brascan purchased this block of shares for $294 million, payable partly in cash and partly in Brascan preferred shares.

Brascan's subsequent open market purchases of Noranda shares triggered a defensive reaction by Noranda's management involving the issue of a large block of treasury shares. In order to deter Brascan or any other major shareholder from increasing its investment in the company, Noranda management created Zinor Holdings to hold these and other Noranda shares owned by its subsidiaries and affiliates. The Zinor structure enabled management to vote a significant block of Noranda shares and thereby dilute the ability of other investors to establish a meaningful voice in Noranda's affairs.

The defensive actions taken by Noranda's management upset the Caisse de dépôt et placement du Québec, which was not only a significant shareholder but also vitally interested in the company's important role in the development of Québec's natural resources. This led to an offer from the Caisse de dépôt to combine its Noranda shareholdings with the shares held by Brascan, and a commitment by the Caisse to invest more than $600 million to hold 30% of Brascade Resources Inc., a new joint-venture holding company. Brascade subsequently made a $287 million cash and share exchange offer to Noranda's public shareholders and purchased $500 million of common shares from Noranda's treasury. As a result of these purchases, Brascade acquired control of approximately 42% of Noranda's common shares. These transactions were completed in October 1981 and shortly thereafter Zinor Holdings was dissolved. Ten years later Brascan acquired full ownership of Brascade.

As Brascan's management became more intimately acquainted with Noranda's assets and finances, they encountered mounting evidence that Noranda had over-extended itself through an aggressive investment program directed at expanding its production capacity and mineral reserves irrespective of the ranking of these operations on the international competitive cost curve. The cash injected into Noranda's treasury by Brascade soon proved to be essential to Noranda's ability to survive the four difficult years which lay ahead for all natural resource companies.

In addition to the strain on its financial resources, Noranda had also acquired ownership of a number of mineral properties, each with its own acute problems. These high-cost mines and partially developed ore bodies had the potential to generate earnings only at peak metal price levels, and over their short lives cost Noranda more than $300 million. A similar amount was lost on Noranda's oil and natural gas ventures in the United States. In the forest products sector, the costly expansion of the Atholville pulp mill in New Brunswick resulted in operating and capital losses of more than $200 million before it was finally shut down and sold.

Because of Brascan's mounting concerns over Noranda's financial stability and investment practices, David Kerr took charge of Noranda's business planning processes in 1986. Shortly thereafter, three important transactions were initiated to generate more than $800 million of much-needed cash. The profits realized from the sale of Noranda's Australian exploration subsidiary, together with the gains recorded on the completion of public share offerings by Hemlo Gold Mines Inc. and Noranda Forest Inc. in 1987, were used to offset a $600 million write-down required on the company's overvalued mining and metallurgical assets.

After the completion of these initiatives in 1987, David Kerr was appointed President of Noranda and assumed responsibility for introducing new management into the corporate, financial and human resources functions. Courtney Pratt joined Noranda in 1988 to help oversee the corporate changes then under way and to assist in making the new management appointments. His role in the group later expanded to advising on most senior group executive appointments. This included assisting Royal Trustco in 1993 at a critical stage in the sale of its trust and financial intermediary operations.

After strengthening Noranda's balance sheet, attention was turned to revitalizing the company's principal operating units by installing executives with the requisite technical expertise to lead the mining, forest and energy businesses.

The minerals sector commanded the most attention, as Noranda's existing mineral reserves were rapidly depleting and exploration results had been unsatisfactory. To re-establish Noranda as a world-class mining company, a three-step process was initiated which led to the acquisition of control of Falconbridge Limited, a company which possessed long-life mines and prospective development properties and was managed by well-regarded mining executives. Shares of Falconbridge were first acquired through open market purchases in 1988 to establish a 23% ownership position at a relatively low cost. A successful public takeover offer was then launched in 1989 in partnership with Trelleborg N.V. of Sweden which entailed paying a premium for control, effectively shared one-third by Noranda and two-thirds by Trelleborg.

The third step was completed in 1994, when Falconbridge was re-established as a public company and Trelleborg sold a portion of its investment through the public markets in what was then a record common equity issue for a Canadian company, totalling $1.3 billion. As a result, Noranda emerged as the controlling shareholder with a 46% ownership position, full management control and an unrealized profit on its investment of well over $1 billion. Finally in August 1995, Trelleborg sold its residual 25% interest to the public, opening the way for Noranda to increase its ownership of Falconbridge over time.

Following the acquisition of Falconbridge, David Kerr assigned the management of Noranda's mining sector to executives with hands-on mining and metallurgical experience. Alex Balogh and David Goldman played major roles in transforming Noranda's mining and metallurgical operations. David Bumstead assumed full responsibility for all major corporate development initiatives and Mike Knuckey brought his considerable exploration experience to Noranda to assist it in replacing its shrinking mineral reserves. This entailed a commitment to acquiring and developing only long-life mining properties which had the potential to rank as low-cost operations in world-wide terms. The late Frank Pickard and his successor, Øyvind Hushovd, together played similar roles at Falconbridge in strengthening its operations and reserves.

Through its solid base in Noranda and Falconbridge, the group proceeded during the early 1990s to initiate one of the largest capital investment programs undertaken by a Canadian-owned mining and metals group. By the end of 1997, over $6 billion of new mining and metallurgical projects had been completed or were in the construction or advanced planning stages. Two major new mines were developed to replenish the group's long-life reserves – the $500 million Raglan nickel mine in northern Québec, which started production in late 1997, and the 44% owned, $2.4 billion Collahuasi copper project in northern Chile, which started production in June 1998. And in 1998, Noranda purchased a 37½% interest in the giant Antamina copper/zinc project in Peru.

In addition, over $500 million is being invested to expand and upgrade the group's extensive copper, nickel and zinc metallurgical facilities in Québec, Norway, the Dominican Republic and Chile, and a further $400 million is dedicated to improvements in the group's aluminum smelting and fabricating business in the United States. Another metallurgical investment involves Noranda's entry into the magnesium business with the construction of a $730 million magnesium refinery in Québec using proprietary technology developed by Noranda's highly ranked Technology Centre. This project should enable Noranda to become one of the world's lowest cost producers of this important metal by the year 2000. These and other similar investments are being made to establish Noranda as a leading international mining and metals company.

∾

In 1990, Linn Macdonald was recruited from Abitibi-Price to assist in rebuilding Noranda Forest's operations. Over the course of the next five years, the relative operating performance of each of the company's forest product plants improved markedly as they were steadily repositioned. A low-cost solid wood business was expanded under the leadership of Dominic Gammiero, to rank, on a production basis, among the top five panelboard companies in North America and one of the most efficient in the world. Tim Price was elected as a director of Noranda Forest in 1991 to provide Edper with a more meaningful voice on this company's board. In so doing, he fulfilled a lifetime ambition of re-establishing a direct link with the forest product industry which his family had previously enjoyed through the Québec-based Price Pulp and Paper Company.

In February 1993, Linn Macdonald completed the sale of Noranda Forest's 49% interest in MacMillan Bloedel. The investment in MacMillan Bloedel had been made in 1981 in exchange for Noranda treasury shares, as one of the measures used by Noranda management to dilute Brascan's ownership position, in the hope of discouraging it from increasing its investment in Noranda. Although efforts had been made to combine Noranda Forest and MacMillan Bloedel, personal relationships and the political environment persuaded Noranda that the capital invested in MacMillan Bloedel could be better redeployed in Noranda Forest's wholly-owned solid wood and specialty paper operations.

∽

By 1986, Noranda had invested nearly $1 billion in the oil and gas sector through Canadian Hunter Exploration Ltd., hoping for a repeat of Jim Gray's and John Master's 1976 success in discovering the Elmworth Deep Basin gas field in Alberta. Canadian Hunter was rich in reserves, but low on production and earnings in relation to the amount invested by Noranda. In order to generate a higher base level of earnings from this sector to cushion the cyclical earnings swings from the mining and forest products sectors, it was decided to expand beyond Canadian Hunter's existing asset base.

David Kerr spearheaded a strategy for materially expanding Noranda's oil and gas operations without draining Noranda's scarce cash resources. He accomplished this by involving Hees International in the accumulation of a 38% interest in Norcen Energy Resources Limited, headed by Eddie Battle, and a 49% interest in North Canadian Oils Ltd., headed by Norm Gish. Both of these executives were professionals of the highest calibre and facilitated the group's expansion of its interest in this sector by working constructively with David Kerr and their boards of directors. By December 1987, effective working control of these companies had been established and Noranda purchased Hees International's investment in these two energy companies in exchange for $696 million of Noranda's common shares. In the process, Noranda materially strengthened its equity base and immediately moved into the top ranks of Canadian natural gas producers.

Next, Norcen acquired the oil and gas operations of Westmin Resources Limited, including its extensive heavy oil and valuable freehold exploration properties. This transaction was structured to increase Noranda's ownership of Norcen and added a further $250 million to Noranda's equity base. In 1994, Norcen completed the purchase of all of the shares of North Canadian Oils and a new management team was installed under the leadership of Grant Billing with a mandate to increase the earnings contribution from the combined company. In a very short period, Grant Billing proved to be one of the group's most capable executives and exceeded all of the objectives set for him by Noranda.

The various initiatives implemented by Grant Billing transformed Norcen into a profitable and highly-regarded international oil and gas company. As a result, when Noranda decided to reduce its involvement in the oil and gas sector, it was possible, thanks to his outstanding leadership, to sell this investment early in 1998 for a substantial gain and generate a large amount of capital to expand Noranda's mining and metals operations.

Meanwhile, Canadian Hunter had regained its operating momentum and re-established itself as one of Canada's most efficient natural gas producers. Production from its British Columbia and Alberta operations had been increased to nearly 300 million cubic feet of gas per day and proven natural gas reserves stood at over 650 billion cubic feet. More important, a new generation of management led by Steve Savidant and Mike Downey had already achieved considerable success in reducing the company's gas finding costs and in improving its reserve replacement ratios. These initiatives have made Canadian Hunter a focused low-cost producer of natural gas, with operating costs 40% below the industry average and excellent prospects for growth.

In the course of rebuilding Noranda, Peter Bronfman took great satisfaction in seeing the company's various operations start to flourish once again. He came to know personally many of the people employed by Noranda in its corporate offices and at its mine sites, metallurgical plants, forest product mills and energy operations around the world.

Since his earliest involvement with Noranda and its affiliates, he had paid particular attention to their environmental performance, recognizing that this was a potentially vulnerable area for all natural resource companies. With his active support, the Noranda board of directors took the lead and formed an Environment Committee on which he sat. Bud Bird, a fellow Noranda director, recalled Peter's sensitivity to this area: "At meeting after meeting, Peter's voice was consistently the first and strongest in support of environmental responsibilities."

Peter Bronfman's long experience in the business world, however, had taught him that it was not enough to be doing the right thing if others were unaware of your efforts. He encouraged and supported the preparation of comprehensive environmental reports each year as a supplement to Noranda's annual report. These received numerous awards for their clear accounts of each operation's environmental stewardship. In 1996, in accepting an Award for Excellence in environmental reporting, Frank Frantisak, Noranda's Senior Vice-President, Environment, recalled Peter Bronfman's long support for Noranda's efforts in this area: "His sincere and deep personal interest in environmental issues has been a great inspiration for me and my colleagues. His inspiration is reflected in the quality of our report. This award also belongs to him."

Despite Noranda's steady progress, by the mid-1990s it was apparent that a rethinking of its structure was needed to improve its financial performance and shareholder returns. Noranda had become a widely diversified company with a corporate office, a number of wholly-owned divisions and several separately managed affiliates, some of which were themselves publicly traded companies. The perception of Noranda as a conglomerate added to the complexity of the Edper group. In addition, since Noranda had operations in three different sectors of the natural resources industry, investors regarded it as a holding company and tended to discount the value of its common shares.

To maximize value for Noranda's shareholders and thereby for EdperBrascan's shareholders, it was decided that there should be only one publicly traded diversified company in the group, and that each of the other companies should focus on one industry segment. With EdperBrascan designated as the group's diversified company, Noranda began the process in late 1997 of repositioning itself as a pure operating company by returning to its roots in the mining and metals sector.

By early 1998, the first step in the new plan was completed with the sale of Noranda's 49% interest in Norcen Energy Resources. This generated $1.8 billion of proceeds to kick-start a major expansion of Noranda's core mining and metals business. Plans were also put in place to distribute Noranda's interests in 67% owned Noranda Forest and wholly-owned Canadian Hunter to its shareholders. EdperBrascan plans to retain a strong ownership position in each of these two companies, holding initially 31% of Noranda Forest and 40% of Canadian Hunter, and will work closely with them to increase shareholder returns.

The extent of the group's investment in the natural resources sector has increased substantially since Peter Bronfman and his colleagues started to move Brascan further down this road in 1981. The largest amount of the group's capital is now dedicated to this sector, and this is likely to increase based on the group's belief that Canada occupies a unique position internationally in the development of major natural resource projects.

Historically, Canada has been one of the world's biggest exporters of natural resource products and has developed strong technical skills. While the ups and downs of commodity prices will always affect short-term returns, the sector is expected to present continuing opportunities over the longer term for superior returns for those companies which are committed to being low-cost producers and can achieve this status by developing long-life production facilities.

Peter Bronfman applied himself to the expansion of the group's natural resource interests in a multi-dimensional way. He wanted to see Noranda competitive in each of its operations by setting low-cost standards in the sector which would benefit Canada internationally, and he wanted to do so in an environmentally responsible way. Many, but not all, of these objectives have been achieved. Noranda today is widely viewed as enlightened, technologically advanced and committed to improving its competitive position. Notwithstanding this, his colleagues recognize that much work has yet to be done to improve Noranda's financial performance. In addition to investing additional capital to apply the latest technologies, programmes are also being put in place to instill a more rigorous performance culture throughout the organization.

To restock Noranda's dwindling mineral reserves, a major exploration and acquisition programme has been launched. Progress has already been achieved through the recent completion of the Raglan nickel mine in Québec and the Collahuasi copper project in Chile, and with construction soon to get under way on the Antamina copper/zinc project in Peru, one of the largest mining projects in the world. The objective of the ongoing world-wide exploration programme is to discover new high-grade ore bodies in order to secure feed for the company's extensive metallurgical facilities located principally in Canada. At the same time, Noranda has set aside significant capital to acquire an interest in one or more additional large-scale, low-cost mining projects of the same size and calibre as the Collahuasi and Antamina projects.

Peter Bronfman's colleagues firmly believe that Noranda has the financial resources, operating facilities, technological base and renewed commitment to be among the very best mining and metals companies in the world. They know full well that Noranda's progress in meeting this goal will greatly influence EdperBrascan's overall performance in the years ahead.

Chapter Twelve

From Water to Energy

What could be more symbolic of Canada than a massive waterfall of pure, cold, fast-moving water glittering in the sunshine as it descends from rocky heights to land with roaring force many feet below? Peter Bronfman saw this as a perfect expression of nature at its powerful best, and he knew that the harnessing and production of hydro-electric power was an industry he would like to be a part of.

There were many aspects of the hydro-electric power industry that appealed to him – its glorious simplicity, its beauty as a natural resource, its undisputed potential for pollution-free power and its usefulness in developing Canada's industrial base.

Hydro-electric power development requires a significant investment of capital in the construction of the water storage, penstock and power production facilities. It also requires faith that water supplies will continue in abundant quantity and that the ingenuity on the part of construction engineers will create a plant that will be efficient, productive and long-lasting. Most people do not spend a great deal of time praying for rain and snowfall, but those who invest in hydro-electric facilities do. Fortunately, Brascan had vast experience in the development and provision of hydro-electric power – dating back to the end of the nineteenth century when Canadian and American engineers electrified Brazil in more ways than one with their imagination, vision and engineering skills.

In fact, the need to produce power to serve Brazil's growing economy was what gave birth to Brascan in the first place. In 1899, Canadian entrepreneurs joined forces with American and European interests to acquire the concession to operate the tramway system in the city of São Paulo. These trams were to be driven not by horses but by the new marvel of the age, electricity. Since there was no power available, the young company proceeded to build power stations in the outskirts of São Paulo to run its trams. Soon it was providing power directly to the citizens and businesses of São Paulo and, in 1904, it extended its tramway and power business to Rio de Janeiro. In order to access the capital needed for its expanding utility operations, the enterprise was renamed Brazilian Traction, Light and Power Company Limited in 1912, and established as a public company based in Toronto and listed on the American and Brussels stock exchanges.

At the height of its operations in the 1940s, Brazilian Traction, Light and Power employed over 50,000 people and provided two-thirds of Brazil's electric power, as well as telephone, transportation and gas services to the people of São Paulo and Rio de Janeiro and surrounding communities. While the people of Brazil did not always understand the company's corporate structure and its Canadian origins, they knew it powered Brazil's burgeoning economy and, as a consequence, the company was always known in Brazil simply as *The Light*.

It was a logical step for Brascan to apply the Brazilian experience to turning a small Canadian company, Great Lakes Power, into a growing source of cash flow and one of the lowest-cost and most reliable producers of electricity in North America.

Like Brascan, Great Lakes Power was formed at the beginning of the twentieth century to develop and generate electricity in northern Ontario. Lake Superior, the most northerly of the Great Lakes, flows into Lake Huron through the St. Mary's River, which forms the border between Ontario and the state of Michigan. This important crossing point was known as the Sault, after a long stretch of rapids on the upper part of the St. Mary's River. In 1916, the Sault Generating Station was built on the Canadian side of the St. Mary's River using the river's strong water flow to generate electricity to serve the city of Sault Ste. Marie, Ontario, and the surrounding district of Algoma.

At the turn of the century, the Province of Ontario had entered the energy business and by the late 1920s had acquired most of the province's privately-owned power companies. However, the people of Sault Ste. Marie and Algoma bucked the trend and, in 1928, voted to retain Great

Lakes Power as a private utility because of its proven capa-bilities and commitment to provide reliable, competitively priced electric power to the region. Great Lakes Power made good on this promise and is today the largest independent producer and distributor of electric energy in Ontario as well as the lowest cost supplier of electricity to industry and residential customers in the province.

For the next forty-five years, Great Lakes Power contin-ued as an independent power company, gradually expand-ing its operations to meet the needs of its service area. Eight hydro-electric generating stations were built and expanded in the Algoma District on two rivers which flow into Lake Superior north of Sault Ste. Marie – the Montreal River and, further north, the Michipicoten River near the town of Wawa. By the early 1970s, Great Lakes Power owned and operated nine power stations.

At this time, Brascan had begun its gradual withdrawal from the utility business in Brazil and was reinvesting a portion of the proceeds received from the sale of these assets in Canada. Early in 1973, Brascan was presented with the opportunity to acquire a large block of shares of Great Lakes Power and by August had secured control of the company.

The acquisition of Great Lakes Power was fully supported by the local community because of Brascan's long history in the power sector. The company was a natural fit for Brascan, since its management was familiar with the power business and had the technical expertise to manage and expand Great Lakes Power's operations. The company's stable cash flow also provided a solid earnings base to complement Brascan's growing Canadian operations.

When Edper acquired its interest in Brascan in 1979, Great Lakes Power had less than 200 megawatts of generating capacity in place, much of which required updating, producing only $39 million of annual power revenues. Over the next eighteen years, Great Lakes Power steadily expanded its power generating capacity to approximately 650 megawatts, and its annual power sales revenues almost five times to $187 million. The first expansion involved the construction of a new generating station on the St. Mary's River to replace the original Sault station built in 1916. The Francis H. Clergue Generating Station became operational in 1982 and was one of the first plants in North America to use technologically advanced bulb-type turbines designed specifically for high water flow applications.

Peter Bronfman took a great interest in Great Lakes Power and enjoyed his visits to Sault Ste. Marie to review these operations. These visits included his attendance in October, 1982 at a board meeting which was held aboard the Algoma Central Railway passenger train en route from Sault Ste. Marie to the Agawa Canyon. The railway provided an outstanding opportunity to view the terrain and river systems of the Algoma District bedecked in glorious fall colours, as well as Great Lakes Power's generating facilities on the upper Montreal River. The northern Ontario vista which Peter Bronfman, a noted art connoisseur, and his colleagues could see from the railroad bridge over the dam at the MacKay Generating Station was the same scene which had inspired the famous Group of Seven landscape *The Solemn Land* by A.Y. Jackson.

An early initiative taken by Peter Bronfman and his colleagues to improve Great Lakes Power's financial results was the expansion of its investment activities. In 1984, the Canadian Imperial Bank of Commerce and Merrill Lynch each acquired large share positions in Great Lakes Power and worked with the company to create a limited market investment dealer. Ken Clarke, a director of Merrill Lynch, joined the company as President and Chief Executive Officer and, while nurturing the company's power generating operations, also built a highly effective investment banking team which earned over $100 million in a five-year period. It was during this period that Great Lakes Power began to play an important financing role for the group.

In 1989, Great Lakes Power's investment banking business was merged into Trilon Financial Corporation, and Ken Clarke and the investment banking team became officers of Trilon Financial. Shortly thereafter, the Edper group acquired the shareholdings in Great Lakes Power held by Canadian Imperial Bank of Commerce and Merrill Lynch, and Bob Dunford and Ed Kress of Brascan assumed full responsibility for expanding the company's power generating business.

The first of these initiatives was the development of three new hydro-electric generating stations on the Magpie River, which flows into Lake Superior near Wawa. These stations began operating in 1990. During the course of the next decade, numerous other improvements were made to upgrade the reliability and productivity of Great Lakes Power's northern Ontario stations, including most recently the redesign and returbining of the Andrews and MacKay generating stations on the Montreal River.

But the Edper group realized that meaningful growth to Great Lakes Power's operating base would require looking further afield, given the limited growth in demand for power in Great Lakes Power's traditional service area in northern Ontario. An opportunity arose in 1989 to participate as a 50% joint-venture partner in the development of a major hydro-electric generating station and flood and sediment control facility in southern Louisiana. Built on a diversion which directs water from the Mississippi River to the nearby Red and Atchafalaya Rivers, the Sidney A. Murray, Jr. Generating Station is one of the largest run-of-the-river stations in the world.

When the new station started full operation in 1991, Louisiana HydroElectric Power, as the joint venture is known, became an important generator of revenue and cash flow for Great Lakes Power, adding 192 megawatts of capacity. Since this operation uses water from a different watershed than the company's northern Ontario stations, it also helps reduce the financial impact of variations in precipitation levels.

Following this success, the joint-venture concept was applied closer to home. In 1993, Great Lakes Power joined with Westcoast Energy in a 50/50 partnership to build the 110 megawatt Lake Superior Power gas-fired cogeneration station in Sault Ste. Marie, Ontario. And in 1994, Great Lakes Power partnered with David Boileau, a local businessman, to develop the Valerie Falls hydro-electric station near Atikokan in northwestern Ontario.

For some time Great Lakes Power had been looking for ways to expand its operations into Québec, where the group, through its metallurgical operations, is one of the largest consumers of electrical power. An opportunity arose in late 1996 when Joey Tanenbaum, an innovative and dynamic Toronto businessman, offered to sell to the group Pontiac Power, a company owned by him, John Bahen and the Canadian Imperial Bank of Commerce. Joey Tanenbaum had been a long-time friend of a number of Peter Bronfman's senior colleagues and someone with whom they had had excellent business dealings over many years. Pontiac Power owned and operated two hydro-electric generating stations in western Québec, located on tributaries of the Ottawa River west of Hull. In addition to contributing an additional 28 megawatts of capacity to Great Lakes Power, Pontiac Power held valuable water power development rights on the Gatineau River and a number of other river systems in Québec.

With the completion of these initiatives, Great Lakes Power expanded its operations well beyond its traditional service area into other parts of Canada and the United States and increased its generating capacity to approximately 650 megawatts.

For the past fifteen years, Bob Dunford has provided continuity of management and strategic direction for the group's power generating operations as Group Chairman Power Generation and as Chairman of Great Lakes Power. Ed Kress, EdperBrascan's Executive Vice-President and one of its longest-serving officers, having joined Brascan in 1974, was appointed President and Chief Executive of Great Lakes Power in 1992. Ed Kress' earlier involvement with Brascan's Brazilian utility operations proved to be of considerable value in leading the expansion of the company. Working together first with Hugh Harris and later with Don Watson, Mike McEwen and Bud Carruthers, he helped establish the group's generating facilities as efficient low-cost producers of electrical power.

Great Lakes Power, like all public and private energy producers, grew for most of its life in an era of regulated power. Governments across North America considered the generation of electric power to be a key element of their industrial strategy. The Province of Ontario was no exception and viewed Ontario Hydro as the jewel in its industrial crown. As in many industries during the 1990s, the tide started to turn away from government monopolies and regulated markets towards increased competition and an enhanced role for the private sector in Ontario's power industry.

Great Lakes Power, as Ontario's largest independent producer and distributor of power, has monitored these developments closely, believing that a more open and competitive environment would enable it to seek additional customers and expand its generating base. Under the regulated system, Great Lakes Power's low-cost structure has allowed it to charge lower rates than those billed elsewhere in Ontario and in the neighbouring regions of the United

States. Freed of these and other regulatory constraints, and with optimal use of its strategically located water storage facilities, Great Lakes Power expects to be very competitive under a deregulated system.

Notwithstanding the fact that the power generating business is capital intensive, requiring long lead times to build and bring new projects into operation, it is considered an attractive area for investment since it provides the stable earnings stream and operating cash flows sought by the group to balance its cyclical natural resource earnings. Considerable value is placed on the financial benefits which flow from owning stable cash generating businesses at the senior level in the group's corporate structure.

In this regard, Great Lakes Power is a particularly attractive investment, as it consistently generates free cash flow which does not need to be reinvested in its plant and equipment to remain competitive, other than for expansion purposes. Since the group acquired its investment in Great Lakes Power in 1979, its operating cash flows have grown from less than $15 million to more than $120 million per annum.

Along with Peter Bronfman's appreciation of nature at work for industry in an environmentally friendly way, the poetic symmetry of the group's continuing involvement in the generation of hydro-electric power for nearly one hundred years held great appeal for him.

Chapter Thirteen

The Glue

From Edper's earliest days, Peter Bronfman realized the central importance of financial management to the group. The constant need to expand its capital base and refine the composition of its investment portfolio required a specialized knowledge of mergers, acquisitions, corporate financing and the overall functioning of the capital markets. This need became increasingly critical as the group started to acquire controlling interests in public companies during the 1970s.

Peter Bronfman had also concluded that the required financial expertise should exist at a senior level and be developed internally, since in many ways effective financial management could well be the glue he was looking for to hold the different parts of the group together and provide it with a competitive advantage. As a result, he encouraged his colleagues, Jack Cockwell, Tim Price and David Kerr during the early 1970s to start honing their skills in this area and commence building a merchant banking arm which would help in keeping abreast of developments in the financial markets.

When Edper acquired control of Brascan, it therefore seemed natural to Peter Bronfman and his colleagues that they should build on Brascan's minority common share investment in London Life in order to broaden the group's window on the financial markets. Peter Bronfman at the time did, however, harbour some doubts about the retail side of the financial services business. It was one thing to provide financial services to corporations, institutions and sophisticated individuals, but quite another to deal with the general public through a multitude of branches and agents across the country. Time would show that he was right to have concerns, since these latter activities would prove to be incompatible with the capital-intensive and cyclical nature of the group's natural resources and real estate businesses, which represented the two largest components of its operations.

Eventually he decided to go along with the plans to create a predominantly retail financial services business using the London Life shareholding as the initial building block. This business, unlike the chartered banks, would conduct a diversified range of operations including mortgage lending, personal trust services and life and casualty insurance. In theory, these separately managed operations would feed business to each other and achieve significant cost savings through the use of common delivery and information systems and in some cases by sharing physical facilities.

To accomplish these grand goals, Trilon Financial Corporation was formed in 1982 and started business by acquiring Brascan's 24% shareholding in London Life, as well as its 18% shareholding in Royal Trustco which Brascan had acquired in 1981 following Robert Campeau's aborted takeover attempt. Trilon Financial then set about increasing both of these ownership positions through market purchases as well as the acquisition of key blocks of London Life shares from The Toronto-Dominion Bank and the Jeffery family of London, Ontario.

Allen Lambert joined the group in 1982 as Chairman of Trilon Financial and quickly assembled a management team which included Mel Hawkrigg as President and Gordon Cunningham as Executive Vice-President. Together with Frank Lochan, Trilon's Chief Financial Officer, they initiated a number of acquisitions with the intention of integrating the marketing and distribution of the various financial products offered by these companies.

Companies acquired by Trilon Financial in the mid-1980s included Wellington Insurance Company, Triathlon Leasing Inc., Eurobrokers Investment Corporation, Meloche Monnex Inc., The Holden Group and Royal LePage Limited. Companies formed by Trilon Financial included Trivest Insurance Agencies, Century Property & Casualty Company and, at a later date, the 20/20 Mutual Fund Group and Trilon Securities Corporation.

A number of these companies were highly successful, in particular, Meloche Monnex, Century Property & Casualty and Trilon Securities. However, the objectives of joint marketing of products and realizing a broad range of cost synergies did not materialize as planned. This was largely because the individuals formulating these programmes were unsuccessful in resolving the territorial conflicts which arose between the senior executives of Trilon Financial's two large partly-owned subsidiaries, London Life and Royal Trustco.

In an attempt to address these problems, changes were made in the management of Trilon Financial. Ken Clarke, who had helped found the successful investment banking joint venture involving Great Lakes Power, Merrill Lynch and the Canadian Imperial Bank of Commerce in 1984, was appointed President and Chief Executive of Trilon Financial in 1989. A team of six investment banking executives, which included Sandy Riley, Hugh Aird and Michael Freund, transferred from Great Lakes Power to Trilon Financial to bolster its commercial financing capabilities. At the same time, Gordon Cunningham was appointed President of London Insurance Group, with responsibility for redirecting the group's insurance operations and, most important, encouraging co-operation between London Life and its affiliates.

The plans to achieve greater co-operation between Trilon Financial's subsidiaries were set back in 1990 when Royal Trustco started to encounter loan loss problems in its operations in the United Kingdom. The objective of achieving group cost and marketing synergies became difficult to achieve as attention turned to more pressing concerns. By late 1992, Royal Trustco's problems were placing significant demands on Trilon Financial's management and financial resources, and at the end of that year, Ken Clarke elected to step down as President of Trilon Financial in order to pursue his long-stated interest in philanthropic work.

The Legacy

∽

In December 1992, George Myhal, who had built an out-standing investment record with Hees International, was appointed President and Chief Executive of Trilon Financial. The mandate given to him by Trilon Financial's board was to assist Royal Trustco in resolving its problems, to improve and then liquidate under-performing operations and generally to reduce risk. It was recognized that Trilon would lose its investment grade credit ratings and access to the capital markets if it did not immediately address these issues.

George Myhal's performance under trying conditions was, by any measure, exceptional, including providing the leadership needed to recover $500 million from Trilon Financial's investment in Gentra Inc., the successor company to Royal Trustco. Other initiatives implemented to reduce risk included selling Eurobrokers' money brokerage and derivative businesses and Triathlon Leasing's equipment and automobile leasing operations. In the process, Trilon Financial repaid over $1 billion of short-term financing, strengthened its financial profile and had its credit ratings upgraded.

Commencing in 1994, George Myhal, closely assisted by Frank Lochan, began the process of expanding Trilon Financial's wholly-owned investment banking capabilities, choosing to attract young executives prepared to work and be rewarded as part of a team. Frank Lochan, who had been hired by Brascan in 1974 as the comptroller of its Canadian operations, moved to Trilon Financial at the time of its formation. As Trilon Financial's longest-serving executive, he provided continuity and played an important role in resolving many of the difficult problems the company encountered during the early 1990s.

In 1995, Aaron Regent and Sam Pollock Jr. assumed direct responsibility for Trilon's underwriting and advisory services and the development of a much broader range of services available to group companies as well as other clients. Trevor Kerr provided valuable continuity in dealing with clients and in helping integrate the new team of younger executives.

The one final area of operation which required Trilon's attention was 54% owned Royal LePage. This company, like many others that depended on the real estate industry for their livelihood, also required a major restructuring. Colum Bastable was appointed President and Chief Executive in 1993 and, with the support of Trilon, implemented a comprehensive plan to reduce costs, improve market share and recruit the best sales agents and managers, including Simon Dean to head up the residential and home relocation operations.

Having re-established its confidence in the leadership of Trilon Financial, the group took steps in 1994 and 1995 to increase its ownership of Trilon Financial from 48% to 65%. This paid off handsomely over the next two years as the value of Trilon Financial's assets recovered and positive earnings momentum was restored leading to a five-fold increase in the stock market price of the company's shares.

Over the course of the first fifteen years of its life, Trilon Financial underwent a gradual but major transformation from being largely a holding company for the group's interests in the retail financial services sector to becoming a focused operating company providing financial and management services to group companies, other corporations, institutions and selected high net-worth individuals. Along the way, the restructuring and disposition of its early investments in Royal Trustco and London Life proved critical to this transformation.

Shortly after Trilon Financial increased its ownership of Royal Trustco to 49% in 1983, Hartland McDougall and Michael Cornelissen were appointed Chairman and President and Chief Executive, respectively. Michael Cornelissen had performed admirably in the early restructuring of Trizec Corporation and had played an important role in its acquisition of the U.S. based Hahn shopping center company. Royal Trustco, under the leadership of Hartland McDougall and Michael Cornelissen, recorded exceptional financial results throughout the 1980s by increasing earnings from $44 million in 1982 to $265 million in 1989. This performance came to an abrupt end in 1990, largely as a result of the worldwide collapse in real estate values and two strategic initiatives which became the cause of serious difficulties.

The first problem related to the acquisition in December 1989 of Pacific First Financial Corporation, a U.S. savings and loan company. What was not foreseen was the response of regulators and policymakers in the United States to the developing crisis in the savings and loan industry. The regulators introduced new rules and proceeded to liquidate foreclosed real estate at fire sale prices, driving down property values, which in turn severely hurt otherwise sound savings and loan companies.

The second problem was caused by Royal Trustco's decision to expand its U.K. operations. Although constrained by conservative head office lending criteria and approval limits, local U.K. management had assembled a large portfolio of real estate loans which, because of their small individual size, escaped head office review.

These two problems came to a head when the worldwide collapse in real estate values first occurred in the United Kingdom, followed shortly in the United States and about two years later in Canada. As Royal Trustco was the only Canadian trust company with a major international presence, the U.K. and U.S. loan loss provisions which it reported early in 1991 took many Canadian investors, including Trilon Financial, by surprise.

Unfortunately for Royal Trustco, Canadians were unaware of the difficulties which lay ahead in their own real estate markets. Even though it was difficult to demonstrate at the time, with the benefit of hindsight it soon became evident that Royal Trustco's balance sheet and lending record were comparable to, or better than, other financial institutions in its three geographic markets.

In order to address the problems faced by Royal Trustco, it was decided in the middle of 1992 to sell Pacific First to reduce the company's real estate exposure and improve its capital ratios. Shortly thereafter, Jim Miller was appointed as

Royal Trustco's President and Chief Executive Officer, replacing Michael Cornelissen. Investors, anxious to hear some good news following Jim Miller's arrival, were unprepared for his decision to "clear the decks" and record large write-offs, even though the nature and extent of, not to mention the need for, these measures were quite uncertain at the time. His sweeping action set off a chain of events starting in January 1993, including negative daily media commentary and difficulties in processing transactions for Royal Trustco's clients through the Canadian payments clearing system.

On top of this situation came a series of unfortunate public and private statements from the Superintendent of Financial Institutions, including remarks to the effect that major shareholders of financial institutions were not, by their nature, helpful. These statements provoked the Canadian financial press into a speculative frenzy that further eroded public confidence and effectively ended Trilon Financial's ability to resolve the crisis on its own.

Reduced to a severely weakened negotiating position, Royal Trustco had no alternative but to accede to an exclusive negotiating arrangement with the Royal Bank of Canada. This led to the sale of its principal operating subsidiaries to the Royal Bank in August 1993, which continued these businesses under the Royal Trust name, leaving Royal Trustco with a large residual portfolio of real estate loans. Stripped of its best assets, Royal Trustco stayed in business under the name Gentra Inc., with a collection of unwanted loans as its main reason for continuing in business.

Trilon supported the sale of Royal Trustco's principal businesses to the Royal Bank to ensure that there would be no loss or disruption in service to Royal Trustco's clients and deposit holders. This was not, however, accomplished without considerable cost to Trilon Financial and to Royal Trustco's other shareholders. These losses were partly mitigated by Gentra's subsequent success in managing its residual loan portfolio to prove up equity values of more than $1 billion for its shareholders. This in itself demonstrated that Royal Trustco had not been short of capital in a regulatory or any other sense throughout this period.

Royal Trustco was the group's most costly business setback. It placed a cloud over Trilon Financial, Brascan and a number of other group companies for several years. However, starting in 1994, after the gradual surfacing of similar real estate loan problems in every other Canadian financial institution and with the steady recovery in the value of Gentra's preferred and common shares, members of the business community and key regulators acknowledged that Trilon Financial had acted responsibly in providing the leadership which ensured that Royal Trustco's depositors and other clients were protected, notwithstanding the high cost to the group and the company's other shareholders.

In 1979, when Edper acquired its first interest in London Life Insurance Company through its acquisition of Brascan, London Life had a sound reputation but lagged the industry in investment returns. It was also facing management succession problems.

By 1982, the ownership of London Life had been increased to 56% in order to strengthen the group's ability to implement a number of necessary changes in its investment policies and other areas of operation. Earl Orser, who had been retained as a consultant to conduct an operational review, was appointed President and Chief Executive Officer, and other management changes followed as London Life redefined its role in the individual financial security market. Tom Allan was one of the new management appointments made at this time and was instrumental in improving the key investment function, enabling London Life to consistently report top quartile returns in most of its investment portfolios.

Following the purchase of the shareholdings of The Toronto-Dominion Bank and the Jeffery family in London Life, Trilon Financial increased its ownership through market purchases to 98%. In 1985, London Insurance Group Inc. (initially called Lonvest Corporation) was launched as a public company, holding all of Trilon Financial's insurance operations, including London Life, Wellington Insurance and, later, The Holden Group.

With Earl Orser approaching retirement and no natural successor immediately available, Gordon Cunningham was appointed President of London Insurance Group in 1989. In 1993, Mel Hawkrigg was appointed Chairman of London Insurance Group to assist him in dealing with the strategic challenges faced by the industry. By 1994, as a result of mounting concerns over the competitive threats posed by the major chartered banks, Trilon Financial became more proactive in working with London Insurance Group to reduce unit costs. This led to the acquisition of Prudential Life's Canadian individual and group life insurance business and the sale of a number of London Life's peripheral insurance operations.

In order to address a number of other critical challenges faced by London Insurance Group, Fred Tomczyk was appointed President and Chief Executive in 1996. Having risen through the company's ranks, he was expected to provide a more effective, hands-on leadership approach and was given a strong mandate to maximize shareholder value. Fred Tomczyk's appointment also facilitated George Myhal working more closely with the company's executives and ensured that London Insurance Group's and Trilon Financial's board policies and strategic plans were closely aligned and promptly implemented. During the following ten months, the value of Trilon Financial's investment in London Insurance Group doubled through a reinvigorated management team, expanded sales force and a judiciously timed sale of its U.S. retail insurance operations.

The business community was quick to notice London Insurance Group's renewed business momentum, leading to an approach by the Royal Bank of Canada to Trilon Financial in July 1997 with an offer to acquire the company at a significant premium to its previous stock market value. Great-West Life shortly thereafter offered a higher price. Trilon Financial accepted this second offer, which provided the company's public shareholders and its senior management team, which held meaningful ownership positions, with significant gains on their investments in London Insurance Group.

The sale of London Insurance Group in 1997 triggered two other restructuring and simplification initiatives later that year. The first initiative involved Gentra, the successor company to Royal Trustco, successfully converting with the help of Trilon its portfolio of loans and mortgages receivable into real estate, at or near the bottom of the property market. Since ownership of real estate was not part of Trilon's mandate, it sold its 43% interest in Gentra to Brookfield Properties. This change aligned all of the group's property operations in North America under one company and allowed Trilon Financial to concentrate on its wholly-owned financial services activities.

The second initiative undertaken late in 1997 involved Trilon Financial's acquisition of EdperBrascan's merchant banking business, which had been conducted through Hees International by a team of financial executives who were ably led by Brian Lawson. The purchase of Hees International's merchant banking business aligned all of the group's financial activities in North America under Trilon Financial – an objective the group had wanted to achieve for many years.

This business unit, which was immediately renamed Trilon Capital Partners Limited, had a thirty-year record of outstanding investment success and had on a number of occasions performed a key role in assisting group companies in the implementation of major strategic acquisition and divestiture initiatives. It had also been responsible for the acquisition of many of the group's most significant investments, including the identification and execution of the purchases of the group's controlling interests in Brascan, Noranda, Norcen Energy Resources and North Canadian Oils. Other examples of this type of assistance include Hees International's role in the refinancing of Great Lakes Power for Brascan, and the restructuring and acquisition of control of World Financial Properties for Brookfield Properties. In each case, operating affiliates were provided with the opportunity for up to five years to purchase any investment acquired in these companies by Hees International once the affiliates had assembled the necessary financial or operating capacity to complete the purchases.

The sale of London Insurance Group and Gentra and the acquisition of Hees International completed the transformation of Trilon Financial from a diversified provider of retail and commercial financial services to a strongly capitalized company providing investment, commercial and merchant banking services to institutions and corporations, including companies within the Edper group. Completing the withdrawal from retail financial services in 1997 to concentrate on the financial activities which had served the group so well in the past would have pleased Peter Bronfman greatly, since it removed one of his main areas of concerns about the group's operations.

By uniting the Edper group's traditional merchant banking business with Trilon Financial's commercial and investment banking activities, the group established a strong, corporately focused financial enterprise intimately familiar with the group's strategic and financial plans. Possession of this knowledge enables Trilon Financial's senior executives to provide timely and relevant financial and management advice to group affiliates. The variety of assignments undertaken each year by Trilon Financial creates a stimulating work environment and an excellent training ground for group financial and investment executives to broaden their knowledge and familiarize themselves with the operations of the group's affiliates.

In this manner, Trilon Financial fulfills its mandate within the group for co-ordinating the group's finances. Trilon is also expected to provide the glue which helps the group's business units to work co-operatively together in exchanging financial knowledge and in promoting best practices. This is intended to be achieved in the context of the group's financing plans, which Trilon Financial executives have responsibility for overseeing.

Trilon Financial, with a capital base of more than $2 billion, is today one of the largest financial companies in Canada outside of the major deposit-taking institutions. It is also one of the most liquid and financially sound, with minimal debt and a capital structure which can support a major expansion of its business. The current objective is to double earnings from operations within five years. In 1997, Trilon Financial became the group's most profitable company, reporting total earnings of $789 million, including gains realized from the sale of Trilon Financial's common share-holdings in London Insurance Group and Gentra Inc.

Trilon's responsibility for developing and maintaining a reservoir of high-calibre financial and management talent to co-ordinate and help expedite the implementation of the group's financial and strategic plans continues this key group function previously performed by Hees International. As a result, the Trilon that emerged in late 1997 bears many resemblances to the financial group which Peter Bronfman had assembled around him a generation or so earlier. As in the early 1970s, it is staffed for the most part by young executives eager for success but strongly committed to teamwork and to the future of the Edper group as a whole. The combination of providing professional in-house financial services to group and third-party clients, which had worked so well for the group in the 1970s, had been successfully reinstated.

Chapter Fourteen

Building on History

By the time Edper became acquainted with Brascan in 1979, it had already shifted its primary focus from Brazil to Canada. While building Brascan's operating base in North America was the main priority for Peter Bronfman and his colleagues, they also realized that Brascan's well-earned reputation in Brazil was a valuable asset which, if nurtured properly, would provide a foothold for the group to expand in South America when the time arrived to venture further afield.

Peter Bronfman was particularly excited about Brascan's Brazilian connection. It may have been the sense of adventure in participating in the building of a vast country that had the potential to become a giant on the world's economic stage. Or perhaps it was the courteous charm of the people themselves that attracted him to Brazil and gave it a special place for him among the group's various investments.

But before serious thought could be given to expanding the group's investment in South America, there were some pressing problems which had to be addressed by Peter Bronfman and his new Brazilian colleagues.

In the 1960s, Brazilian Traction, Light and Power was facing mounting difficulties with its utilities in Brazil. The growing inflation of costs and regulatory restrictions on increasing revenues had caused diminishing returns. At the same time, dynamic growth in the Brazilian economy created a demand for expansion of the company's services and the capital investments required to provide them. Also at this time, the apparent success of a number of government-owned utilities provided a ground swell for nationalizing the country's privately-owned utilities.

For these reasons, Brazilian Traction, Light and Power agreed to start negotiating the sale of its telephone company to the Brazilian Government. The sale was completed in 1966, for US $96 million, payable over twenty years. The Brazilian Government of the day was determined to keep as much foreign capital as possible invested in the country, and wrote into the terms of the deal a requirement that approximately two-thirds of the sale price be reinvested in Brazil. The balance of the proceeds was returned to Canada and invested in a number of Canadian companies, including John Labatt and London Life. In recognition of the emerging importance of Canada to the company, its name was changed in 1969 to Brascan Limited.

A small investment group was set up in Brazil under Roberto de Andrade to initiate a diversification programme using the non-remittable proceeds due to Brazilian Traction, Light and Power. Banco Brascan was created with these funds as a registered investment bank and became the core of this first diversification effort. Over the course of the next twelve years, a diverse group of assets was acquired which, with the exception of the wholly-owned investment bank, comprised minority equity interests in a variety of agricultural, consumer goods and industrial companies. Among the unrelated group of companies which appeared in Brascan Brazil's portfolio during this period were a sardine cannery, a lobster fishery, a pineapple plantation, meat packing operations, a food processor, a tin mine and a tropical pine forest. In 1978, Roberto de Andrade also established a real estate group led by Jacky Delmar, which soon became a major contributor to Brascan Brazil's earnings and equity values.

When Peter Bronfman and his colleagues first reviewed this portfolio in 1979, they were reminded of the problems of Edper's early investment activities during the 1950s and 1960s. From their experience in bringing order and purpose to their own holdings, they quickly realized that the Brazilian investment group would need a dose of similar medicine – a guiding strategy, a focus on a few sectors where a high level of competence could be achieved, and a greater degree of control exercised over individual investments.

Looming on the horizon was another problem – the developing economic crisis in Brazil and many other South American countries which would lead to that continent's "lost decade." Inflation in Brazil moved to hyper-levels, government deficits soared and economic growth ground to a halt. Many of these problems had been caused by the nationalization programmes adopted by Brazil and many other governments during the 1960s and 1970s and by the notion that they could develop their economies better in isolation from the rest of the world. But it would take another fifteen years and much pain and lost potential growth before these countries realized their mistakes.

Faced with the twin problems of a diverse investment portfolio and destructive fiscal policies, Peter Bronfman and his colleagues quickly went to work with their Brazilian counterparts to bring some order to the investments held. The strategy which was put in place would focus in the future on three main sectors – natural resources, real estate development and financial and business services. These mirrored the areas which Edper planned to concentrate on in Canada, the only exception being the electrical power sector, which would remain firmly in the Brazilian government's hands for the next sixteen years. These operations, which by their nature included hard assets, were also expected to provide a fair degree of protection against Brazil's high inflation rate. The corporate office in Rio was trimmed down to a smaller, tighter group focused on results, under the very capable leadership of Roberto de Andrade.

The process of whittling down Brascan Brazil's investment portfolio to a manageable size also provided some early opportunities to recover additional capital for reinvestment in Canada. In 1980, the group's wholly-owned investment bank, Banco Brascan, and its interest in a local brewer, Skol Caracú, were both sold. And over the next two years, joint-venture partners bought 50% interests in the group's forestry and mining operations. Through the sale of these interests, over $160 million was repatriated to Canada during the early 1980s.

❧

Knowing the importance of developing hands-on personal relations with his senior executives throughout the group, Peter Bronfman looked for a way to relate effectively to his Brazilian team, even though they were more than 5,000 miles away. Regular visits to Brazil were instituted to discuss their current initiatives and business plans. These meetings, which were held in Rio de Janeiro, generally involved Peter Bronfman, Trevor Eyton, Jack Cockwell, Bob Dunford and Ed Kress and helped to build a strong relationship between the management groups in both countries. They were supplemented by the regular participation of Roberto de Andrade at Brascan's quarterly board meetings, as well as frequent communication by telephone. The group of executives in Brazil immediately welcomed the active participation of Peter Bronfman and his colleagues and were pleased to be part of the new team.

It was during the earliest of these visits that Peter Bronfman developed his affection for Brazil. At first his casual approach surprised his new Brazilian friends, who were used to a greater degree of formality from their Canadian shareholders. In fact, on one early occasion he was denied access to a Brascan Brazil review meeting by an over-eager executive who felt that this friendly gentleman in a sweater and slacks could not possibly be the principal shareholder of their Canadian parent company.

It was also during these early visits that Peter Bronfman began his close friendship with Jacky Delmar, who was and continues to be the driving force behind Brascan Brazil's real estate operations. Jacky Delmar had joined Brascan Brazil in the late 1970s after an extensive stint in the real estate business in Montreal. Possibly their common roots and their mutual interests in real estate provided the special bond which first brought together two quite different personalities. Peter Bronfman grew to greatly admire his sense of humour, his warm outgoing personality and his tremendous energy. Jacky Delmar in turn valued his concern for others, his sensitivity and his capacity for deep and enduring friendship.

The friendship between these two men developed over the years to the point that Peter Bronfman would, whenever possible, arrive in Rio a few days early for the annual January business meetings so that he could spend time with Jacky Delmar, his family and friends at their beachfront cottages over the holiday period before becoming immersed in the scheduled work sessions. It was through these contacts that he cultivated a deeper understanding of Brazil's many challenging social problems and the natural warmth of its people. Jacky Delmar remained particularly close to Peter Bronfman and soon after his death wrote these words in testimony to his departed friend: "Peter had a heart big enough to contain all of us and wrap us in his mantle of warmth and love. He was the fairest of men, a father, a friend and a leader. What a blessing to have entered his tender and marvelous world and what a pain to leave it."

When Peter Bronfman and his colleagues in Toronto and Rio de Janeiro set about developing a new business strategy for Brascan Brazil in the early 1980s, there was an overriding objective – to preserve and build on the excellent reputation that Brascan had earned in Brazil over the preceding eighty years. Since then, Roberto de Andrade, Jacky Delmar and their Brazilian colleagues have carefully built a diversified company with solid business operations in the natural resources, real estate and financial and business services sectors. In the natural resources sector, two large ranches have been developed in central Brazil where some 26,000 head of cattle graze and on which over two million coffee, citrus and rubber trees have been planted. Further expansions of farming operations into western central Brazil are now under way. A tropical pine plantation has been developed in southern Brazil to provide wood fibre for a new large-scale panelboard mill the company is building in partnership with the Sonae group of Portugal.

From a modest start in 1979, the group's real estate operations have been expanded in Rio de Janeiro and São Paulo to include three shopping centres, two Inter-Continental five-star hotels and a condominium construction group which has the capacity to develop and sell over 500 units each year. The group's financial services operations, which comprise advisory services and brokerage, were recently expanded into investment management through a partnership with the Pittsburgh-based Mellon Bank. Another key operation is 40% owned Accor Brasil, which issues over one million restaurant, food, fuel and transportation vouchers each day. Roberto de Andrade and his Vice-President, Trigo de Negreiros, have both worked closely with Firmin Antonio, the exceptionally capable and energetic chief executive of

Accor Brasil, in developing the successful partnership with the Accor Group from France. Together, they have built this dynamic business services company into the largest and most profitable of its kind in South America.

Over the past eighteen years, the value of Brascan Brazil's operations has increased significantly from $100 million in 1979 to approximately $900 million by the end of 1997. In addition, throughout this period Brascan Brazil has safeguarded and significantly enhanced the reputation it earned early in the twentieth century for being innovative and for making a positive contribution to Brazil's growth. As a result, Brascan Brazil's record and business relationships today provide a solid base for the group to grow in its principal areas of operation as Brazil realizes its enormous potential.

While the Brascan Brazil team was working on nurturing its legacy in Brazil, the group was also gaining confidence to expand its operations into other parts of South America. Having well-established operations in Brazil provided a valuable learning experience and a natural base from which to explore opportunities in other countries on this vast continent. Brazil represents approximately half the continent's land mass, population and economic activity, ranking it as the sixth-largest economy in the world. Given the advantage of having long-established operations in the largest country on the continent and with an enviable reputation for delivering on commitments, it was natural for Peter Bronfman and his colleagues to choose South America, rather than Europe or Asia, as a key area for future growth.

Along with its enormous mineral, forestry and energy potential, South America has the added advantage of lying within the same time zones as much of North America. Moreover, Canadians are generally held in high regard in the region, partly because of the infrastructure and other projects they helped to construct in the early part of the twentieth century. Canada is also viewed as a well-respected and helpful middle power on the world stage.

After acquiring Norcen in the 1980s, Edper was quick to encourage its management team to place a high priority on South America in building its international oil and gas operations. Over the next decade, Norcen's operations in this region were expanded through the development of oil fields in Venezuela and the acquisition of the largest oil and gas production company in Guatemala. The successful growth of Norcen's South American operations contributed meaningfully to the group's ability to realize a significant gain on this investment when Norcen was sold early in 1998.

Through Noranda and Falconbridge, in the early 1990s, the group began its aggressive pursuit of mining and metallurgical investments in this region. The first major foray in the mining sector outside Brazil was Falconbridge's development, in partnership with Minorco S.A., of the massive Collahuasi copper mine in northern Chile, one of the world's largest copper projects, which started initial production in June 1998. The Refimet copper smelter near Antofagasta, also in northern Chile, was acquired by

Noranda in 1996 and is being expanded in order to process a portion of the copper concentrates produced by group companies in the region.

Continuing on this path in 1998, Noranda acquired a 37½% interest in the massive Antamina copper/zinc deposit in Peru. The Collahuasi and Antamina deposits rank among the largest ore bodies in the world and meet the group's objective of increasing its ownership of long-life mineral reserves of the highest quality. However, given the magnitude of the upfront capital investment required and engineering and other technical challenges to develop these projects in the high Andes, joint ventures have been formed with other leading mining and metals companies to share expertise and spread risk. Noranda has also launched grassroots exploration programs throughout South America, including working closely with Brascan Brazil on exploring the region's largely untapped mineral potential.

The group's diversified operations in Brazil, combined with its new operations elsewhere in South America, provide the potential for a larger presence on this continent. Long experience in Brazil is a valuable asset and, no doubt, will help immeasurably in achieving the group's broader growth objectives in South America. In all likelihood, each of the different operations conducted by Brascan Brazil will eventually become more closely aligned with its counterpart in North America in order to share and draw on the group's combined technical base and, in the case of the mining sector, to provide a secure source of concentrates for its expanding Canadian metallurgical processing facilities.

Lynda Hamilton and Peter Bronfman at home in the early 1990s, with a favourite Group of Seven painting by Lawren Harris in the background

A portrait of Peter Bronfman's family taken shortly before his death in 1996

The expansion of Woodsworth College at the University of Toronto, completed in 1994, was partly funded by a personal gift from Peter Bronfman

Peter Bronfman receiving an Honorary Degree from the University of Toronto in November 1996 with representatives of the University. From the left: Lionel Schipper, Rose Wolfe, Peter Bronfman, Wendy Cecil-Cockwell, Rob Prichard and Alex Waugh

*University of Toronto Chancellor Rose Wolfe addressing the Dedication Ceremony
for the Peter Bronfman Courtyard at Woodsworth College in June 1997*

*A plaque on the courtyard
wall at Woodsworth College
commemorates Peter
Bronfman's contribution to
the college*

Brenda Bronfman receiving her father's posthumous Order of Canada from Governor General Roméo LeBlanc in February 1997

Peter Bronfman's Order of Canada medal and portrait hang in a place of honour in the EdperBrascan boardroom

Book Five

The Mind of the Man

In these final chapters, Peter Bronfman's concerns for the unquantifiable risks of business as well as his financial and market theories are described against the background of his family's experience and the undulating fortunes of Canadian business. His deeply held personal values and his goals for providing assistance to the less fortunate are also noted. Having met with considerable success on a variety of fronts, Peter Bronfman had ample opportunity to celebrate, and that he did, but often in unusual and quite modest ways. His concept of leadership, its joys and its responsibilities are examined and the reasons for the passionate dedication of his team to the preservation of his philosophy and values are shown. Being as much a philosopher as a businessman, a great deal of thought went into the development of his personal and business values, which should be of meaningful benefit to his colleagues, his friends and students of business.

Chapter Fifteen

Harnessing the Unknowns

The vicissitudes of business life can be punishing and brutal, rarely leaving a sensitive participant unmarked. Like the incessant and erosive action of the water on the shore, events through the years carved their own significant and telling lines in Peter Bronfman's view of the world. As a thinking man, there was little that escaped his notice, evaluation and eventual incorporation into his assessment of risk and his approach to business life.

Perhaps because he began his business career when he was young and with little practical experience, he showed early signs that he would be an inveterate worrier. It was not concern about his own abilities or, for that matter, his limitations, but rather what he came to refer to as the "Unknowns". These were the imponderables which he could not measure, predict or nail down with any degree of precision. Ranking foremost among these unknowns were the short-term machinations of the stock market, uninsurable business risk and the unpredictability of governments, which at any time could arbitrarily change the rules which businesses had to follow.

He took some delight in describing his trait for worrying about these unquantifiable events and other risks by commenting: "My colleagues do the work and I worry enough for all of us." Similarly, when asked what he did for a living, he would invariably say: "My job is to do the worrying."

His deep concern about the unknowns originated with his first understanding of his father's and uncles' early business dealings. At the bottom of every business assessment he made was his concern that he must never do anything that would reflect badly on his family. Washing away the memories of the prohibition days was important to him, and he assiduously avoided any actions that could bring back old ghosts.

Once he and his businesses had ventured on to a larger playing field, they were, by virtue of the Bronfman name, destined to be in the spotlight. As his business interests grew he became increasingly careful to ensure that his activities were never a source of embarrassment to his family or his cousins' business at Seagram. Every public act put him further out on a limb and he felt that any failure would be extremely visible and uncomfortable, not only for himself but for his extended family as well.

Alloyed with these basic concerns was his desire to make his own mark in the community, to do something positive, noteworthy and admirable. But aiming for such lofty accomplishments always entails the assumption of some risk, and at the mention of risk, he felt the fingers of worry. He knew the unknowns could never be eliminated, but he believed there had to be a way to reduce the overall risk in any venture and sought to find a formula to do just that.

To begin with, he sensed that the stock market, that sometimes volatile, cyclone-like whirlwind of activity which can suck you up into its vortex only to drop you down like useless debris later, was a particularly erratic creature – powerful, uncontrollable and quite intangible. The downside possibilities in any stock market transaction always loomed far larger in his deliberations than any upside potential.

For years he had listened attentively to his father's colourful but chilling tales of the stock market crash of 1929. It had occurred the very month and year in which Peter Bronfman was born. The young boy, spellbound by his father's recollections, was steeped in horror by the unforeseen tumbling of market values and the ensuing destructive repercussions.

Because of his grudging respect for the stock market and fear of the ruin it could cause, he encouraged his colleagues to become students of its frequently capricious behaviour and to manage the business and their personal financial affairs accordingly. He constantly urged them to confine their stock market exposure to investing for the long term and only in companies in which they were personally and actively involved. At the same time he knew that, for Edper to achieve its growth objectives, he and his colleagues would have to learn to live with the many different facets of the investment community and, in particular, the tendency for some to claim success at the peaks and minimize any responsibility for the troughs.

It was the troughs that worried him, especially when the stock market had been volatile and confused as occurred in 1929. He had first- hand experience of the market collapses of the early 1970s and 1987, but it was the unruly Canadian markets of the early 1990s that proved to be the most agonizing period for him. The pain was at its worst early in 1993 when, in what seemed to be an uncontrolled fury, the market placed vicious downward pressure on the shares of Edper and a number of its affiliates.

During the long and dreary months of the early 1990s, as the recession seeped into every crevasse of the Canadian economy, he was concerned with the growing pessimism he saw throughout the financial sector, governments and industry in general. Formerly dynamic leaders were being humbled by unanticipated and unseen powers which were beyond their control. They could feel any influence and security they had so recently known slipping through their fingers with each month's steady slide further into the recession. The unknown forces at work were showing that they could be grim reapers indeed.

Peter Bronfman was fully cognizant of the Edper group's need for strong leadership at a time when almost everyone was bowing to the tyranny of the market. One will never know the psychological cost to him in having to display confidence, each and every day, to bolster the spirits of his colleagues. It was during this time that he started to take long, solitary walks around his neighbourhood, often stopping in for brief visits with family, colleagues and friends – a cup of tea, a piece of pie or just a chat, then off again. On the sidewalks and ravine paths of his adopted city, he spent hours thinking as he wandered, refueling his own ability to present a confident countenance to those who looked to him for guidance.

He knew it was his responsibility to energize his team and supplement their will to overcome the challenges that were toppling many enterprises which had once seemed so secure. It was critically important to him that his team set out each day unequivocally certain of his trust and confidence in them. This, combined with their known abilities to get the job done, reinforced his belief that they could out-manoeuvre the recession and outlast the tenacious stranglehold it exerted on a number of their businesses.

Life had taught him that attitude was paramount in determining the outcome of any undertaking, small or large, personal or corporate. He knew that, even in the midst of the most hostile environment, adopting a positive attitude was the one choice that was available to anyone. It had worked for his grandparents on the cold, grim Saskatchewan prairie, it had worked for his father and uncle in the dangerous and topsy-turvy world of the liquor business, and he believed it could also work for him in the equally depressing and threatening Canadian recession of the early 1990s.

While he was fully prepared to carry a disproportionate share of the burden of worry for the group's affairs himself, he was not alone in using a positive approach in tackling problems because he had always endeavoured to surround himself with people he trusted to be positive and loyal. He had consistently sought out individuals for his team who were inquisitive in a practical, solution-seeking way.

Another quality which he valued, particularly in difficult times, was decisiveness. He did not want his businesses to be encumbered with philosophical executives who dithered over decisions and could not stake out a path and follow it. His style of management required individuals who could seize a problem, examine it thoroughly and come to him with a strong and logical recommendation well supported by reasonable arguments. At the same time, these executives would also have to be prepared to see their game plans undergo the piercing analysis of their colleagues and not feel undermined or threatened by the process.

During what was a very trying time for him, he drew great comfort from knowing that he had relied on the correct characteristics in selecting his key colleagues and that they would remain absolutely loyal to him under even the direst of circumstances.

In leading his colleagues through the recession, he had been determined to be ever present with them and, throughout the bleak years, he steeled himself to putting on the positive face required of any brave captain of a ship caught in the middle of a violent storm. He was disciplined enough to seldom show any cracks in his countenance and to constantly reassure colleagues that he could see a light at the end of the tunnel. Whether he could or not – no one knew for certain – but his loyalty to them and the confidence he displayed spurred them to try harder. Throughout, his own resolve was reinforced by his wife Lynda Hamilton who, because she had been a successful business woman in her own right, was always a tower of strength for him, but never more so than during these periods of difficulty.

Beyond this, where did the worry find its most fertile ground? It was his concern for others that really caused it to take root and grow. Although he had never known want, his tastes had always been down-to-earth and simple. He and Lynda Hamilton kept two modest residences, a cosy town home in Toronto and a small, converted school house in Palgrave, sixty kilometres northwest of the city. They had no interest in building, owning or living in a mansion.

His fears of losing all the material success he had worked for were not based on concern for how he could manage to do without, because he believed that he and his wife would have no problem scaling back their lifestyle. His most treasured pleasures away from business had always come from reading, thinking, writing poetry and enjoying the company of his family and friends. Being with others and the art of good conversation held more appeal for him than private planes, lavish parties or exotic vacations.

He always, however, believed he carried a personal responsibility for the thousands of employees and their families who depended on his leadership for the successful continuance of their employer companies. He took his responsibilities very deeply to heart, and this sense of duty added greatly to the wearying travails of the recession and any perceived threat to the health of the corporate enterprise.

Once the group had steered its way to safety through the hazards of the early 1990s, the mending and then the rebuilding could begin again. But for Peter Bronfman, it had been a watershed experience. The anxiety of those years caused him to collect his thoughts, examine the lessons learned and then sift through the facts to crystallize his thinking about the needs and the future of the enterprise. Having been witness to numerous business cycles over the previous forty years, he recognized that the group's emergence from the recession of the 1990s, stronger than before, did not mean that it had somehow found a way to shelter itself from being swept away by unknown or uncharted currents in the future.

Recessions are cyclical and the timing not always predictable, but their eventual recurrence is a certainty. He was determined to make structural changes to the organization to fortify its defences for the next time the cycle turned against it. His objective was to make the unknowns which had been the group's nemesis in the past into an ally by harnessing their power and converting them into a force to strengthen and secure what was important to the group and its plans for the future.

He believed that the group had to be reinforced and made resilient enough to withstand the roughest of shocks coming from unexpected directions. It would also have to be shaped so that it would never need to draw on any one of its core holdings during times of deep distress in order to hold the enterprise together. As well, the entire organization had to be both strong and, equally important, be seen to be strong, so that people would seek out the group as the partner of choice during difficult periods in the economy. It had to be so firmly based, so well financed and unshakeable that it could be relied upon as a source of stability for others in search of an anchor to steady them in rough patches or a life preserver to keep them afloat in case of sudden disaster.

The key objectives of his plan, which were not fully implemented until after his death, included three main initiatives – significantly expanding Brookfield Properties' capital base, withdrawing completely from retail financial services by selling London Insurance Group, and increasing the financial returns from the group's natural resource investments by transforming Noranda into one of the world's leading and most profitable mining and metallurgical companies. It was from Peter Bronfman's worrying nature that these demanding objectives were born.

In another important respect, the worrier in him focused on devising the optimum structure for each business deal. He believed that even a sweet deal would turn quite sour if badly structured. Over the years he had become a keen student of how best to put a deal together so that the risks taken on by each party closely matched its level of tolerance for loss. For his part, he preferred to have the risks clearly constrained in order to quell his natural worries and allow him to sleep comfortably at night. Thus, together with his colleagues, he developed the concepts of "structured partnerships" and "fair sharing". He was always happy to share generously any upside potential in exchange for a reduction in downside risk. In many cases this would entail providing a disproportionate amount of capital to a venture in return for the other party providing the additional downside protection he sought.

Even though every colleague had a specific role to play in the organization, with interchangeability always in the wings, some, more frequently than others, were assigned the task of presenting the dissenting case and the risks associated with any proposal as part of testing its mettle. In this respect, Bob Harding more often than not was asked to play the devil's advocate in fulfilling his key responsibility for managing the group's overall risk profile. Peter Bronfman placed great value on this role, especially during the early 1990s when it was extremely important to ensure that no plan went into action without being fine-combed for potential problems and weighed carefully for the appropriate balance of risks and rewards.

He expected the group's annual strategic business plans and project proposals to deal candidly with all manner of risks likely to be faced. He questioned those responsible for monitoring risks even more carefully than those championing new project proposals. Because of his desire to be kept informed about potential problems long before they became an issue, he encouraged his colleagues to gather industry intelligence constantly, test the winds of change and then identify the safe harbours in which to ride out pending storms.

In his business plan reviews, he invariably asked those responsible for monitoring risks for the five most ominous threats to the group's plans that they had been able to identify. As a result, early on in the group's development a tradition was born. If a colleague wanted to guarantee Peter Bronfman's priority attention, even for the most mundane section of a plan or a specific project proposal, he would accompany it with what became known as "Peter's wall of worry". He would then demonstrate how it could be scaled, preferably with appropriate safety nets, if he hoped to get not only Peter Bronfman's attention but also his blessing and approval for the undertaking.

This tradition goes on unabated, often leading to intensive debates that can continue well into the night. For example, the business plans prepared in the mid-1990s took this tradition to a new level by intentionally listing a number of disconcerting facts related to the economy and the stock market. This was done partly to stimulate debate, but also to instill a sense of urgency and to spur executives to take immediate steps to strengthen the group, so that it could ride through any future recession or major stock market downturn with ample surplus resources available to benefit from the opportunities which would be sure to arise.

One of the questions examined and debated at length was whether North America was heading down a path which could lead to a stock market correction similar to the one which took place in Japan from December 1989 through to August 1992. During this period, the Nikkei stock market index declined from 39,000 to 14,000 and five years later had recovered only 20% of this loss. This was a major factor in deciding to reconfigure the management and operations of London Insurance Group in order to enhance the group's chances of selling the investment. A particular concern was the fact that, in the normal course of business, London Insurance Group invested large sums of money in the stock market both for its own account as well as for its customers. It was felt that, if the group proceeded with its aggressive growth plans for its cyclical natural resource and real estate operations, it would need to be liquid and not be inhibited by the cries of dismay sure to come from the multitude of investment clients and insurance policyholders, should the amount of their dividends and the values of their policies decline as a result of a future stock market correction.

The role of equity mutual funds and their impact on the stock market was another possible threat examined in reviewing these business plans. The mutual fund industry, like the stock market, was viewed by Peter Bronfman as a potentially powerful but unpredictable creature of finance that had the propensity to unwind investment assets back into the market at much lower prices and at a faster pace than they could ever be accumulated. Two previous instances were used to illustrate how mutual funds or the equivalent financial vehicles had significantly exaggerated the rise in stock market prices and compounded the losses once a meaningful market correction took root.

When the market corrected in 1929, investment trusts, the predecessors to today's mutual funds, dumped shares to meet margin calls, thus compounding the decline in share prices, leading to a drop of more than 80%. Similarly, the unravelling of the freewheeling mutual fund industry in the 1960s was another illustration given of how these investment vehicles created, or at least aided, the 60% decline in stock market prices which took place in the early 1970s.

The rapid growth in Canadian equity mutual funds from $1.2 billion in 1980 to $70 billion in 1997 was also identified as a potential concern. The ability of mutual fund investors to withdraw their funds at short notice and the illiquidity of many of the investments held by the mutual funds were seen as potential areas of danger, requiring careful monitoring of the group's financing initiatives and corporate acquisition plans. In particular, attention would be directed to expediting the planned refinancing of the group's real estate operations held through Brookfield Properties with additional equity and long-term property mortgages, each having recourse to a specific property only and not to Brookfield Properties' own credit. The urgency applied to this task reflected the group's concerns that a collapse in the equity markets could retard the growth of the financial services industry, which had been a major force behind the increased demand for office space during the mid-1990s.

Worry and experience can lead to empathy in some people, and Peter Bronfman was one of these. From time to time, the game of business presents a participant with a flashing moment of opportunity when a high score can be made with one shot. But his sympathy for those facing a financial crisis made him reluctant to take advantage when competitors and others were in a weakened position and vulnerable to a nasty blow.

This occurred, for example, late in 1987 when Wood Gundy was backed against the wall as a result of the sudden collapse in the price of the shares of British Petroleum. Wood Gundy had assumed a disproportionately high underwriting position in this issue, the largest British privatization to that time. When Wood Gundy found itself seriously short of financing and without the time and allies to put it in place, the Edper group backed them with a $140 million loan, based essentially on a handshake with Ed King, the firm's President and Chief Executive Officer at the time, and a couple of his other partners, and saw them through to more stable times. There was no discussion or thought of exacting a fee or any other special consideration for saving the company from possible ruin.

Though many business people pride themselves on a reputation for being invincible at the bargaining table and never taking less than they could, again Peter Bronfman had always preferred a slightly different, some might say softer, approach to the thrust, parry and stab of high finance and business deals. Because relationships and the longer view were so important to him, he did not regard each single deal as the make-or-break test. Over the years, he had taught his colleagues to have the courage of their convictions when doing the right thing did not necessarily follow the conventional business wisdom of maximizing financial returns at each and every opportunity.

The concept of fair dealing, of give and take in the pattern of transactions, seemed to him a more reasonable approach than thinking of each external partner or competitor as an adversary and each deal as a fight to the finish. If there were special circumstances which made a particular transaction unique in his opinion, then a less conventional approach might be the best one. Two examples of his taking the broader issues and longer-term benefits into consideration and then consummating a deal which was not the most rewarding choice in the shorter term can be found in the sale of the Montreal Canadiens, as described in Chapter Five, and the disposition of the group's investment in Canadian CableSystems.

The sale of the group's 25% interest in Canadian Cable-Systems to Ted Rogers was a particularly good example of Peter Bronfman's sense of what was right and appropriate. Knowing in 1978 that Ted Rogers was committed to integrating his goals in the communications industry with his vision of the country, he believed Ted Rogers was the appropriate buyer for the group's shareholdings. At the time, he likened Ted Rogers to the man who chipped away each day at granite building blocks, not as a mere stone mason but rather as the builder of a cathedral. Later in life, Ted Rogers recalled Peter Bronfman's role in selling him the critical 25% of Canadian CableSystems, with the following words: "Peter had a role in building many successful Canadian companies which created tens of thousands of jobs in Canada and made a real mark on the country. He was also a fabulous partner and a real team player." The association with Ted Rogers continues to this day through the participation of his long-time and equally accomplished associate, Phil Lind, as a director of EdperBrascan.

❧

Peter Bronfman's worries and concerns for others had a broader community application as well. A privileged life can have a soporific effect on the social conscience and it can numb what would otherwise be the natural human tendency to kindness, sympathy and helping those who need a boost. It is an effortless activity to keep one's eyes averted from the poor, the homeless, the uneducated and the underprivileged or even from those who are down just a few rungs too many on life's ladder of comfort and status.

He was not, however, a man who could pretend not to see or who could turn away when he witnessed a need. For all his privileges, he never grew scales over his eyes or put his emotions in a tough, protective carapace that could let him shut out the suffering of others or even the acknowledgment that some small assistance could make a great difference. It is not that he was a bleeding heart, open to any sadness and every plea for help, for he was a practical man who knew his own limits as well as those of others. He understood that he could never absorb and cure all the world's sadness and poverty, but he did want to help in a meaningful way.

An important part of what he had learned at his father's knee while growing up in Montreal was the value of involvement in community work. He would not be the first, nor would he be the last, to enter the world of volunteerism out of a sense of duty and obligation and, during the course of immersion in good work, come to find it deeply rewarding in a personal sense. He would also discover at an early age and much to his surprise that he could learn skills and develop a network of relationships which would be valuable in a business context and, at a later date, happily influence his life. In essence, he believed that the privilege which comes with wealth and influence is accompanied by its twin – an obligation to do something to help those less fortunate.

His goal was not to solve other people's problems but rather to help provide them with the means to find their own solutions, to elevate themselves out of their difficulties so they would not feel beholden and so that they too would ultimately have the self-respect, confidence and resources to be of help to others. He was always vigilant about never stealing that vital elixir of independence and initiative from those whom he assisted, because he realized it was essential for their continued success.

In spite of his worrying nature, he was not a man to let this hobble his ambitions or inhibit his actions. Instead he tried to put his tendency to worry to work for him, using it to inflame his drive for success while keeping his activities within manageable boundaries and relying on it at times as an effective test of new people, new ideas and new proposals.

Closely linked to worry is relief when worries prove to have been for naught, and following relief often comes a sense of celebration that the challenge has been met. There are times when even the most profound worrier puts his frowns and beads aside and decides to celebrate his relief and his great joy at victory. It is said that the tougher the climb up the mountain, the more rewarding the view from the peak. As a climber of so many business and personal mountains, Peter Bronfman also had his own unique but modest ways of recording his appreciation and celebrating success.

Chapter Sixteen

Celebrating Success

If ever there was a person who sought balance in his life it was Peter Bronfman. Long before the self-improvement gurus and lifestyle advisers found eager readers for their tomes on how to get more joy from living and how to find the path to happiness, he had discovered, or perhaps invented, his own formula for enjoying the gift of life.

While his approach to business may often have appeared deceptively relaxed and casual, he knew, as all great builders do, that hard, steady work is the only reliable way to construct a sturdy, long-lasting foundation, whether for a home, commercial property or business enterprise. But at the same time, he was frequently quoted – and often chided his colleagues with the saying: "All work and no play makes Jack a dull boy." For him, the magic lay in sensing when to push harder and when to put down the tools, wash up and change the pace.

Within the first year of melding the Brascan personnel with the Edper team, a fresh approach to having company gatherings entered the group culture. Hours had been long and progress had been made, but they knew it would be some time before tangible rewards became evident. Peter Bronfman and his Edper colleagues were eager to show the new members of the team that their efforts were appreciated, and so the company picnic was born.

First, it must be remembered that virtually everyone was young, reasonably fit and energetic. It must also be noted that company gatherings under the former Brascan regime had been quite formal affairs and were rarely used to celebrate anything, much less mix executives with the junior staff. The first summer picnic was an eye opener for all concerned. The office was closed for part of the afternoon and a motor-launch was rented to ferry everyone across to a pre-selected site on the Toronto Islands. People who had worked together for years and had only seen one another in business attire were decked out in shorts, T-shirts and running shoes. Baseball caps and sun hats were the order of the day and a jolly mood prevailed.

The games began with an egg tossing contest, in which almost everyone was splattered with raw eggs, getting events off to a rather slimy but hilarious start. Water balloon tossing was one of a number of other goofy games which had people messy and laughing and served to prepare them for the real test to come – the soccer game.

Men and women were divided into teams and no one escaped. The game was fast, physical and fun but there could be no doubt that each side was committed to winning. It took courage at first for some of the shyer members to take the plunge into the full come-hell-or-high-water spirit of the competition, but it did happen. People threw themselves into the game with so much gusto that it continued unabated until the sun was finally sinking into Lake Ontario.

By that time, the picnickers were tuckered out, happy and ravenous. It was time for an enchanted repast complete with rib-sticking good food set out in the rustic environment just across the water from the glittering office towers of Toronto's downtown. Unknown to most, arrangements had been made for a truly elegant meal to be served at the wooden picnic benches further along the shore. As the sky turned pink and orange, the unmistakable aroma of steak and salmon grilling on the barbecue wafted across the island. White linen-covered tables greeted the grubby and limping players as they hobbled to the supper scene lit by flickering candles. Caesar salad, baked potatoes and garlic bread also awaited the starving teams. For dessert, they tucked into apple pie and ice cream. With dirt-streaked and sunburnt faces, bruises on their shins and stained clothes, the group shared hearty fare and laughter, told jokes and stories and realized their leaders knew there was a time to leave work behind and have a little fun.

The curious juxtaposition of the pastoral Toronto Islands and the twinkling lights of the city, the tired and dirty guests with the elegant dinner presentation, all bathed in the rich amber glow of a summer evening sunset, made it a night to remember and put in place the beginnings of a shared history and a new culture. Peter Bronfman was pleased that the people he would be working with found so much pleasure in one another and in the evening that had been provided. It was a little bizarre, somewhat eccentric, a lot of fun and it made everyone present feel special and part of the team.

Each time thereafter, whether the picnic was hosted by Tim Casgrain at Bronte Park in Oakville or held at Trevor Eyton's Caledon farm, everyone insisted that the soccer game was the highlight of the day. Peter Bronfman also took his share of physical punishment in these games, once badly twisting his knee. His involvement and enthusiasm for the company picnic had taken on a life of its own – as so many of his other ideas did over the years.

It was not only at these picnics that Peter Bronfman's colleagues found a sociable outlet for their energies and high spirits. There was the annual tennis tournament inspired and meticulously organized by Tim Price. Also, every few weeks or so it seemed someone would have a birthday. The office pace would slow down a few beats while everyone ate ice cream cake and made jokes about the celebrant, but then, it was back to work probably even harder than before owing to a sugar-induced high!

Peter Bronfman's encouragement of these traditions within the office came from his belief that they celebrated the team rather than praised any one individual. High-calibre performance was expected from everyone, but he felt it was important to give witness to the value of working together, for that kind of recognition really belonged to the whole team.

Peter Bronfman found a wonderful partner in his wife Lynda Hamilton, for she too believed in celebrating success and life itself in an understated but warm and personal way.

Often referred to by him as well as others as his "angel", Lynda Hamilton made their home in the country a peaceful refuge for quiet pleasures where proximity to their animals and the verdant beauty of nature created its own kind of celebration. She also avoided the limelight and gave him the comforts of home and serenity. This peace of mind and the contemplative environment which they created and shared was the true expression of their personal characters and love for each other.

Lynda Hamilton's understanding that her partner celebrated success in a quiet and modest way – and usually by helping someone else – sprang from her own approach to appreciating what they had. They often worked together to make a difference to a particular individual, a family or an organization as a private, personal celebration of some special accomplishment or occasion in their lives. Most people would never know the genesis of the gesture, but it was their preferred way of celebrating and demonstrating their gratitude for success and good fortune. Sue McGovern, Peter Bronfman's devoted personal assistant for twenty-five years, witnessed many examples of this generosity and played a key role in helping him and Lynda express their appreciation and bring pleasure to others.

When he turned sixty in October 1989, Lynda and his three children arranged a surprise circus-themed party for his friends and colleagues to enjoy with him. At the party he was quick to exclaim: "This party isn't about me – it is about all of us being together and enjoying everything the carnival of life presents to us!" From the circus tent erected at his country home to the clowns, the balloons, the games, the jokes, the popcorn machines, the magicians and the buttons, the party was a joyful celebration of friendship. The speeches that night were entertaining and moving. It was evident to all that his birthday party, as with all the many dinners and other events he had a hand in arranging, was not about what he had but rather what he could share. His gratitude for life itself was overwhelming and contagious. He was fond of proclaiming that love was like germs – only powerful when spread around.

As much as he embraced and enjoyed these celebrations, as a rule he shied away from any publicity that would increase his or the Edper group's public profile. He liked privacy, for himself and his colleagues, and believed they would do better work if they kept themselves out of the limelight to the extent appropriate and possible as substantial owners of public enterprises. Every particle of him felt this to be true.

No matter what the accomplishment or victory, he was not one to pull out all the stops and gush with self-satisfaction and boastful pride either privately or publicly. He believed such behaviour was immodest and unbecoming and it even made him jumpy when he saw it in others. He held to the belief that "Pride goeth before a fall", and used it as a guiding principle in his life. His vision of what he wanted to do and should do for his companies and his country was vast, and so every major success was, in his eyes, only a tiny step in the desired direction, not the *pièce de résistance* that some might think.

When Edper successfully completed the takeover of Brascan, Peter Bronfman suddenly found himself swimming in a sea of praise, congratulations and compliments and felt he could drown. He sought dry land where his feet could be firmly planted on something solid because he knew that there was still a very long way to go in realizing his dreams and that laudatory noises would only serve to distract him and his colleagues from their goals. A quote from an interview with Peter Newman on the subject of the Brascan takeover, which appeared in the July 1979 issue of *Maclean's* magazine, succinctly captures his attitude: "We shook hands, grinned for about eleven seconds and then got back to work. We are not gloaters. Jack Cockwell is too smart to gloat and I'm too nervous." Anyone who knew him well cannot help but smile at that comment for it contains the essence of his style and his disdain for the prideful posturing that often accompanies victory.

∽

As the owner of two championship sports teams – the Montreal Canadiens hockey club from 1972 to 1978 and the Toronto Blue Jays baseball team from 1979 to 1993 – he became more familiar than most with the experience of winning. While many team owners revel in the public spotlight and delight in having a high personal profile replete with flamboyance and panache, he usually managed to keep his own name out of the lavish press coverage of team victories. He was committed to the players, coaches and staff, but most people, even serious fans, might not have known of his connection with their beloved team.

Although no one else could claim to be the holder of four Stanley Cup championships for hockey and two World Series championships for baseball, he drew his most tangible pleasure from his association with these teams in the pervasive joy that spread through Montreal and Toronto when the Canadiens and later the Blue Jays captured the top spot in their respective sports. The pennants, cups, trophies and various other awards that were presented to him as the owner always found their way into the clubhouse or corporate office where they could be shared with everyone. He believed that the success of the team was something to be celebrated, a joy to be cast around to everyone who cared to share in the excitement of the home team's accomplishments.

In the broadest sense, it meant more to him that the city as a whole celebrated and basked in the glory of its championship team. This was particularly the case when the Toronto Blue Jays, during the depths of a major recession, brought home two successive World Series championships in 1992 and 1993. Toronto badly needed a boost to its sagging morale and the baseball championships were just the tonic the citizens of the city yearned for. Whether a corporate titan, a struggling student, a plumber, a nurse, a mailman, a homemaker or a child in school, no one could escape the burst of elation and delight which showered down on an otherwise miserable Toronto for two glorious autumns when the Blue Jays worked their incredible magic with their bats and gloves. For Peter Bronfman the real reward was in witnessing the elevated mood and celebration of his fellow citizens and knowing he had played a small part in bringing it about. In fact all the members of the Edper team shared this private pleasure in seeing the fruits of their investment so thoroughly enjoyed by so many.

Peter Bronfman's firm conviction that it was always the team rather than any one individual which should be recognized when success was achieved met with an occasional exception. Cito Gaston, the General Manager of the Blue Jays, was a man Peter Bronfman held in the utmost esteem and, therefore, it pleased him immensely to have had a small role to play in the University of Toronto's unusual and bold decision to award this sports figure an honorary degree. Cito Gaston's record of personal achievement and dignity in the face of a multitude of challenges over the years made him not only a popular but also a very worthy recipient of the University's highest honour.

Often called a "force for good" in the world of baseball specifically and sports generally, Cito Gaston had risen above many barriers during his career as a player to enter the ranks of management and then to lead the Blue Jays in winning two successive World Series championships. Loved and respected by players, owners, fans and the general public as well, he became Dr. Cito Gaston at a ceremony that overflowed Convocation Hall at the University of Toronto. Peter Bronfman was, in a word, thrilled that he should receive such recognition. The honour would enhance not only Cito Gaston's life but all who believed in what he had achieved and represented. That too was a true celebration of success.

In looking back at the factors which had made his success possible, Cito Gaston noted Peter Bronfman's support in the following words: "While not particularly vocal or excitable, the laid back and common sense approach he brought to our meetings ensured that reason and objectivity were part of every decision. As a man of high morals he ensured that all members of the organization were treated with the utmost integrity."

✍

Throughout his life, Peter Bronfman was known to measure everything in the long term. As a result of his voracious reading and life-long study of market trends, he placed little credence in short-term market swings. Rather, he believed strongly in long-wave market theories, having become intrigued at an early age with the fact that the stock indices plus dividends had historically yielded a ten-fold return to shareholders every thirty to forty years. It fascinated him that this had occurred without exception and with surprising symmetry since the year 1800 – nearly 200 years, a substantial test period in anyone's estimation. He also noted that there was one hitch – although the quantum and overall time span of the ten-fold increases were predictable, the performance in any one year or over several years could vary tremendously from the long-term trend line. This was one of the reasons why he felt it was wrong to measure and celebrate the success of any enterprise by reference to stock prices in terms of one-year or even five-year periods of performance.

If the Edper group were measured by its performance from 1987 to 1992 alone, it would probably have been close to the bottom quartile, whereas if measured from 1992 to 1997, its performance would place it in the very top decile. But neither analysis could tell an accurate story or represent a useful assessment of the group's real performance.

Over a twenty-five-year period, however, from 1972 when Peter Bronfman set out with the nucleus of his new team in place until 1997, the group's performance comfortably exceeded the ten-fold increase the market indices historically took thirty to forty years to achieve. But he was adamant that an even longer time was required to tell if the group had been properly structured, staffed and provided with the necessary direction and values to consistently exceed the historical benchmarks. In any event, to be a true performer in his mind, the group's results would need to surpass the historical benchmarks consistently by a significant amount.

Perhaps because Peter Bronfman shunned personal attention and even managed to keep the spotlight from lingering too long on his corporate achievements, he never lost his sense of the big picture. His reach always exceeded his grasp, and so every successive accomplishment was kept in perspective and was never allowed to swell out of proportion relative to the overall goals he set for himself and his enterprise.

When success came, his need to celebrate more often than not found an outlet in the exploration of how he could help others achieve their dreams. In his association with Woodsworth College at the University of Toronto, he found hope and promise, courage and determination in abundance. During the early years of his growing intimacy with the mission and goals of Woodsworth College, he spent time talking with the students and developed a profound admiration for their brave resolve to educate themselves, as he termed it, *the hard way*, that is – on a part-time basis.

In June 1995, Peter Bronfman was asked by Dr. Noah Meltz, the principal of Woodsworth College, to address the graduating class on the subject of success. Though he normally declined such requests, this was one he wanted to accept because of his respect for Noah Meltz and his affection for Woodsworth College, its administration and the students. True to character, he began his remarks with the question "Who am I to talk to you about success? You, who have overcome so many obstacles in earning your degrees, are an inspiration to me! You have chosen to come to the university as adults, so many of you are balancing the demands of family, work and academic studies while also living a life and volunteering too! I am amazed and overwhelmed by your courage and I know that for you there is so much more in the future because you possess the intelligence, the creativity and the determination to achieve and enjoy. Tonight I am here not to advise you on how to achieve success, but rather to celebrate your success with you."

His own modesty allowed him to see and appreciate fully the success of others, particularly those who had had to try harder, for whatever reason, to achieve their victories. He obtained great enjoyment from seeing others do well and he knew that Woodsworth College could be the key to helping many reach beyond their present circumstances and expand their horizons.

For this reason, after his death, his wife Lynda Hamilton, friends, colleagues and The Edper Group Foundation chose to honour his memory with a major gift to the University of Toronto for scholarships to Woodsworth College students.

His colleagues recognized that for Peter Bronfman a true celebration of success is the one which allows and encourages others to achieve their dreams. Because of his faith in the part-time students at Woodsworth College and his confidence that their education would be an important key in making a better world, generations of future Woodsworth College students will be given a helping hand to ensure that success will be within their reach. The ability to give that assistance was, for him, the sweetest reward of success.

A true indication of the deep personal regard in which he was held is the fact that without any solicitation, individuals continue to make donations to the University of Toronto in his memory. These include not only his colleagues and executives of professional firms he had worked with, but also others "down the line" who had been touched by him in some way.

These commitments to Woodsworth College continue Peter Bronfman's life-long interest in education and have reinforced the Edper group's focus on this area of philanthropy. Through The Edper Group Foundation, senior group companies and executives have joined together on a number of related initiatives in this field, including the Peter Bronfman International Graduate Scholarships for children of group employees and a new, broad ranging group scholarship program at York University. By combining resources and applying them in a focused way, the group hopes to make a meaningful contribution and continue Peter Bronfman's tradition of community service.

The Mind of the Man

❧

Real builders, busy and active though they are most of the time, also have a dreaming side, an invisible part of them that resides in the soul and that requires quiet, peaceful solitude to foster creativity and growth. Peter Bronfman, the builder was also a dreamer. He sought time at his country home for refreshment of the spirit, for reflection on what had been achieved in the past and ultimately for renewal of purpose in what he dreamed and hoped was still to come.

As a perpetual student, Peter Bronfman devoted a good portion of his free time to reading widely on business matters and many other subjects, including literature, music, art and philosophy. He also wrote a great deal himself, including essays and poetry. He often said that his love of poetry was based on a simple fact of economics – fragmented poetic expression could capture more truth in just a handful of words, offering up a concept for inspection and appreciation of more concise perfection than even the most eloquent prose could ever do. It is not surprising that, given this evaluation of poetry, he was particularly fond of the Japanese poetic form called *haiku*.

But he did not limit himself to one particular style. He indulged in writing many different forms from devilishly playful limericks to formal sonnets, blank verse and song lyrics depending on his mood, inspiration and the occasion which prompted him to pull out his pen and write. One evening in late summer he was strolling in Montreal, his city of birth, and found himself quite moved by the early evening light wrapped around Mont Royal, nature's place of peace and solitude for so many of the city's dwellers over the years. When he got home, he wrote the following paean:

Oh God
When I climb these steps
to this beautiful mountain
and see and hear the sights and sounds
of years gone by
I pray thee
preserve this beloved mount
so others still to come
may suckle at its breast
and so be nurtured
by nature at its best.

Arthur MacKenzie, one of his many long-time friends, shared his passion for poetry and music. As a renowned concert pianist, he made the perfect partner by composing music for Peter Bronfman's lyrics, and together they created and recorded songs which marked significant events and experiences in each other's lives. Arthur MacKenzie and other close friends from his personal life were drawn into his business world and served with diligence and distinction on the boards of several public companies formed and managed by Peter Bronfman and his colleagues.

A large part of his sense of his own life was rooted in a deep gratitude for all that Canadians have to be thankful for – one another, a fine and tolerant country, and abundant opportunities to get away from the hustle and bustle of urban life and enjoy the beauty and peace of the countryside.

Also, like any good builder, he valued balance and proportion in his life. He enjoyed simple, quiet contemplation in the country and yet in his city life he was happy to celebrate success in the creative company of his business colleagues, long-time friends and family. In this way he embraced each day, week and month and the joys and challenges they brought to him according to the ancient and time-tested motto *Vivemus vivamus!* – *"While we are alive - Let us live!"*

Chapter Seventeen

The Road Ahead

For any organization to form itself into a unit which survives beyond a few decades, it must have a leader capable of transforming his or her vision from a dream into reality. The leader must ignite the first few sparks of activity and then create sufficient momentum to enable the fledgling body to overcome its early challenges. After this it requires determination, discipline and constant caring to achieve sustainable success.

When the inevitable minor shortcomings and unexpected major challenges emerge, they have to be dealt with speedily before they get out of hand or else the organization will crumble and fail. When serious problems do occur and the obstacles seem insurmountable, leaders must be able to find within themselves the strength to set the course and give the words of inspiration to sustain, motivate and urge their colleagues to try harder.

Leadership can be a joy as well as a challenge. It requires good judgement to select and attract the right colleagues, a thorough knowledge of the business to coach them in well-tested ways, a sense of fairness and patience to foster loyalty, and sufficient creativity and respect to keep them working constructively together. Foresight is essential to know when to let some of them go to make room for new people to forge ahead. Leaders must also know how to balance the daily routine needs of their organization with fresh opportunities to keep the best of their colleagues challenged and stretched to their potential.

Most important of all, a good leader must be the first to identify and adapt to the shifting times and new environments, and when it is time, the leader must devise a succession plan. Guideposts for the future need to be a key part of the leader's legacy.

All of these elements of leadership were integral to Peter Bronfman's concept of building a lasting enterprise, elements that he developed and refined throughout his business career. From the outset he found inspiration in history and the books he read, but he was also the kind of man who usually put a personal twist on any old or new idea.

By 1995, the Edper group had put in place a team of loyal colleagues based on trusting relationships and a solid foundation of capital permanently dedicated to the group's business. With this accomplished, the time had arrived to complete the final steps for ensuring stability in the ownership of the enterprise. For a number of years, Peter Bronfman had been exploring his options to determine what would best serve the corporate entity, the investors and the many other constituencies which were part of the Edper group's broad reach.

After forty years of building, facing setbacks and reaping successes, he decided it was at last time to lock in the ownership and management succession plans he had been slowly refining. In his mind, this required an ownership structure based on the trust and values that had been so integral to what had been achieved, complemented with carefully devised checks and balances which would allow the Edper group to continue to grow and flourish. It was essential to him that the structure preserve the very best of their ways of doing business because these management practices and shared values would, he firmly believed, be crucial to the group's continued success.

The combination of his shareholdings in the Edper group with those held by his long-standing colleagues through EdperPartners Limited in December 1995 represented the formal passing of the reins from Peter Bronfman to his colleagues. Since they had worked together for so long and were totally committed to sharing and teamwork, little in effect changed in how they went about their business and how they related to each other in the days, weeks and months that followed.

Most other company founders and builders would have found this a difficult step to take, for from that point onward his vote on many of the key issues would carry merely the same weight as any one of his other twenty-five colleagues who participated in the ownership of EdperPartners Limited. He, however, had built his enterprise based on loyalty and trust and he was committed to reducing his involvement based on these same principles.

~~

During the twenty-four months which followed, the Edper group reported record financial results and achieved major advances on virtually all fronts. While Peter Bronfman was able to witness only the accomplishments of 1996, these together with a successful 1997 fulfilled many of the immediate objectives he had sought for the group before his death. The general tempo of the economy had picked up and the business environment provided opportunities both to harvest and to lay down the seeds for future growth.

In the process, the group extended its long-term record for building shareholder value. By the end of 1997, the twenty-five year annual compound rate of return earned by an original shareholder of Mico Enterprises (the first publicly listed company in the Edper group and an important predecessor to Hees International and EdperBrascan Corporation) was once again well above 20% – more than twice the Toronto Stock Exchange average. This was achieved by stringing together four years of 30% plus performance to offset the four dismal years of substandard performance recorded in the early 1990s.

During the first nine months of 1997, the group's corporate structure, which had been both a strength and a weakness, was significantly simplified through the combination of The Edper Group Limited, Hees International Bancorp Inc. and Brascan Limited to form EdperBrascan Corporation. In the process, three public and four private holding companies were eliminated and, even after cancelling the group's shareholdings in these companies, the capital base of EdperBrascan alone approached $5 billion.

Also during this two-year period, Brookfield Properties doubled its holdings of premier North American office properties and tripled its capital base to more than $3 billion. This was made possible by Brookfield Properties' successful conclusion in November 1996 of the largest and most profitable merchant banking deal ever undertaken by the group, which involved assembling a blue-ribbon group of investors to acquire 11 million square feet of prime office properties in the United States. Fortunately the timing was almost perfect, whether by good judgement or by chance – the real estate markets turned around within a few months and property values increased significantly.

In the financial services sector, Trilon Financial revamped the management of London Insurance Group and helped it increase its share of the Canadian life insurance market to nearly 20%. In the process, London Insurance Group attracted the envious attention of a number of other financial institutions. These carefully timed and executed steps doubled the value of London Insurance Group and enabled Trilon Financial to sell its shareholdings in this company in November 1997 for $1.6 billion and a substantial gain, well ahead of the group's most optimistic plans.

EdperBrascan itself reported record earnings of $625 million in 1997, including net investment gains of $325 million. Most important, group executives were still keenly aware of the very high price that they had paid when they strayed from some of the group's essential values during the early

1990s. They were therefore careful to low-key the release of news on these ground-breaking achievements, content to have investors assess the results for themselves.

The rebuilding of Brookfield Properties, the sale of London Insurance Group and record financial results were only a few of the notable achievements recorded during 1996 and 1997. By the end of 1997, the group had ownership interests in over 120 production facilities including 23 mines, 27 metallurgical and fabricating plants, 34 forest product mills, 10 major producing oil and gas properties and 17 power generating stations, as well as 58 office buildings and retail centres containing 32 million square feet of rentable space and 30 large land tracts on which 50,000 homes will eventually be constructed. Among the properties owned is BCE Place in Toronto, the Edper group's corporate headquarters since 1992 and the most attractive and technologically advanced office complex in Canada. Other major developments have been planned and the construction of a number of new production facilities are well advanced. In aggregate, plans are in place to invest more than $10 billion prior to the turn of the century, largely under an internally generated capital investment program. These investments are expected to provide considerable additional growth in the group's production capacity, revenues and shareholder earnings.

Although some of the group's most meaningful successes were completed after Peter Bronfman passed away at the end of 1996, the groundwork had been carefully laid before his death and it is a great source of sadness for his colleagues that he was unable to see more of the fruits of his years of labour. He could be reassured, however, that though he may not be with them to provide direction as their leader, in so many ways he is present in spirit because his values continue to act as the guideposts they seek. Teamwork, sharing credit, leading by example and fair dealing are deeply ingrained, and they are committed to following the path carefully laid down by their mentor, partner and friend.

A couple of weeks before he died, Peter Bronfman garnered his strength and asked that his wife Lynda Hamilton take him to the Edper group offices to attend what would turn out to be his last business planning session with his colleagues. Frail but determined, he engaged in the usual challenging of the assumptions underlying the plan with keen interest. It was clear he had a full heart and was enjoying every minute of the verbal jostling.

One of his usual traits, however, had disappeared. Senior colleagues had always taken care to alert new executives that although he might give the impression of not understanding something and would ask the same question from different angles over a period of days or weeks, they should not make the mistake of assuming he did not fully grasp a concept. His approach was actually useful to him as a means of testing the answers for consistency over time. He had also discovered that this little quirk made others more confident in opening up and sharing views with him, rather than holding back because they feared his intellect or judgement. Finally, his method of asking questions also served as a practical antenna for detecting duplicity and insincerity and allowed him to separate those he could trust and believe from those he would choose to keep at a friendly distance.

During his last business planning session there was no evidence on his part of asking any question a second time. Nor did he demonstrate any inability to remember even the smallest details of plans or transactions going back to the very beginning of the group's development, despite his life-long claim to having a poor memory. The twinkle in his eye could not be missed as his colleagues teased him on that day about his remarkably improved abilities in the memory department. At this point in his life, he was simply not going to waste any time and was determined to get right to the point on every topic he touched.

At the meeting, his partners and colleagues unveiled the portrait of him which they wanted to hang on the main wall of the EdperBrascan boardroom. "No," said Peter Bronfman to his assembled team. "It must be hung on a side wall as we stand beside one another in partnership. I am only the first of many who will help make this a great enterprise." The portrait was placed as he had wished, and now beside it also hangs his Order of Canada medal, which was presented posthumously to his daughter Brenda in February 1997.

Although Peter Bronfman's four principal values were simple, straightforward and well known – teamwork, sharing credit, leading by example and fair dealing – he was frequently asked to explain how he applied them to achieve his success in the world of industry and finance. Invariably these requests could be boiled down to one recurring question – What is the secret?

As a private and modest man who by his nature always appreciated what others had to offer, he could never be comfortable giving advice. He would politely decline the flattering requests to spread his wisdom and tell stories of his experiences. This book has endeavoured to describe some of the reasons for his success and to record this thoughtful and caring man's views on life and how his values have been, and continue to be, helpful to his family, friends and business colleagues.

The extent to which his values led to success in his own business life or can be of assistance to others in the future is a question which he would have been the first to say that only others can judge – and not yet. He knew that each person would have his own way of measuring success and only with the passage of time could any meaningful conclusions be reached. For him the short-term tally of wins and losses was separate from the assessment of a lasting business enterprise.

He believed that winning by an arbitrary goal, whether it entailed achieving the highest score on the ice rink, baseball field or in any other game or competition, or accumulating the most assets in a business context at a particular point in time was a shallow measure of success. Only by formulating and executing plans firmly rooted in shared values which pass the test of time can real long-term success be achieved.

Peter Bronfman worked hard to put the mechanism for corporate longevity in place within the Edper group. He then exercised diligence in fulfilling his responsibility as a leader to ensure that there would be generational depth with individuals of various ages demonstrably committed to his values. Furthermore, and perhaps most important, it was by his own example that he set a high standard for the future leaders of the Edper group to follow. He reinforced this by constantly reminding them of the words carved on the wall of the Montreal Canadiens' locker room, urging them *"to hold the torch high"* in their dealings with each other and the world at large.

Appendices

I. **Closing Reflections**
    Words from Peter Bronfman   . . . 327

II. **Chronology**
    Development of EdperBrascan . . 337

III. **Corporate Chart** 348

Appendix One

Closing Reflections

Early in 1996, Peter Bronfman's colleagues prepared a brief history of the Edper group as a gift to him. Among other things, The Edper Story contained a compendium of lessons learned in the development of the group over more than forty years. Before this document was released to a wider audience, Peter Bronfman added a Foreword which set out in his own words the important values which shaped his thinking in building the group. This Foreword is reproduced in full below.

When my colleagues first approached me to write an introduction to *The Edper Story*, my initial response was that it was too soon to be recording the history of the Edper group. They persisted, and explained that the book was essentially for internal use to help new board members and to facilitate younger executives learning about our ways. Furthermore, my colleagues reminded me that, when reviewing current business issues, we often draw upon lessons learned along the way without stopping to refer to the past events which shaped and continue to affect our business dealings. *The Edper Story* attempts to record many of the lessons learned in the course of the group's development.

Appendix One

Once I accepted the task of writing the introduction, I started my own walk down memory lane. I did this in order to sift through the important experiences that have had a profound impact on my business life, so that I could piece them together in a logical form. In all of this, good fortune has played an important part.

My early memories of business go back to my childhood when I first became aware of my father's preoccupation with building the family's liquor business. Throughout our early years at home, my brother Edward and I assumed that we would one day, together with our cousins, play a role in the management of the Seagram Company. It therefore came as a shock to learn, soon after I graduated from Yale, that we would have to make it on our own — albeit with a nest egg to ease the way. Our Seagram Company shareholdings representing the nest egg were, however, substantially reduced to secure my father's continuing role with that company.

Initially, we were hurt by our Uncle Sam's rejection, but being young and somewhat defiant we did not take long to bounce back. Naively, I felt we could build our own company in a relatively short period of time, particularly since we did have some start-up capital. In any event, that was our mission in 1954.

Our next big decision was to locate our business in Canada, rather than in New York where my father had spent much of his time. We both saw opportunities in this country to build the infrastructure needed to accommodate this country's generous immigration policies and high growth rates relative to the rest of the world.

In short order, my brother and I began to assemble land and build apartment buildings for both ends of the market, as well as the first modern office building in Montreal. We also built recreation centres and ski facilities in the Laurentian mountains. At the time, we were favoured with low interest rates and good profit margins, which led us to believe we could replicate these early successes in the industrial sector. We proceeded to acquire minority equity interests in a variety of industrial businesses only to find out too late the significance of size and competitive advantage. As each of our industrial businesses began to prosper, larger competitors from the United States would enter our markets and force us either to sell out or accept indefinite substandard returns, a tough but good lesson to learn early in our careers.

However, we did survive and after a brief but enjoyable and highly profitable involvement in the sports business through our ownership of the Montreal Canadiens, I began to think once again about building a truly great Canadian company. Our big chance came in 1979 when we acquired control of Brascan Limited and, through it, started to expand into the natural resources business. By this time, we were doing very well with our real estate and merchant banking activities and felt it was time to diversify our operations in a meaningful way. Wanting to stay in Canada narrowed the field down to mining, forest products and the petroleum businesses, three sectors where we felt the country had distinct competitive advantages over our neighbour to the south.

Well before this time, it became clear to me that we could not achieve our objectives by working alone or by hiring individuals who thought of themselves primarily as employees who might not stay through the inevitable rough patches. I also recognized there were many aspects of business of little interest to me which required specialized skills and training.

With this in mind, and in order to further our growth, we set out to attract some very special people with the skills and inclination to work as partners and members of a team with common goals. This process goes on today as younger individuals rapidly earn their way through our senior management ranks while building their ownership interests in the group, sharing equally in key decisions and the formulation of business strategies.

In operating as a team, it has always been important to me that each member recognize his colleagues' special talents as well as their weaknesses. This makes it possible to tackle what sometimes seem to be insurmountable problems. By forming project teams, which disband on completion of their tasks, we have all had the opportunity to enjoy a wide variety of business experiences and to work closely with a broader range of individuals than is normally the case. A secondary benefit of this approach, particularly for myself, has been the opportunity for day-to-day working contact with top flight executives whose ages range across three generations, including many younger people. Under most other corporate structures, I would have long ago been completely isolated from our best young executives.

Through these experiences, I have come to learn that each successive generation is better equipped to adapt to the rapid technological and other changes taking place in the world.

This has given me tremendous comfort in passing the reins to David Kerr and Jack Cockwell, and from my own viewpoint left me freer to concentrate on the areas where I derive the most personal satisfaction. This does not mean that I have any intention of retiring, and God willing, I hope to be active in the business for many years to come.

Once management succession was taken care of, I turned my mind to dealing with the sensitive issue of ownership succession. As a founder, I viewed it as one of my principal responsibilities. And while resolving the ownership matter was important for my own purpose, lenders and investors were also looking for assurances that they could count on consistency in our dealings and business values. In essence, they wanted to know that the special relationships of trust, commitment and fair dealing would continue into the future.

I am well aware that many family corporations fail in the transition to becoming more widely owned. In my case, I was fortunate to have a large number of long-standing business colleagues who owned major share positions in the group and who were ready and willing to step forward and increase their investment, along with our younger colleagues. I believe it was largely because of their ability and willingness to commit their capital to the business that we were able to avoid the public discord that has plagued so many other family corporations. Nevertheless, in order to accomplish the ownership changes I believed were necessary, I was confronted with a number of difficult decisions I feel should be explained.

One of these related to the timing and manner in which my brother Edward's advisers persuaded him to withdraw his family's capital from the business. These actions strained the group's financial resources during the last economic downturn and as a consequence we found ourselves having to improvise and scramble. Fortunately, these events never affected our personal feelings and affection for each other.

Edward's departure opened the way to bringing my children into the business. My colleagues readily embraced my son's involvement, believing he would provide the long-term continuity sought by them and our principal backers in the financial community. However, the onset of the recession in the early 1990s set my plans awry as my son and two daughters began to have serious concerns about the business, especially after seeing my brother Edward withdraw his capital. As a result, they became understandably apprehensive and, acting on the advice of their personal advisers, decided to withdraw their capital from the business.

I knew in my heart by this time that the best way to deal with succession and remove any concerns over the group's ownership and future direction was to combine my shareholdings with those of my long-standing business colleagues who shared my vision and goals. Perhaps to some degree I was helped by not being a believer in family dynasties where you often hear about the success stories but rarely about the attendant rivalries and heartaches. Accordingly, I decided to liquidate many of my personal assets and distribute the proceeds to my children in order to give them their capital so they could determine their own destinies.

By combining my Edper group shareholdings with those held by my colleagues, we were able to demonstrate to our financial backers that control would remain firmly in hands committed to the Edper group and its values and business perspectives. This took place during 1995 when, at the same time, we put in place long-term governance mechanisms with input from twenty-five of my senior colleagues. As a result, I am confident today we have accomplished something unique, which will allow my colleagues and the executives in each of our operating affiliates to concentrate on building long-term values for their respective shareholders un-distracted by concerns over control of their companies.

There is one further business experience which at the time proved very difficult for me and my colleagues. For various reasons, we have always been reluctant to assume a great deal of debt. As a result, we decided at an early stage to finance our long-term equity investments with equity capital and to reserve debt for the purposes of financing financial assets. This gave us a strong financial structure, albeit a somewhat complex one. Even with this structure, we, like many other Canadian companies, were severely tested when the Canadian corporate sector faced a massive contraction of credit following the collapse of a number of major Canadian companies excessively leveraged with debt.

Fortunately, our policy of financing our operating affiliates with substantial equity had been carefully followed by most of our group companies, and this gave us the ability to refinance in an orderly manner. I am now able to be philosophical about this experience, believing that we needed to be tested before being more broadly accepted. We have, however, taken steps to simplify ourselves and do spend more time than before explaining the merits of our financial structure to a wider audience, partly to ensure that we are better understood in the future.

I have dwelt on some of the tough situations we have lived through in recent years — which contrast with what in essence is a good news story. This is perhaps because these experiences remain fresh in my mind. Putting them aside, I cannot imagine how anyone could wish for a more satisfying business career, including four Stanley Cups and two World Series wins along the way.

Today, I am blessed with the good fortune of still being in a position to contribute to the business, and to enjoy the loyalty and close friendship of my long-standing business colleagues, as well as daily contact with many bright young executives. Together with them, I have been part of making a dream come true.

I would like to believe that my encouragement of individual initiatives and team building have been among the more important contributions I have made to the group's development. By working together as a team, a great deal has been accomplished which is well chronicled by my colleagues in the pages that follow. However, I must record that they have been very generous in describing my role, as I was only one member of a large team. But, as a founder of the group, I was fortunate to lead the team and I have derived immense personal satisfaction from the support and loyalty afforded me by my colleagues. Briefly stated, I could not have asked for more.

In the future, I hope to spend more of my time helping others beyond our group make their own dreams come true. I am an absolute believer in the limitless opportunities provided by this country, not only because of its ability to be competitive, given its vast and varied resources, but also because our basic decencies extend to the way business is conducted. Canada also offers the opportunity for all of us to upgrade our skills throughout our working lives, with excellent on-the-job training programs and continuing education offered by some of the world's best universities.

I am acutely aware that a missing ingredient in this country is the lack of capital available to young entrepreneurs whose businesses have not yet matured. In this regard, it has been a point of pride for me that our merchant banking operations help others in building their businesses, particularly in their hours of greatest need. In the process, we have helped foster their entrepreneurial spirits and save a number of enterprises and many valuable jobs. Watching these businesses prosper after we have been repaid provides some of the best memories of my career. And, I will naturally encourage my colleagues to continue with this tradition while maintaining an open door for those starting their journey down the road I have been so fortunate to travel.

Before closing, I must make special mention of just a very few of my business colleagues with whom I go back many years. It has been a real pleasure for me to see the manner in which Tim Price and David Kerr have taken on challenging corporate responsibilities over the years. In particular, as a fellow board member of Noranda, I have had the advantage of being able to follow David Kerr's progress in reshaping our natural resources interests. I never cease to admire his growth and maturity, and the way in which he and his colleagues handle this vital role. Jack Cockwell and Trevor Eyton have in many respects been two of my closest colleagues. Frankly, without their guidance and unflagging energy, our group could not have achieved all that it has.

In this foreword, I have not mentioned the many other people and financial institutions who have helped us over the years, largely for fear of leaving some out. They each know how appreciative and thankful I am for their counsel and assistance along the way. Their help has been invaluable.

Finally, together with my colleagues, I look forward to furthering the Edper group's business and community goals and to fulfilling our dreams as they continue to evolve.

Peter F. Bronfman
January 24, 1996

Appendix Two

Chronology

EdperBrascan's Roots	**1899**	São Paulo Tramway, Light and Power Company is incorporated
	1912	Brazilian Traction, Light and Power Company Limited is incorporated in Toronto as a public company to develop hydro-electric power operations and other utility services in Brazil
	1916	Great Lakes Power Company Limited is incorporated to provide hydro-electric power in Sault Ste. Marie and the Algoma District in Ontario
	1922	Noranda Mines Limited is incorporated to develop and operate the Horne copper-zinc -gold mine in Rouyn-Noranda, Québec
	1923	Canadian Arena Company is incorporated to own the Montreal Forum and Montreal Canadiens Hockey Club
	1954	Edper Investments Limited, owned by the Peter, Edward and Mildred Mona Bronfman trusts, is incorporated in Montreal to hold a one-third interest in Seco Limited, the holding company for the Bronfman family interests in Seagram

Appendix Two

Early Edper Investments	**1954-56**	Investments made in industrial companies and real estate joint ventures
	1957	Edper completes the development of the Peel Centre office building in Montreal
	1960	Edper sells its interest in Seco and acquires a smaller but direct holding in Seagram
	1961-67	Edper makes further investments in real estate joint ventures and small privately held financial and industrial companies
New Direction	**1968**	Edper introduces a new business plan to restructure its investment portfolio
		Edper exchanges its commercial real estate properties for 60% of Great West Saddlery Limited (GWS) and its recreational real estate properties for 20% of Marigot Investments Limited
		GWS acquires shares in four technology companies
		GWS acquires Edper's and Sam Hashman's commercial real estate holdings
		Edper acquires 46% of National Hees Industries Limited from GWS
Great-West Life Investment	**1969**	GWS launches attempted takeover of Great-West Life Assurance, purchasing a 20% interest
		GWS abandons takeover of Great-West Life and sells its shares to Power Corporation
		Following the sale of its telephone operations to the Brazilian Government, Brazilian Traction, Light and Power is renamed Brascan Limited
	1970	GWS is renamed Great West International Equities Ltd.
		National Hees Industries is restructured as National Hees Enterprises Limited

Canadian Arena Acquisition	1971	Edper merges Great West International with Trizec Corporation and receives a 10% interest in Trizec
		Edper acquires a 58% interest in Canadian Arena Company, owner of the Montreal Forum and the Montreal Canadiens hockey club
	1972	Edper increases its interest in Marigot to 66%, which is restructured as Mico Enterprises Ltd. to conduct the group's merchant banking activities
		Edper sells its shares of Seagram to finance its acquisition of Canadian Arena
	1973	Edper acquires the Mildred Mona Bronfman Trust's shareholdings in Edper Investments Limited
		Brascan acquires Great Lakes Power
Management Partnership	1974	Management partnership formalized with a substantial ownership of Mico Enterprises
		Mico Enterprises acquires controlling interest in Westmount Life Insurance
		Canadian Arena renamed Carena Bancorp Inc. and acquires a 20% interest in IAC Limited
	1975	Mico Investments Limited formed with Mercantile Bank of Canada to participate in the preferred share market
Trizec Acquisition	1976	Edper pools its shares in Trizec with English Property Corporation, giving Carena a 50.1% controlling interest in Trizec
		Major restructuring of Trizec commences
		Mico Enterprises sells its interest in Westmount Life for a substantial gain
Cash Generation	1977	Mico Enterprises sells its interests in recreational real estate properties and restructures Astral Bellevue Pathé

Appendix Two

Cash Generation (continued)	**1977**	Mico Enterprises acquires a 25% interest in Canadian CableSystems and participates in various transactions with S.B. McLaughlin & Co.
	1978	Carena sells its interests in the Montreal Canadiens in anticipation of making a major investment in the natural resource sector
		Edper Resources Limited is formed, owned by Edper (66%) and the Patiño family (34%)
		Edper sells its interests in Canadian CableSystems, S.B. McLaughlin and other companies to raise cash for investment in the natural resource sector
Brascan Acquisition	**1979**	Edper moves its head office from Montreal to Toronto
		Olympia & York acquires English Property Corporation and its interest in Trizec
		Brascan sells *The Light*, its Brazilian electric utility, to the Brazilian Government
		Brascan launches a hostile takeover of F.W. Woolworth Company
		Edper acquires, through Edper Resources, a 48% controlling interest in Brascan, which abandons the Woolworth takeover
		Major restructuring of Brascan's Canadian and Brazilian operations is initiated
		Brascan acquires a 13% interest in Noranda Mines Limited from Argus Corporation
Expansion and Restructuring	**1980**	Mico Enterprises merges with National Hees Enterprises Limited (Hees), a TSE listed company, which commences a rapid expansion of its business and capital base
		Brascan increases its interest in John Labatt Limited from 24% to 42% and in London Life Insurance Company from 29% to 39%

Expansion and **Restructuring** (continued)	**1980**	Brascan combines its oil, gas and coal assets with Western Mines to increase its interest to 84% and renames the company Westmin Resources Limited
Growth Period	**1981**	Noranda Mines acquires a 49% interest in MacMillan Bloedel in exchange for shares
		Brascade Resources Inc. is formed by Brascan (70%) and the Caisse de dépôt et placement du Québec (30%) to hold their interests in Noranda Mines
		Brascade increases its interest in Noranda Mines to 42%
		Brascan acquires a 20% interest in Scott Paper
		Brascan acquires an 18% interest in Royal Trustco
	1982	Hees expands its group financing role and merchant banking business
		Brascan increases its interest in London Life to 56%
		Trilon Financial Corporation is formed to acquire Brascan's interest in London Life and increases ownership in London Life to 98%
		Brascan increases its ownership of Scott Paper to 24%
		Great Lakes Power Inc. acquires a 17% interest in Union Energy
	1983	National Hees is renamed Hees International Corporation
		Brascade acquires Brascan's interest in Westmin
		Trilon acquires Brascan's interest in Royal Trustco and increases its ownership in Royal Trustco to 49%

Appendix Two

Growth Period (continued)	**1984**	Hees acquires an interest in Dexleigh Corporation and other investments
		Great Lakes Power's investment activities are restructured and expanded in partnership with CIBC and Merrill Lynch
	1985	Brascan sells its 25% interest in Scott Paper and receives warrants for a 10% interest
		Trilon launches 65% owned London Insurance Group as a public company, which holds its interest in London Life and later acquires Wellington Insurance
		Carena acquires a 50% interest in Coscan Development Corporation
Capital Accumulation and Further Acquisitions	**1986**	Group companies focus on increasing their capital bases mainly through equity issues
		Hees acquires a 38% interest in Norcen Energy Resources Limited and increases its interest in North Canadian Oils Ltd.
		Noranda acquires and develops the Golden Giant Mine in Hemlo, Ontario
		London Insurance Group acquires 60% of The Holden Group
	1987	Noranda sells 12% of Hemlo Gold and 19% of Noranda Forest Inc. through initial public offerings
		Noranda acquires Hees' 38% interest in Norcen and a 49% interest in North Canadian Oils, in exchange for its shares
		Hees exchanges its Noranda shares for Brascan shares
		Hees receives assignments to restructure Versatile Corporation and a number of other corporations
		Carena acquires a 45% interest in Carma Corporation

Capital Accumulation and Further Acquisitions (continued)	1988	Hees acquires a 50% interest in Canadian Corporate Services, owner of a 60% voting and 4% common share interest in The Pagurian Corporation Limited
		Hees receives an assignment to manage and restructure National Business Systems
		Hees is renamed Hees International Bancorp Inc.
		Noranda acquires a 23% interest in Falconbridge Limited
Establishment of Edper Enterprises Ltd. as a Public Company	1989	Edper Investments Limited is renamed Edper Enterprises Ltd. and launched as a public company
		EdperPartners Limited, owned by senior Edper executives, acquires control of Pagurian
		Edper Holdings Inc., owned 65% by the Peter Bronfman family and 35% by Pagurian, is formed to hold the controlling interest in Edper Enterprises
Consolidation of Holdings	1989	Noranda and Trelleborg each increase their interests in Falconbridge to 50% and take the company private
		Norcen acquires Westmin's oil and gas assets
		Brascan acquires a 28% interest in M.A. Hanna and sells its Scott Paper warrants
		Trilon acquires Great Lakes Power's investment banking business and forms Trilon Securities Corporation
		Carena, together with Hees, receives an assignment from BCE to manage BCE Development Corporation (BCED)
		Carena acquires a one-third interest in three World Financial Center properties

Appendix Two

Severe Recession	**1990**	In response to the recession, Edper group companies adopt plans to withdraw from non-core businesses, improve productivity and conserve cash
Restructuring	**1991**	Brascan increases its interest in Brascade to 99% and sells its 29% interest in M.A. Hanna for cash and warrants
		Labatt sells its food division and increases its ownership of the Toronto Blue Jays to 90%
	1992	Royal Trustco records a loss and decides to seek a strategic alliance with a major financial institution
	1993	Edper and Hees start to implement group simplification plans
		Noranda Forest sells its 49% interest in MacMillan Bloedel
		Norcen acquires Noranda's 50% interest in North Canadian Oils
		Brascan sells its 38% interest in John Labatt and its M.A. Hanna warrants
		Royal Trustco sells its operating subsidiaries to the Royal Bank of Canada and continues in business under the name Gentra Inc.
Strong Recovery	**1994**	Noranda initiates a major capital investment program
		Falconbridge is re-established as a public company, owned 46% by Noranda
		Norcen acquires all the outstanding shares of North Canadian Oils
		Trilon sells Eurobrokers Investment Corporation and Triathlon's fleet leasing business in order to reduce financial risk
		Brascan increases its ownership of Trilon from 48% to 56%

Strong Recovery (continued)	1994	The Brazilian Government introduces an economic stabilization plan to reduce inflation, liberalize trade and accelerate investment
Simplification	1994	Hees acquires Edper's ownership interests in Brascan and Carena
		Hees increases its effective ownership of Carena to 87% by subscribing for treasury shares
		Carena's 32% ownership in Trizec is reduced to a nominal level following the restructuring of Trizec
		Carena increases its ownership interests in Brookfield Commercial Properties to 100%, in Coscan to 90% and in Carma to 75%
Group Ownership	1995	Pagurian is renamed The Edper Group Limited and becomes the most senior public company in the group by acquiring the publicly-owned shares of Edper Enterprises Ltd.
		Peter Bronfman combines a portion of his shareholdings in The Edper Group Limited with EdperPartners Limited
Further Simplification Initiatives	1995	Noranda acquires the public's shareholdings in Brunswick Mining and Smelting Corporation and other subsidiaries
		Brascan increases its ownership of Trilon to 65%
		Brascan sells its 76% interest in Westmin for a substantial gain
		London Insurance Group sells wholly-owned Wellington Insurance
		Hees increases its interest in Carena to 94%

Appendix Two

Further Simplification Initiatives (continued)	1995	Carena and Royal LePage form Brookfield LePage Management Limited by combining their property management operations
Growth and Consolidation	1996	Brascan increases its ownership of Great Lakes Power to 93% by acquiring shares accumulated by Hees
		London Life acquires Prudential Insurance Company's Canadian life insurance operations
		Carena changes its name to Brookfield Properties Corporation, and Coscan Developments is renamed Brookfield Homes Ltd.
		Brookfield forms 45% owned World Financial Properties Inc. with CIBC, Li Ka-shing and Citibank to hold its interests in the World Financial Center and other properties
		Great Lakes Power acquires Pontiac Power
		The Edper Group Limited merges with Hees, continuing in business as The Edper Group Limited
Significant Value Creation	1997	Brookfield completes four equity issues to increase its capital base by $1.7 billion and acquires CIBC's and Li Ka-shing's interests in World Financial Properties
		Trilon restructures and sells its investment in London Insurance for $1.6 billion and a significant gain
		Noranda announces its intention to divest its non-mining assets in order to concentrate on its mining and metals business
		EdperBrascan, Brookfield, Great Lakes and Trilon report record earnings

Corporate Simplification	**1997**	The Edper Group Limited and Brascan Limited combine to form EdperBrascan Corporation
		EdperPartners Limited emerges as EdperBrascan's principal shareholder
		Brookfield acquires Trilon's 43% interest in Gentra to align all the group's real estate operations in North America under Brookfield
		Trilon acquires EdperBrascan's merchant banking operations, previously conducted through Hees International, to align all of the group's financial and management services outside Brazil under Trilon
Recent Developments	**To August 1998**	Noranda sells its 49% interest in Norcen for $1.8 billion and a significant gain
		Noranda commences development of the Magnola magnesium project in Québec and acquires its partners' shares of the Refimet copper smelter in Chile
		Noranda acquires a 37½% interest in the Antamina copper-zinc project in Peru
		Brookfield increases its interest in World Financial Properties to 89%

Appendix Three

Corporate Chart

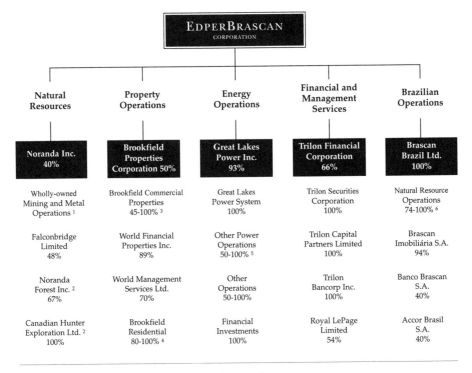

1. *Includes wholly-owned Noranda Copper, Noranda Zinc and Noranda Aluminum*

2. *During 1998, Noranda plans to distribute its interest in Noranda Forest and Canadian Hunter to EdperBrascan and its other shareholders*

3. *Includes wholly-owned Brookfield Commercial Properties and 45% owned Gentra Inc.*

4. *Includes wholly-owned Brookfield Homes Ltd. and 80% owned Carma Corporation*

5. *Includes wholly-owned Pontiac Power, 65% owned Valerie Falls Power, 50% owned Lake Superior Power and a 50% residual interest in Louisiana HydroElectric Power*

6. *Includes wholly-owned Companhia Estanifera do Brasil and Brascan Agro Industrial Ltda. and 74% owned Comfloresta S.A.*

August 1998

Index

A

Accor Brasil S.A   270-1, 348
Accor Group   271
Aird, Hugh   251
Allan, Tom   258
Allen, Lowell   130
Allen, Tom   175
Allen Lambert Galleria   135
American Stock Exchange   121, 124
Andrews Generating Station   244
Antamina copper-zinc project   229,
   237, 273, 347
Antonio, Firmin   270
Apex Press Inc.   81
Apollo Real Estate Fund   218
Argus Corporation Limited   144, 225
Arnell, Gordon   134-5, 159, 193,
   206-9, 216
Arthur, David   135, 207
Astral Bellevue Pathé Inc.   104-5, 339
Astral Communications   104
Atholville pulp mill   226

B

Bahen, John   245
Baillie, Charles   155
Baker, Neil   82, 84-8
Balogh, Alex   228
Banco Brascan S.A.   265, 267, 348

Bank of Montreal   85-6, 98, 110, 173
Bank of Nova Scotia, The   94-5, 103,
   154, 165
Bassett, Isabel   156
Bassett, John, Sr.   94
Bastable, Colum   253
Baton Broadcasting Incorporated
   94-5, 165
Battle, Eddie   231
BCE Development Corporation
   (BCED)   207, 210-12, 215, 343
BCE Inc.   161, 207, 210-12
BCE Place   135, 192, 221, 320
Béliveau, Jean   53-4, 70
Bellevue Photo Labs. Inc.   81, 104
Benson, Kevin   213, 215
Bérard, André   156
Beutel, Austin   59-60, 79, 82, 100-1
Billing, Grant   232
Bird, Bud   233
Bishop's College   69
Black, Conrad   144-5, 225
Blake, Toe   70
Blanchard, James   156
Boileau, David   244
Bowden, John   154
Bowman, Scotty   72
Boyd, Michael   99-100
Boyd Stott McDonald   99, 110, 165
Bramalea Limited   213

Brascade Resources Inc. 145, 225-6, 341, 344

Brascan Brazil 133, 200, 266-71, 273, 348

Brascan Imobiliária S.A. 348

Brascan Limited 2, 52, 57-64, 75, 96, 110-147, 165, 172, 178, 191, 201, 224-7, 230, 235, 239-43, 246, 249-50, 252, 257, 261, 264-5, 268, 299-300, 304-5, 318, 329, 338, 340-7

Brazilian Traction, Light and Power Company Limited 2, 113-114, 239, 265, 337-8

British Petroleum 294

Bronfman family
 origins in eastern Europe 11-14
 in Saskatchewan 15
 in Brandon, Manitoba 16-18
 in hotel business 18-19
 in liquor business 19-25

Bronfman, Abe 14, 17

Bronfman, Allan 14, 16, 25, 27, 30, 33, 67, 79, 80

Bronfman, Bessie 14

Bronfman, Brenda 176, 277, 322

Bronfman, Bruce 176

Bronfman, Charles 27

Bronfman, Edgar 27

Bronfman, Edward 27-8, 30, 53, 67-8, 73, 75, 78-81, 96, 170-2, 175, 328, 332

Bronfman, Harry 14, 16

Bronfman, Jean 14

Bronfman, Laura 14

Bronfman, Linda 176

Bronfman, Lucy 67

Bronfman, Mildred Mona 67, 80, 95-6, 165

Bronfman, Minnie 9, 14, 67

Bronfman, Paul 172

Bronfman, Rose 14

Bronfman, Sam 14, 26-8, 79-80, 85-6, 328

Bronfman, Yechiel (Ekiel) 9, 13-18, 22, 30-1, 33, 67

Brookfield Commercial Properties Ltd. 207, 211-12, 345, 348

Brookfield Homes Ltd. 205-6, 212, 221-2, 346, 348

Brookfield Management Services Ltd. 346, 348

Brookfield Properties Corporation 2, 52, 54, 102, 134-5, 142, 159, 161, 201, 205-22, 260-1, 289, 293, 319-20, 346-8

Brunswick mine 194

Bumstead, David 228

Burke, Michael 98

C

Caisse de dépôt et placement du Québec 145, 165, 225, 341

Callwood, June 34, 73

Campeau, Robert 250

Canada Development Investment Corporation 132

Canadian Arena Company 2, 53-4, 94-7, 102, 104, 165, 205, 339

Canadian CableSystems 104, 110, 295, 340

Canadian Express Limited 174

Canadian Hunter Exploration Ltd. 39, 231, 233, 235, 348

Canadian Imperial Bank of Commerce (CIBC) 154, 174, 218-9, 243, 245, 251, 346

Canary Wharf 215

Cane, Charles 69
Carena Bancorp Inc. 102-3, 111, 141, 339-40, 342-3, 345-6
Carena Developments Limited 2, 205
Carena Properties Inc. 205
Carma Corporation 206, 212, 221, 342, 345, 348
Carruthers, Bud 246
Casgrain, Tim 104, 140, 302
Cecil-Cockwell, Wendy 130, 275
Cemp Investments Ltd. 27
Century Property & Casualty Company 250
Churchill, Gill 130
CIBC Wood Gundy 162
Citibank, N.A. 218, 220, 346
Clarke, Ken 243, 251
Cockwell, Ian 98, 104, 209-10
Cockwell, Jack 7, 88-9, 97-8, 103-4, 120, 123, 126, 128, 144, 186, 194, 200, 248, 268, 305, 331, 336
Collahuasi copper mine 195, 229, 236-7, 272-3
Connacher, Jimmy 85, 87, 120
Cork, Ken 144
Cornelissen, Michael 103, 205, 254, 256
Corzine, Jon 155
Coscan Development Corporation 205, 342, 345-6
Costain Limited 206
Courtois, Jacques 94
Craw, Don 140
Cressy, Gordon 34, 38
CS First Boston 154
Cunningham, Gordon 250-1, 258
Curtin, Jack 155

D

Davidson, Ken 218
Davies, Picton 79
Davis, William 156
Dean, Alan 6, 130
Dean, Simon 253
de Andrade, Roberto 131, 133, 200, 265-8, 270
Delmar, Jacky 200, 266, 268-70
Deloitte & Touche 90
de Negreiros, Trigo 270
Design Precision Castings 81, 99
Desmarais, Paul 86-7
Dimma, Bill 156
Distillers Corporation Limited 23
Dixon Hall 34
Douglas, Steve 135, 197, 207
Downey, Mike 233
Dryden, Ken 51
Dunford, Bob 130-3, 144, 182, 191, 200, 243, 245, 268

E

EdperBrascan Corporation 1-2, 5, 162, 178-9, 185, 199, 201, 222, 235, 237, 246, 260, 277, 318-9, 322, 346-8
Edper Enterprises Ltd. 35, 141-2, 171-5, 178, 343, 345
Edper Group Foundation, The 38, 131, 186, 310-11
Edper Group Limited, The 2, 178, 318, 345-7
Edper Holdings Inc. 174-6, 178
Edper Investments Limited 2, 27, 79-80, 141, 165, 171, 337-8, 343
EdperPartners Limited 173-4, 177-9, 184-90, 317, 343, 345, 347

Edper Resources Limited   109-10,
     124, 340
Elmworth Deep Basin   196, 231
English Property Corporation   102,
     111, 205, 213, 339-40
Eurobrokers Investment Corporation
     250, 252, 344
Exchange Place   220
Exchange Tower   220
Eyton, J. Trevor   109, 120, 123, 126-8,
     144, 194, 200, 268, 302, 336

F

Falconbridge Limited   146, 224,
     228-9, 272, 343-4, 348
Far Hills Resort   105
Farmilo, Bill   130
Fifth Avenue Place   220
Finestone, Barney   43, 81
Flatt, Bruce   134-5, 142, 197, 207,
     209, 216
Flemming, Brian   194
Flood, Al   154
Francis H. Clergue Generating
     Station   198, 242
Frantisak, Frank   234
Freeman-Atwood, Ted   125
Freund, Michael   251
Fullerton, Don   154
F.W. Woolworth Company   117-22,
     124-5, 340

G

Gainey, Bob   52
Gallotti, Antonio   116
Gammiero, Dominic   230
Garrity, Judge James L.   219

Gaston, Cito   307
General Electric Company   130
Gentra Inc.   220, 252, 256-7, 260-1,
     263, 344, 347-8
Geo. W. Bennet Bryson & Co. Ltd.
     89
Gish, Norm   231
Godsoe, Peter   103
Goldgut, Harry   131
Goldman, David   228
Goldman Sachs   154-5
Goldsmith, Marvin   81
Goodman, Eddie   124
Goodman, Ned   59, 79, 82
Goodman and Carr   156
Gordon Capital   154
Gordon Securities Limited   87
Gray, Jim   39, 196, 231
Great Lakes Power Inc.   2, 137, 147,
     162, 177, 201, 240-7, 251, 261, 337,
     339, 341-3, 348
Great West International Equities
     Ltd.   92, 338-9
Great West Saddlery Limited   82-7,
     89, 92, 99, 338
Great-West Life Assurance Company
     84-7, 89, 92-3, 112, 259, 338
Greenberg brothers (Harold, Harvey,
     Sidney and Ian)   105
Grundman, Irving   70, 94, 104

H

Hahn Company, The   205, 254
Halco Leasing Ltd.   81, 99
Hamilton, Lynda   8, 37, 274, 287,
     302-3, 310, 321
Harder, Lew   124

Harding, Bob   140-2, 167, 179, 197, 212, 216, 290
Hardy, Peter   124
Harris, Hugh   246
Hashman, Sam   84, 92
Hawkrigg, Mel   250, 258
Hees International Bancorp Inc.   2, 83, 93, 99, 106, 134, 140-3, 150, 158, 169-70, 172, 174, 177-8, 197, 209, 212, 231-2, 252, 260-1, 263, 318, 340-6
Hemlo Gold Mines Inc.   227, 342
Holden Group, The   250, 258, 342
Holland, Alfred   99
Horsham Corporation   214
Horton, Diane   6
Hunkin, John   154
Hushovd, Øyvind   229

I

IBM Corporation   129
Indigo Books and Music   155
Investo-Plan   81
Investors Group Inc.   87

J

James, Bill   144
Jeffery family   250, 258
Jessie's Centre for Teenagers   34, 73
John Labatt Limited   52, 147, 162, 265, 340, 344
Joseph P. Seagram & Sons   23

K

Ka-shing, Li   218-19
Kassie, Humphrey   99
Kauser, Lowenstein and Meade   87

Keenan, Patrick J.   109-10, 123
Kenning, Brian   140
Kerr, David   89, 94, 97, 104-7, 109-10, 123, 126, 140, 144, 146, 186, 196, 227-8, 231-2, 248, 331, 335
Kerr, Trevor   253
Killi, Joe   216-17
King, Ed   294
Knuckey, Mike   228
Kress, Ed   130, 243, 246, 268

L

Lake Superior Power   244, 348
Lambert, Allen   86, 133-5, 155, 191, 250
La Reserve Resort   105
Laurentian Lanes Limited   81, 94, 104
Laurin, Marcel   70
Laval, Judge Pierre   124
Lawson, Brian   140-2, 197, 260
Learning Partnership, The   38
LeBlanc, Roméo   277
L'Heureux, Bill   140, 159
Light-Serviços de Eletricidade S.A. (*The Light*)   115-16, 201, 240, 340
Lind, Phil   296
Lochan, Frank   6, 130, 250, 252
London Insurance Group Inc.   87, 251, 258-61, 263, 289, 292, 319-20, 342, 345-6
London Life Insurance Company   135, 147, 249-51, 254, 257-9, 265, 340-2, 346
Lonvest Corporation   258
Lougheed, Peter   156
Louisiana HydroElectric Power   244, 348

Lowenstein, Paul 82, 84-5, 87
Lumley, Ed 168
Lyon, Blake 131
Lyons, Terry 140

M

Macdonald, Linn 230
MacKay Generating Station 243-4
MacKenzie, Arthur 313
Maclaren, Roy 156
Maclean's 191, 305
MacMillan Bloedel Limited 230-1, 341, 344
M.A. Hanna Company 162-3, 343-4
Marigot Investments Limited 83, 89, 92-3, 338-9
Marshall, Don 140
Marshall, Paul 130-2, 144, 191
Masters, John 231
Matoff, Paul 22
McAlpine, Duncan 130
McDonough, Brian 218
McDougall, Hartland 254
McEwen, Mike 246
McFarlane, Paul 218
McGoey, Gerry 211
McGovern, Sue 303
McGregor Pine Estates 81
McJannet, Bryan 140
Meade, Ron 87
Mellon Bank 270
Meloche Monnex Inc. 250
Meltz, Dr. Noah 310
Mercantile Bank of Canada 103, 170, 339
Merrill Lynch 154, 217, 243, 251
Mico Enterprises Ltd. 2, 83, 93, 97-9, 104-6, 140, 318

Mico Investments Limited 170, 339
Milavsky, Harold 92, 103, 135, 191, 205, 213
Miller, Jim 255-6
Minorco S.A. 272
Molson Breweries 108-9
Montreal Canadiens (Le Club de Hockey Canadien) 34, 47, 50-3, 70-2, 94-5, 97, 108-9, 112, 204-5, 295, 305-6, 324, 329, 337, 339-40
Montreal Forum 70, 94-5, 108, 205, 339
Montreal Jewish General Hospital 35, 73
Moore, Jake 116, 120-1, 124-6, 129
Munk, Peter 159, 214
Murphy, Peter 69
Myhal, George 140, 142, 169, 197, 252, 259

N

National Business Systems 343
National Hees Enterprises Limited 140, 338, 340-1
National Hockey League 52, 108
Natofin 81
Nesbitt, Michael 156
Newman, Peter 305
Nikkei 292
Noranda Forest Inc. 227, 230-1, 235, 342, 348
Noranda Inc. 2, 132, 137, 145-6, 165, 177, 201, 225-37, 261, 272-3, 289, 342-8
Noranda Mines Limited 2, 124, 144, 224-5, 340-1
Norcen Energy Resources Limited 132, 146, 231, 235, 261, 272, 342-4, 347

Nordholm, Ed 216
Norris, Alan 135, 207
North Canadian Oils Ltd. 146,
   231-2, 261, 342, 344

O
Olympia & York 110, 213, 215-7,
   219, 340
Ondaatje, Christopher 173-4
Onex Corporation 155
Ontario Hydro 246
Ontario Securities Commission 120
Orser, Earl 258
Ortiz-Patiño, Jamie 109, 123
Oxford Properties Limited 193

P
Pacific First Financial Corporation
   254-5
Pagurian Corporation, The 173-6,
   178, 343, 345
Partners Limited 173
Patiño N.V. 109-10, 165, 340
Patrick, Ken 92-3
Peel Centre 79
Peter Bronfman International
   Graduate Scholarships 6, 311
Peter Bronfman Woodsworth
   Scholarships 5, 310-11
Pickard, Frank 229
Place Ville Marie 92
Pollock, Sam 51-2, 70, 72, 94-5, 108,
   159
Pollock, Sam, Jr. 52, 142, 178, 253
Pontiac Power 245, 346, 348
Power Corporation of Canada 86,
   338

Powis, Alf 144
Pratt, Courtney 227
Price Pulp and Paper Company 230
Price, Tim 88-9, 91, 97, 104, 120-1,
   123, 126, 140, 186, 197, 230, 248,
   302, 335
Prichard, Rob 36-7, 275
Pringle, Bill 135, 207
Prudential Life Assurance Company
   of Canada 259, 346

Q
Québec Student Inter-Exchange
   Program 34

R
Raglan nickel mine 195, 229, 236
Refimet copper smelter 272, 347
Regent, Aaron 142, 178, 253
Regent Packaging 81
Reichmann family 111, 215
Reichmann, Paul 193, 215-6
Reisman, Heather 155
Republic Plaza 193, 221
Riley, Sandy 251
Rio Sul 200
Ritchie, Cedric 103
Rogers, Ted 295
Royal Bank of Canada 160, 256-7,
   259, 344
Royal LePage Limited 250, 253, 348
Royal Trust 160-1, 256
Royal Trustco Limited 147, 160, 227,
   250-2, 254-7, 260, 341, 344
Rubin, Tony 140, 197

S

Sardachuk, Ed   92, 103, 205
Sardachuk, Grant   140
São Paulo Tramway,
   Light and Power Company   2,
   199, 337
Sault Generating Station   240
Savidant, Steve   233
S.B. McLaughlin & Company
   Limited   104, 110, 340
Schipper, Lionel   156, 275
Schwartz, Gerry   155
Scott Paper Company   147, 162,
   341-2
Scrymgeour, John   156
Seagram Company Ltd., The   23,
   26-8, 78-80, 95, 282, 328, 337-9
Seco Limited   27, 79-80, 337-8
Senate of Canada   128
Sheckman, Zöe   95
Shiff, Dick   218
Shulman, Saul   156
Siblin, Herb   81
Sidney A. Murray, Jr. Generating
   Station   244
Siller, Phillip   73
Simon, Bob   130
Skol Caracú   267
SkyDome   128
Sonae Investimentos S.A.   270
Space Research Corporation   84
Spilfogel, Lenny   82, 88
Sprague, Henry   69
St. Michael's Hospital   132
St. Stephen's Community House   34
Sun Youth Organization   34

T

Tanenbaum, Joey   245
Taylor, George   162
Thomson, Dick   134, 155
320 Bay Street   221
Tomczyk, Fred   259
Toronto Blue Jays Baseball Club   47,
   50, 52, 72, 204, 305-7, 344
Toronto-Dominion Bank, The   86,
   110, 134, 154-5, 174, 210, 250, 258
Toronto Stock Exchange, The   83-4,
   87, 99, 140, 318
Tory Tory DesLauriers & Binnington
   127
Touche Ross   89-90
Trelleborg N.V.   228, 343
Tremayne, John   142, 178
Triathlon Leasing Inc.   250, 252
Trilon Bancorp Inc.   348
Trilon Capital Partners Limited
   260, 348
Trilon Financial Corporation   2, 52,
   87, 137, 142, 168, 201, 220,
   243, 249-63, 319, 341-8
Trilon Securities Corporation   250,
   348
Trivest Insurance Agencies   250
Trizec Corporation   92, 97, 102-3,
   106-7, 111, 135, 159, 161, 172, 205,
   208, 212-15, 220, 254, 339-40, 345
20/20 Mutual Fund Group   250
Turmell, Antoine   194

U

United Way of Metropolitan Toronto
   34
University of Toronto   5, 8, 36-8,
   275, 307, 309-11

V

Valerie Falls Generating Station 245
Vance, Cyrus 219

W

Walker, Skip 162
Walt, Manfred 140, 142, 197, 216
Waltham Generating Station 198
Watsa, Prem 155
Watson, Don 246
Waugh, Alex 37, 275
Wellington Insurance Company 250, 258, 342, 345
Wells, Don 89
Westchester Estates 81
Westcoast Energy Inc. 244
Western Mines Limited 224, 341
Westmin Resources Limited 132, 194, 224, 232, 341, 345
Westmount Life Insurance Company 99, 104, 165, 339
Widdrington, Peter 124

Wilson, Red 211
Winnipeg Supply and Fuel 87
Wolfe, Rose 275-6
Wood Gundy 85, 294
Woodsworth College 5, 37-8, 275-6, 309-11
World Financial Center 193, 215, 221, 343, 346
World Financial Properties Inc. 215, 217-20, 261, 346-8

Y

Yale University 69
Yeoman, Bob 130, 144
Yorkdale Shopping Centre 92
York University 311

Z

Zimmerman, Adam 144
Zinor Holdings Limited 144-5, 225-6
Zittrer, Sheila 35, 73
Zuccotti, John 219